Introduction to Maple®

David I. Schwartz

State University of New York at Buffalo

Prentice Hall
Upper Saddle River, NJ 07458

Library of Congress Cataloging-In-Publication Data

Schwartz, David I.
  Introduction to Maple / David I. Schwartz
    p.   cm.
  Includes bibliographical references and index.
  ISBN 0–13–095133-1
  1. Maple (Computer file)   2. Mathematics—Data processing.
QA76.95.S33   1998
515′.078′55369—dc21   98-50147
                                                             CIP

Editor-in-chief: **MARCIA HORTON**
Acquisitions editor: **ERIC SVENDSEN**
Director of production and manufacturing: **DAVID W. RICCARDI**
Managing editor: **EILEEN CLARK**
Editorial/production supervision: **ROSE KERNAN**
Cover director: **JAYNE CONTE**
Creative director: **AMY ROSEN**
Marketing manager: **DANNY HOYT**
Manufacturing buyer: **PAT BROWN**
Editorial assistant: **GRIFFIN CABLE**

The author and publisher of this book have used their best efforts in
preparing this book. These efforts include the development, research,
and testing of the theories and programs to determine their effective-
ness. The author and publisher shall not be liable in any event for inci-
dental or consequential damages in connection with, or arising out of,
the furnishing, performance, or use of these programs.

Printed in the United States of America

10 9 8 7 6 5 4 3 2 1

ISBN 0-13-095133-1

Prentice-Hall International (UK) Limited, *London*
Prentice-Hall of Australia Pty. Limited, *Sydney*
Prentice-Hall Canada, Inc., *Toronto*
Prentice-Hall Hispanoamericana, S.A., *Mexico*
Prentice-Hall of India Private Limited, *New Delhi*
Prentice-Hall of Japan, Inc., *Tokyo*
Prentice-Hall (Singapore), Pte., Ltd., *Singapore*
Editora Prentice-Hall do Brazil, Ltda., *Rio de Janeiro*

Macintosh is a registered trademark of Apple Computer, Inc.
ManOwaR is a registered trademark of the band Manowar. Maple and
Maple V are registered trademarks of Waterloo Maple, Inc. MATLAB
is a registered trademark of The MathWorks, Inc. PostScript is a registered trademark of Adobe Systems, Inc. Unix is a registered trademark
of the Open Group. Windows and Windows NT are registered trademarks of Microsoft, Inc. Other product and company names men-
tioned herein may be the trademarks of their respective owners.

About ESource

The Challenge

Professors who teach the Introductory/First-Year Engineering course popular at most engineering schools have a unique challenge—teaching a course defined by a changing curriculum. The first-year engineering course is different from any other engineering course in that there is no real cannon that defines the course content. It is not like Engineering Mechanics or Circuit Theory where a consistent set of topics define the course. Instead, the introductory engineering course is most often defined by the creativity of professors and students, and the specific needs of a college or university each semester. Faculty involved in this course typically put extra effort into it, and it shows in the uniqueness of each course at each school.

Choosing a textbook can be a challenge for unique courses. Most freshmen require some sort of reference material to help them through their first semesters as a college student. But because faculty put such a strong mark on their course, they often have a difficult time finding the right mix of materials for their course and often have to go without a text, or with one that does not really fit. Conventional textbooks are far too static for the typical specialization of the first-year course. How do you find the perfect text for your course that will support your students educational needs, but give you the flexibility to maximize the potential of your course?

ESource—The Prentice Hall Engineering Source
http://emissary.prenhall.com/esource

Prentice Hall created ESource—The Prentice-Hall Engineering Source—to give professors the power to harness the full potential of their text and their freshman/first year engineering course. In today's technologically advanced world, why settle for a book that isn't perfect for your course? Why not have a book that has the exact blend of topics that you want to cover with your students?

More then just a collection of books, ESource is a unique publishing system revolving around the ESource website—http://emissary.prenhall.com/esource/. ESource enables you to put your stamp on your book just as you do your course. It lets you:

Control   You choose exactly what chapters or sections are in your book and in what order they appear. Of course, you can choose the entire book if you'd like and stay with the authors original order.

Optimize   Get the most from your book and your course. ESource lets you produce the optimal text for your students needs.

Customize   You can add your own material anywhere in your text's presentation, and your final product will arrive at your bookstore as a professionally formatted text.

ESource Content

All the content in ESource was written by educators specifically for freshman/first-year students. Authors tried to strike a balanced level of presentation, one that was not either too formulaic and trivial, but not focusing heavily on advanced topics that most introductory students will not encounter until later classes. A developmental editor reviewed the books and made sure that every text was written at the appropriate level, and that the books featured a balanced presentation. Because many professors do not have extensive time to cover these topics in the classroom, authors prepared each text with the idea that many students would use it for self-instruction and independent study. Students should be able to use this content to learn the software tool or subject on their own.

While authors had the freedom to write texts in a style appropriate to their particular subject, all followed certain guidelines created to promote the consistency a text needs. Namely, every chapter opens with a clear set of objectives to lead students into the chapter. Each chapter also contains practice problems that tests a student's skill at performing the tasks they have just learned. Chapters close with extra practice questions and a list of key terms for reference. Authors tried to focus on motivating applications that demonstrate how engineers work in the real world, and included these applications throughout the text in various chapter openers, examples, and problem material. Specific Engineering and Science **Application Boxes** are also located throughout the texts, and focus on a specific application and demonstrating its solution.

Because students often have an adjustment from high school to college, each book contains several **Professional Success Boxes** specifically designed to provide advice on college study skills. Each author has worked to provide students with tips and techniques that help a student better understand the material, and avoid common pitfalls or problems first-year students often have. In addition, this series contains an entire book titled **Engineering Success** by Peter Schiavone of the University of Alberta intended to expose students quickly to what it takes to be an engineering student.

Creating Your Book

Using ESource is simple. You preview the content either on-line or through examination copies of the books you can request on-line, from your PH sales rep, or by calling(1-800-526-0485). Create an on-line outline of the content you want in the order you want using ESource's simple interface. Either type or cut and paste your own material and insert it into the text flow. You can preview the overall organization of the text you've created at anytime (please note, since this preview is immediate, it comes unformatted.), then press another button and receive an order number for your own custom book . If you are not ready to order, do nothing—ESource will save your work. You can come back at any time and change, re-arrange, or add more material to your creation. You are in control. Once you're finished and you have an ISBN, give it to your bookstore and your book will arrive on their shelves six weeks after the order. Your custom desk copies with their instructor supplements will arrive at your address at the same time.

To learn more about this new system for creating the perfect textbook, go to **http://emissary.prenhall.com/esource/**. You can either go through the on-line walkthrough of how to create a book, or experiment yourself.

Community

ESource has two other areas designed to promote the exchange of information among the introductory engineering community, the Faculty and the Student Centers. Created and maintained with the help of Dale Calkins, an Associate Professor at the University of Washington, these areas contain a wealth of useful information and tools. You can preview outlines created by other schools and can see how others organize their courses. Read a monthly article discussing important topics in the curriculum. You can post your own material and share it with others, as well as use what others have posted in your own documents. Communicate with our authors about their books and make suggestions for improvement. Comment about your course and ask for information from others professors. Create an on-line syllabus using our custom syllabus builder. Browse Prentice Hall's catalog and order titles from your sales rep. Tell us new features that we need to add to the site to make it more useful.

Supplements

Adopters of ESource receive an instructor's CD that includes solutions as well as professor and student code for all the books in the series. This CD also contains approximately **350 Powerpoint Transparencies** created by Jack Leifer—of University South Carolina—Aiken. Professors can either follow these transparencies as pre-prepared lectures or use them as the basis for their own custom presentations. In addition, look to the web site to find materials from other schools that you can download and use in your own course.

Titles in the ESource Series

Introduction to Unix
0-13-095135-8
David I. Schwartz

Introduction to Maple
0-13-095133-1
David I. Schwartz

Introduction to Word
0-13-254764-3
David C. Kuncicky

Introduction to Excel
0-13-254749-X
David C. Kuncicky

Introduction to MathCAD
0-13-937493-0
Ronald W. Larsen

Introduction to AutoCAD, R. 14
0-13-011001-9
Mark Dix and Paul Riley

Introduction to the Internet, 2/e
0-13-011037-X
Scott D. James

Design Concepts for Engineers
0-13-081369-9
Mark N. Horenstein

Engineering Design—A Day in the Life of Four Engineers
0-13-660242-8
Mark N. Horenstein

Engineering Ethics
0-13-784224-4
Charles B. Fleddermann

Engineering Success
0-13-080859-8
Peter Schiavone

Mathematics Review
0-13-011501-0
Peter Schiavone

Introduction to C
0-13-011854-0
Delores M. Etter

Introduction to C++
0-13-011855-9
Delores M. Etter

Introduction to MATLAB
0-13-013149-0
Delores M. Etter with David C. Kuncicky

Introduction to FORTRAN 90
0-13-013146-6
Larry Nyhoff and Sanford Leestma

About the Authors

No project could ever come to pass without a group of authors who have the vision and the courage to turn a stack of blank paper into a book. The authors in this series worked diligently to produce their books, provide the building blocks of the series.

Delores M. Etter is a Professor of Electrical and Computer Engineering at the University of Colorado. Dr. Etter was a faculty member at the University of New Mexico and also a Visiting Professor at Stanford University. Dr. Etter was responsible for the Freshman Engineering Program at the University of New Mexico and is active in the Integrated Teaching Laboratory at the University of Colorado. She was elected a Fellow of the Institute of Electrical and Electronic Engineers for her contributions to education and for her technical leadership in digital signal processing. IN addition to writing best-selling textbooks for engineering computing, Dr. Etter has also published research in the area of adaptive signal processing.

Sanford Leestma is a Professor of Mathematics and Computer Science at Calvin College, and received his Ph.D from New Mexico State University. He has been the long time co-author of successful textbooks on Fortran, Pascal, and data structures in Pascal. His current research interests are in the areas of algorithms and numerical compuitation.

Larry Nyhoff is a Professor of Mathematics and Computer Science at Calvin College. After doing bachelors work at Calvin, and Masters work at Michigan, he received a Ph.D. from Michigan State and also did graduate work in computer science at Western Michigan. Dr. Nyhoff has taught at Calvin for the past 34 years—mathematics at first and computer science for the past several years. He has co-authored several computer science textbooks since 1981 including titles on Fortran and C++, as well as a brand new title on Data Structures in C++.

Acknowledgments: We express our sincere appreciation to all who helped in the preparation of this module, especially our acquisitions editor Alan Apt, managing editor Laura Steele, development editor Sandra Chavez, and production editor Judy Winthrop. We also thank Larry Genalo for several examples and exercises and Erin Fulp for the Internet address application in Chapter 10. We appreciate the insightful review provided by Bart Childs. We thank our families—Shar, Jeff, Dawn, Rebecca, Megan, Sara, Greg, Julie, Joshua, Derek, Tom, Joan; Marge, Michelle, Sandy, Lori, Michael—for being patient and understanding. We thank God for allowing us to write this text.

Mark Dix began working with AutoCAD in 1985 as a programmer for CAD Support Associates, Inc. He helped design a system for creating estimates and bills of material directly from AutoCAD drawing databases for use in the automated conveyor industry. This system became the basis for systems still widely in use today. In 1986 he began collaborating with Paul Riley to create AutoCAD training materials, combining Riley's background in industrial design and training with Dix' s background in writing, curriculum development, and programming. Dix and Riley have created tutorial and teaching methods for every AutoCAD release since Version 2.5. Mr. Dix has a Master of Arts in Teaching from Cornell University and a Masters of Education from the University of Massachusetts. He is currently the Director of Dearborn Academy High School in Arlington, Massachusetts.

Paul Riley is an author, instructor, and designer specializing in graphics and design for multimedia. He is a founding partner of CAD Support Associates, a contract service and professional training organization for computer-aided design. His 15 years of business experience and 20 years of teaching experience are supported by degrees in education and computer science. Paul has taught AutoCAD at the University of Massachusetts at Lowell and is presently teaching AutoCAD at Mt. Ida College in Newton, Massachusetts. He has developed a program, Computer-Aided Design for Professionals that is highly regarded by corporate clients and has been an ongoing success since 1982.

David I. Schwartz is a Lecturer at SUNY-Buffalo who teaches freshman and first-year engineering, and has a Ph.D from SUNY-Buffalo in Civil Engineering. Schwartz originally became interested in Civil engineering out of an interest in building grand structures, but has also pursued other academic interests including artificial intelligence and applied mathematics. He became interested in Unix and Maple through their application to his research, and eventually jumped at the chance to teach these subjects to students. He tries to teach his students to become incremental learners and encourages frequent practice to master a subject, and gain the maturity and confidence to tackle other subjects independently. In his spare time, Schwartz is an avid musician and plays drums in a variety of bands.

Acknowledgments: I would like to thank the entire School of Engineering and Applied Science at the State University of New York at Buffalo for the opportunity to teach not only my students, but myself as well; all my EAS140 students, without whom this book would not be possible—thanks for slugging through my lab packets; Andrea Au, Eric Svendsen, and Elizabeth Wood at Prentice Hall for advising and encouraging me as well as wading through my blizzard of e-mail; Linda and Tony for starting the whole thing in the first place; Rogil Camama, Linda Chattin, Stuart Chen, Jeffrey Chottiner, Roger Christian, Anthony Dalessio, Eugene DeMaitre, Dawn Halvorsen, Thomas Hill, Michael Lamanna, Nate "X" Patwardhan, Durvejai Sheobaran, "Able" Alan Somlo, Ben Stein, Craig Sutton, Barbara Umiker, and Chester "JC" Zeshonski for making this book a reality; Ewa Arrasjid, "Corky" Brunskill, Bob Meyer, and Dave Yearke at "the Department Formerly Known as ECS" for all their friendship, advice, and respect; Jeff, Tony, Forrest, and Mike for the interviews; and, Michael Ryan and Warren Thomas for believing in me.

Ronald W. Larsen is an Associate Professor in Chemical Engineering at Montana State University, and received his Ph.D from the Pennsylvania State University. Larsen was initially attracted to engineering because he felt it was a serving profession, and because engineers are often called on to eliminate dull and routine tasks. He also enjoys the fact that engineering rewards creativity and presents constant challenges. Larsen feels that teaching large sections of students is one of the most challenging tasks he has ever encountered because it enhances the importance of effective communication. He has drawn on a two year experince teaching courses in Mongolia through an interpreter to improve his skills in the classroom. Larsen sees software as one of the changes that has the potential to radically alter the way engineers work, and his book Introduction to Mathcad was written to help young engineers prepare to be productive in an ever-changing workplace.

Acknowledgments: To my students at Montana State University who have endured the rough drafts and typos, and who still allow me to experiment with their classes— my sincere thanks.

Peter Schiavone is a professor and student advisor in the Department of Mechanical Engineering at the University of Alberta. He received his Ph.D. from the University of Strathclyde, U.K. in 1988. He has authored several books in the area of study skills and academic success as well as numerous papers in scientific research journals.

Before starting his career in academia, Dr. Schiavone worked in the private sector for Smith's Industries (Aerospace and Defence Systems Company) and Marconi Instruments in several different areas of engineering including aerospace, systems and software engineering. During that time he developed an interest in engineering research and the applications of mathematics and the physical sciences to solving real-world engineering problems.

His love for teaching brought him to the academic world. He founded the first Mathematics Resource Center at the University of Alberta: a unit designed specifically to teach high school students the necessary survival skills in mathematics and the physical sciences required for first-year engineering. This led to the Students' Union Gold Key award for outstanding contributions to the University and to the community at large.

Dr. Schiavone lectures regularly to freshman engineering students, high school teachers, and new professors on all aspects of engineering success, in particular, maximizing students' academic performance. He wrote the book *Engineering Success* in order to share with you the *secrets of success in engineering study*: the most effective, tried and tested methods used by the most successful engineering students.

Acknowledgments: I'd like to acknowledge the contributions of: Eric Svendsen, for his encouragement and support; Richard Felder for being such an inspiration; the many students who shared their experiences of first-year engineering—both good and bad; and finally, my wife Linda for her continued support and for giving me Conan.

Scott D. James is a staff lecturer at Kettering University (formerly GMI Engineering & Management Institute) in Flint, Michigan. He is currently pursuing a Ph.D. in Systems Engineering with an emphasis on software engineering and computer-integrated manufacturing. Scott decided on writing textbooks after he found a void in the books that were available. "I really wanted a book that showed how to do things in good detail but in a clear and concise way. Many of the books on the market are full of fluff and force you to dig out the really important facts." Scott decided on teaching as a profession after several years in the computer industry. "I thought that it was really important to know what it was like outside of academia. I wanted to provide students with classes that were up to date and provide the information that is really used and needed."

Acknowledgments: Scott would like to acknowledge his family for the time to work on the text and his students and peers at Kettering who offered helpful critique of the materials that eventually became the book.

David C. Kuncicky is a native Floridian. He earned his Baccalaureate in psychology, Master's in computer science, and Ph.D. in computer science from Florida State University. Dr. Kuncicky is the Director of Computing and Multimedia Services for the FAMU-FSU College of Engineering. He also serves as a faculty member in the Department of Electrical Engineering. He has taught computer science and computer engineering courses for the past 15 years. He has published research in the areas of intelligent hybrid systems and neural networks. He is actively involved in the education of computer and network system administrators and is a leader in the area of technology-based curriculum delivery.

Acknowledgments: Thanks to Steffie and Helen for putting up with my late nights and long weekends at the computer. Thanks also to the helpful and insightful technical reviews by the following people: Jerry Ralya, Kathy Kitto of Western Washington University, Avi Singhal of Arizona State University, and Thomas Hill of the State University of New York at Buffalo. I appreciate the patience of Eric Svendsen and Rose Kernan of Prentice Hall for gently guiding me through this project. Finally, thanks to Dean C.J. Chen for providing continued tutelage and support.

Mark Horenstein is an Associate Professor in the Electrical and Computer Engineering Department at Boston University. He received his Bachelors in Electrical Engineering in 1973 from Massachusetts Institute of Technology, his Masters in Electrical Engineering in 1975

from University of California at Berkeley, and his Ph.D. in Electrical Engineering in 1978 from Massachusetts Institute of Technology. Professor Horenstein's research interests are in applied electrostatics and electromagnetics as well as microelectronics, including sensors, instrumentation, and measurement. His research deals with the simulation, test, and measurement of electromagnetic fields. Some topics include electrostatics in manufacturing processes, electrostatic instrumentation, EOS/ESD control, and electromagnetic wave propagation.

Professor Horenstein designed and developed a class at Boston University, which he now teaches entitled Senior Design Project (ENG SC 466). In this course, the student gets real engineering design experience by working for a virtual company, created by Professor Horenstein, that does real projects for outside companies—almost like an apprenticeship. Once in "the company" (Xebec Technologies), the student is assigned to an engineering team of 3-4 persons. A series of potential customers are recruited, from which the team must accept an engineering project. The team must develop a working prototype deliverable engineering system that serves the need of the customer. More than one team may be assigned to the same project, in which case there is competition for the customer's business.

Acknowledgements: Several individuals contributed to the ideas and concepts presented in Design Principles for Engineers. The concept of the Peak Performance design competition, which forms a cornerstone of the book, originated with Professor James Bethune of Boston University. Professor Bethune has been instrumental in conceiving of and running Peak Performance each year and has been the inspiration behind many of the design concepts associated with it. He also provided helpful information on dimensions and tolerance. Several of the ideas presented in the book, particularly the topics on brainstorming and teamwork, were gleaned from a workshop on engineering design help bi-annually by Professor Charles Lovas of Southern Methodist University. The principles of estimation were derived in part from a freshman engineering problem posed by Professor Thomas Kincaid of Boston University.

I would like to thank my family, Roxanne, Rachel, and Arielle, for giving me the time and space to think about and write this book. I also appreciate Roxanne's inspiration and help in identifying examples of human/machine interfaces.

Dedicated to Roxanne, Rachel, and Arielle

Charles B. Fleddermann is a professor in the Department of Electrical and Computer Engineering at the University of New Mexico in Albuquerque, New Mexico. He is a third generation engineer—his grandfather was a civil engineer and father an aeronautical engineer—so "engineering was in my genetic makeup." The genesis of a book on engineering ethics was in the ABET requirement to incorporate ethics topics into the undergraduate engineering curriculum. "Our department decided to have a one-hour seminar course on engineering ethics, but there was no book suitable for such a course." Other texts were tried the first few times the course was offered, but none of them presented ethical theory, analysis, and problem solving in a readily accessible way. "I wanted to have a text which would be concise, yet would give the student the tools required to solve the ethical problems that they might encounter in their professional lives."

Reviewers

ESource benefited from a wealth of reviewers who on the series from its initial idea stage to its completion. Reviewers read manuscripts and contributed insightful comments that helped the authors write great books. We would like to thank everyone who helped us with this project.

Concept Document
Naeem Abdurrahman- University of Texas, Austin
Grant Baker- University of Alaska, Anchorage
Betty Barr- University of Houston
William Beckwith- Clemson University
Ramzi Bualuan- University of Notre Dame
Dale Calkins- University of Washington
Arthur Clausing- University of Illinois at Urbana-Champaign
John Glover- University of Houston
A.S. Hodel- Auburn University
Denise Jackson- University of Tennessee, Knoxville
Kathleen Kitto- Western Washington University
Terry Kohutek- Texas A&M University
Larry Richards- University of Virginia
Avi Singhal- Arizona State University
Joseph Wujek- University of California, Berkeley
Mandochehr Zoghi- University of Dayton

Books
Stephen Allan- Utah State University
Naeem Abdurrahman - University of Texas Austin
Anil Bajaj- Purdue University
Grant Baker - University of Alaska - Anchorage
Betty Barr - University of Houston

William Beckwith - Clemson University
Haym Benaroya- Rutgers University
Tom Bledsaw- ITT Technical Institute
Tom Bryson- University of Missouri, Rolla
Ramzi Bualuan - University of Notre Dame
Dan Budny- Purdue University
Dale Calkins - University of Washington
Arthur Clausing - University of Illinois
James Devine- University of South Florida
Patrick Fitzhorn - Colorado State University
Dale Elifrits- University of Missouri, Rolla
Frank Gerlitz - Washtenaw College
John Glover - University of Houston
John Graham - University of North Carolina-Charlotte
Malcom Heimer - Florida International University
A.S. Hodel - Auburn University
Vern Johnson- University of Arizona
Kathleen Kitto - Western Washington University
Robert Montgomery- Purdue University
Mark Nagurka- Marquette University
Ramarathnam Narasimhan- University of Miami
Larry Richards - University of Virginia
Marc H. Richman - Brown University
Avi Singhal-Arizona State University
Tim Sykes- Houston Community College
Thomas Hill- SUNY at Buffalo
Michael S. Wells - Tennessee Tech University
Joseph Wujek - University of California - Berkeley
Edward Young- University of South Carolina
Mandochehr Zoghi - University of Dayton

Contents

1

Introduction to Maple

1.1 PROBLEMS

People solve problems. However, what distinguishes ***engineering*** and ***science*** problems from other types of problems? Certainly not all tasks require an engineer or scientist! Loosely stated, scientists *develop* theoretical concepts of the physical world. Engineers then *apply* these theories to create physical systems for people. This section introduces the concept of problem solving.

1.1.1 Tools

Tools assist the processes of thinking about, analysis of, and testing for problem solving. Tools include physical *devices* and abstract *methods*. Physical tools, like machinery, extend human physical capabilities. Abstract tools, like algorithms, enhance problem solving.

1.1.2 Modeling

Models are tools that analyze and predict physical behaviors. Science and engineering models combine physical prototypes with algorithms and equations. Well-devised models reasonably and efficiently predict accurate behaviors.

1.1.3 Experimentation

Experimentation yields good models. For instance, consider a building and a model of it, as shown in Figure 1.1. Over many years, laboratory testing and theoretical development have provided engineers with idealized mathematical models that assist in structural design. Continued testing of idealized and actual behaviors improves the understanding and development of better models.

OBJECTIVES

After reading this chapter, you should be able to:

- Relate engineering and science to problem solving
- Discuss the role of mathematics and computers as tools
- Understand how Maple operates
- Review the problem-solving process
- Describe the notations employed in this text

Throughout all generations, engineers have strived to construct the world's tallest building. The Petronas Towers in Kuala Lumpur, Malaysia currently hold the title with an uppermost height of 592.4 meters. Courtesy of Thornton Thomasetti Engineers.

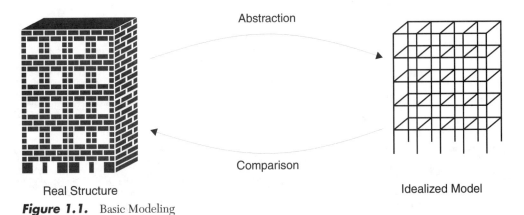

Figure 1.1. Basic Modeling

1.1.4 Mathematics

Mathematics provides abstract models. Scientists and engineers represent physical values as variables and constants inside mathematical equations. Equations are not perfect, but equations based on experimentation yield reliable models.

1.1.5 Computers

Tools, like **computers**, assist in complex mathematical analysis and other burdensome tasks. Hardware and software make up the "body" and "mind" of a computer. Hardware consists of the physical devices of computers. Software provides the "intelligence" for computations and communication.

1.1.6 Black Boxes

Application software implements mathematical models for analysis and design. Understand, however, a computer program's assumptions and limitations as you would with any model! Never let computer applications become **black boxes**, programs that shield users from processing methods of input and output. Always check your output with simpler "textbook" models.

1.2 MAPLE

Maple is a powerful software tool for symbolic and numerical analysis. This section reviews the basics of the Maple program.

1.2.1 Computer Algebra System

Maple, which is a **computer algebra system** (CAS), implements symbolic mathematics. A CAS provides commands for manipulating and deriving symbolic equations from other equations. The symbolic approach is often described as analytical. **Analytical methods** seek exact, symbolic answers to mathematical problems. Many CASs, like Maple, commonly employ numerical methods as well.

1.2.2 History of Maple

Computer-based symbolic analysis was introduced in the late 1960s. After years of development, Maple appeared in the early 1980s for academic applications. Eventually, the Waterloo Maple, Inc. corporation commercially released Maple. Maple remains popular in both academic and commercial environments.

1.2.3 Why Maple?

Maple is very useful for a number of reasons:

- It performs symbolic and numerical analysis for a wide variety of tasks.
- It contains a rich library of over 2500 functions.
- You can construct customized programs by using Maple commands.
- Newer features of Maple include spreadsheets and Web-page publishing.

PROFESSIONAL SUCCESS: A STUDENT'S PERSPECTIVE OF MAPLE

Durvejai Sheobaran is a former student of mine who struggled with Maple as a freshman. Here is his tale and some advice:

"When I first started learning Maple in my Introductory Engineering class, I struggled with syntax errors and unexpected output. Dave told me to practice, so practice I did. Do yourself some favors. Seek help from your instructors. Use Maple's Help functions. Check your input, and make sure to have correctly entered all necessary options. Keep practicing . . . the more I practiced, the easier it was to work with Maple.

I also struggled with not knowing why we were learning Maple. Have a little faith. If your class uses Maple, expect it to appear in other classes as well. My differential equations class required Maple for all homework. For a mechanical-design project, we had to model a golf ball's trajectory. Without Maple, I would have been stranded!

Learn Maple. Never just copy the commands. Assure yourself by contemplating the logic behind the commands, and try to predict the results beforehand. Checking and analyzing will help reduce those blasted syntax errors! Try working with some classmates, too. Now, back to you, Dave!"

1.2.4 How Does Maple Work?

The **kernel**, **libraries**, and an **interface** make up the structure of Maple, as shown in Figure 1.2:

Figure 1.2.   The Structure of Maple

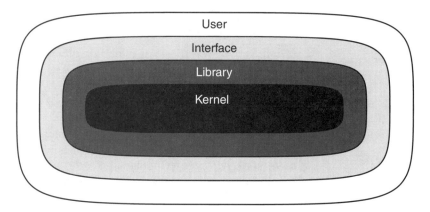

- **Kernel**: About 10% of Maple functions make up the Maple kernel, the core command group. These functions interpret and process input, evaluate numerical quantities, and manage memory. Maple provides both *shared* and *parallel* kernels, as discussed in Chapter 4.

- *Library*: About 90% of Maple functions are written in Maple code and kernel operations. Some functions automatically load when Maple is started. Others must be manually loaded. Consult Appendix D for more information.
- *Interface*: The user communicates with Maple through the interface. Maple interprets commands and evaluates the desired procedures. Although Maple provides a text-based interface, this text focuses on the **graphical user interface** (GUI) version of Maple. These interfaces are discussed in the next chapter.
- *User*: That's you!

1.3 OVERVIEW

This text covers Maple V Release 5 (VR5). Important distinctions between VR5 and Release 4 (VR4) are noted throughout the text. Beware that not all platforms support the same features.

1.3.1 Problem-Solving Methodology

Each chapter applies Maple to the solution of a variety of problems. As you work through these problems, follow a general problem-solving methodology, as illustrated in Figure 1.3. In general, break problems down into smaller, more manageable subproblems. Also, when steps fail, go back to previous steps and iterate for better solutions.

1.3.2 Notation

Before attempting anything, thoroughly review the notation in Table 1-1. Computer manuals and textbooks are typically awash with such notation.

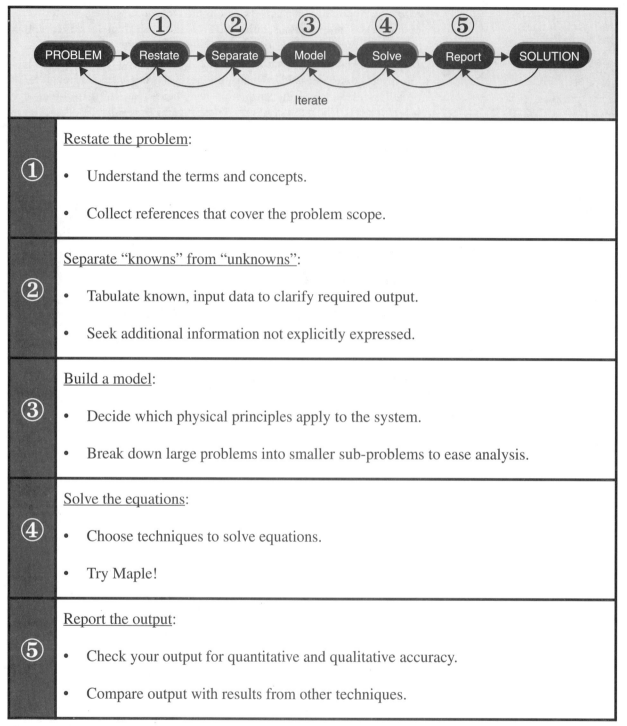

Figure 1.3.   Problem-Solving Methodology

TABLE 1-1   Notation

NOTATION	DESCRIPTION
Key Terms	These **terms** involve important concepts and are shown in boldface italics. Key terms are summarized at the end of each chapter.
`Input`	Computer **input** and **commands** are shown in boldface Courier font.
`Arguments`	Many Maple commands take *arguments*, which are values that can vary. Never type the literal name "***argument***"! Always type the value of "***argument***" instead. Arguments are indicated in boldface italic Courier font.
Maple Output	GUI Maple reports most output in *italics*. Numerical values are usually shown in plain font. Mathematical expressions and equations are commonly shown in *italics*. Beware that you must enter mathematical expressions like sin x as `sin(x)`.
`Computer Output`	Maple sometimes produces output in plain Courier font, usually as error messages. Text-based Maple also uses this font.
commentary	*Comments* are shown in this small italic font. Never enter these comments into Maple commands!
↵	Press the Enter or Return key on your keyboard.
Menu1 → Menu2	Select Menu items by pointing and clicking your mouse. For instance, the sequence Edit→Execute→Worksheet indicates for you to select Edit. You can now select sub-menus. Point your mouse on Execute. Finally, select Worksheet. You can also press the Alt key along with the first underlined letter to select a particular menu item. Do not press Alt again to activate sub-menus.
Topic . . . Subtopic	Point and click your mouse inside the Help Browser for help on specific topics. Consult Appendix B for more information on getting help in Maple.

SUMMARY

A variety of tools help solve science and engineering problems. Tools include both physical devices and abstract methods. Computer programs implement models derived from scientific principles and experimentation to ease analysis and improve accuracy. However, many programs hide methods by acting as black boxes. Check your work! Computer algebra systems provide methods for both symbolic and numerical analysis. Three basic components—the kernel, libraries, and the interface—form Maple.

KEY TERMS

analytical methods
black boxes
computer algebra system
computers
engineering

experimentation
graphical user interface (GUI)
Maple
Maple interface
Maple kernel

Maple library
mathematics
models
science
tools

2

Maple Overview

2.1 MAPLE ENVIRONMENT

Maple provides a robust environment for mathematical computations, graphing, and report writing. This section introduces Maple's user interface.

2.1.1 Starting Maple

Maple provides two basic environments. Its most common environment is that of the graphical user interface (GUI) version. Double-click on the Maple V icon in the Windows and MacIntosh environment to start up this version of Maple. A Unix user typically enters **xmaple** or **maple -x** at the command prompt for the GUI version.

OBJECTIVES

After reading this chapter, you should be able to:

- Use the Maple GUI interface
- Demonstrate Maple worksheets
- Demonstrate input and output
- Demonstrate execution groups
- Understand essential Maple functions

Sometimes, big engineering problems come in small packages . . . perhaps millions of them. Zebra mussels have infested North-American waterways. These remarkably sturdy creatures clog pipes and foul water. Much research is devoted to dealing with these pests. Courtesy of U.S. Geological Survey, Great Lakes Science Center

2.1.2 Command-Line Interface

Maple's text-based command-line version is shown below in Figure 2.1.

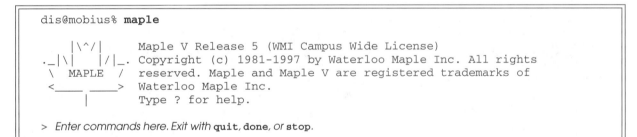

```
dis@mobius% maple

     |\^/|      Maple V Release 5 (WMI Campus Wide License)
._|\|   |/|_.  Copyright (c) 1981-1997 by Waterloo Maple Inc. All rights
 \  MAPLE  /   reserved. Maple and Maple V are registered trademarks of
 <____ ____>   Waterloo Maple Inc.
      |         Type ? for help.
```
> *Enter commands here. Exit with* **quit**, **done**, *or* **stop**.

Figure 2.1.   Command-Line Maple Interface

2.1.3 GUI Interface

This text focuses on the GUI interface of Maple, as shown with annotations in Figure 2.2:

- <u>Menu Bar</u>: Select commands with your mouse or the Alt key.
- <u>Tool Bar</u>: Click on these icons for shortcuts. Icons change for text, plots, and help.
- <u>Context Bar</u>: Change input and output formats, halt execution, and edit commands.
- <u>Maple Worksheet</u>: Enter commands to produce output.
- <u>Maple Workspace</u>: Open multiple worksheets and help windows.
- <u>Window Operations</u>: Click on the title-bar icons for resizing, iconifying, and closing.

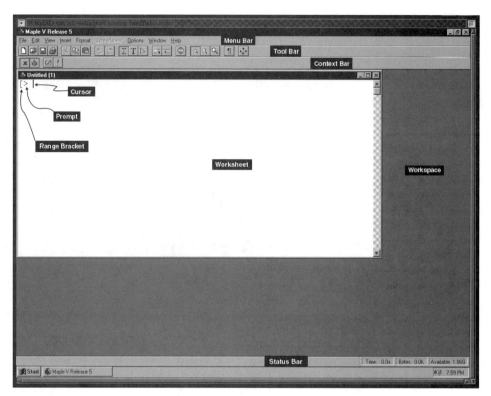

Figure 2.2. Maple Window

PROFESSIONAL SUCCESS: LEARNING ABOUT MAPLE

No matter how exciting and engaging Maple, or any material, may be, the nitty-gritty details might drag you down. But, learning need not bore you! Pique your interest and motivation with these tips:

❑ Familiarize yourself with the text:

Successful professionals never know everything. They just know where to look. Quickly flip though all chapters and appendices. Compare your course syllabus with the organization of the text.

❑ Learn the notation:

Thoroughly understand all notation! Otherwise, lost shall you ever be!

❑ Set goals:

Carefully read your assignments and text, but never try to learn everything at once! Attempt only a few sections at a time.

❑ Practice reading:

Learning requires both *understanding* and *practice*. Study the text and practice the commands. After reviewing the notation, skim the text a few times. Periodically remind yourself of chapter objectives. Improve your retention by rereading the material.

❑ Practice implementing:

Follow the suggested examples in the book. Always try to understand the reasoning behind each exercise, and guess the possible output before attempting the commands. Read the text above and below each command for explanations of syntax and behavior.

❑ Be Patient!

Expect some frustration that will eventually subside. With enough practice and patience, you can learn almost anything in this world.

PRACTICE!

1. Locate and activate Maple on your system. Which version do you use?
2. Select <u>H</u>elp→<u>N</u>ewUser'sTour for a quick overview. Also, review Appendix B.
3. Select <u>H</u>elp→<u>B</u>alloonHelp. Point your mouse on an icon and on a menu. What happens?
4. Check if <u>F</u>ile→<u>A</u>utoSaveSettings is set. What does this option perform?
5. Open a new worksheet with <u>F</u>ile→<u>N</u>ew. Now close the worksheet.
6. Open the Help Browser.
7. Select Worksheet Interface . . . Reference . . . Menus . . . Standard Menus in the Help Browser. What is the role of the <u>W</u>indow menu?
8. Now, close the Help Browser.

2.2 MAPLE INPUT AND OUTPUT

The Maple *worksheet* provides your main interface for communicating and working with Maple. This section introduces important features of the worksheet.

2.2.1 Help

To find help on a Maple command, enter **?command** at the Maple prompt (>) for help on a command name called **command**:

- First, type a question mark (**?**) followed by the command name **command**.
- Next, press the Enter key (⏎).

For instance, for help on the **sqrt** command, you would type **?sqrt** and then press ⏎ at the prompt. Also, review Appendix B for information on help.

2.2.2 Moving Around Your Worksheet

Point and click the mouse, or press the arrow keys to change the position of the cursor. Avoid moving the cursor with the Backspace, Del, and ⏎ keys. Advanced users should investigate **?hotmac**, **?hotunix**, or **?hotwin** for keyboard shortcuts.

2.2.3 Maple Input

Enter *Maple input* after the Maple prompt, which is the right angle bracket (>):

[> *Enter Maple input here. But never type the Maple prompt (>)!*

Maple input consists of commands and mathematical expressions that Maple executes and evaluates. Maple displays all executable input in red.

2.2.4 Input Modes

Maple provides two input methods—*Maple Notation* and *Standard Math*—as shown in Table 2-1:

- <u>Maple Notation</u>: Input is one dimensional. Maple reproduces keyboard-character input for mathematical expressions. Terminate input with a semi-colon (**;**) or colon (**:**)
- <u>Standard Math</u>: Input is two dimensional. Maple converts keyboard-character input into typeset textbook notation. Terminate input by pressing ⏎ twice.

TABLE 2-1 Maple Input Modes

INPUT	PROMPT	EXAMPLE
Maple Notation	[>		(a+b)/c
Standard Math	[> ❓	$\dfrac{a+b}{c}$

2.2.5 Choosing Input Modes

This text employs Maple Notation. You may switch input modes for a particular expression by first highlighting that expression with your mouse. You can then either:

- Select the Notation/Math Toggle icon 🅇, or
- Press the right mouse button, and select or unselect StandardMath.

You can also set a default mode with Options→InputDisplay:

- Choose either MapleNotation or StandardMath, then
- Press ↵ at the Maple prompt (>) to activate the new mode.

Maple preserves your choice for future sessions if you have selected File→AutoSave Settings. Consult **?worksheet[expressions]** for more information.

2.2.6 Maple Output

After you enter commands, Maple executes input and produces results called **Maple output**, which is shown in blue. Maple produces some output, like the symbols Σ, lim, and ∂, is written in black. To see an example of the output produced by Maple, compute the sum 1 + 1:

STEP 1:
MAPLE INPUT
AND OUTPUT

Practice with input and output.

> 1+1;↵   *RED INPUT: Enter* 1+1; *and then press Return to evaluate the expression* 1+1.

2   *BLUE OUTPUT: Maple produces the output* 2.

Note that you should never terminate help commands like **?command** with a semicolon or a colon.

2.2.7 Error Messages

What happens if you forget to enter a semicolon or colon?

STEP 2:
ERROR
MESSAGES

What should you do if Maple reports an error?

> 1+1↵   *Enter* 1+1 *without a terminating semicolon or colon.*

Warning, premature end of input   *Maple reports a common error message.*

To fix the error, place the cursor *after* the input **1+1**. Next, type a semicolon and then press ↵. Maple then computes 2.

2.2.8 Multiple Inputs

Semicolons and colons terminate and separate input command statements:

- A semicolon (**;**) signals the end of input. Maple evaluates the input and *shows* the output.

- A colon (**:**) tells Maple to not only perform the computations, but to *suppress* the results. However, Maple still stores the results from assignments. (See Section 2.4 and Chapter 4.)

You can separate commands on the same input line by using semicolons and colons:

STEP 3:
MULTIPLE
INPUTS

> 1+1: 1+2;↵   *Enter more than one input command on the same line.*

                                               Compute 1+1 but do not show output. Next, compute and show 1+2.

                      3   *The colon suppresses the output of 1+1.*

Consult **?separator** for more information.

2.2.9 Text

Document your work! ***Text*** is composed of inert, nonexecutable input. Enter text by moving the cursor one space to the left of the prompt, as shown in Figure 2.3. The worksheet is now primed for text entry, so start typing. When you are finished, press ↵ and a new Maple prompt (>) will appear. You can also enter text by selecting Insert→ Te̱xtInput or the text icon **T**. However, Maple does not insert a new prompt after you press ↵. Click on the icon ▷ to get a new prompt. (The next section shows you how to combine the new execution group that forms.) Beware that *text* differs from *Maple text*, a format in which you save worksheets.

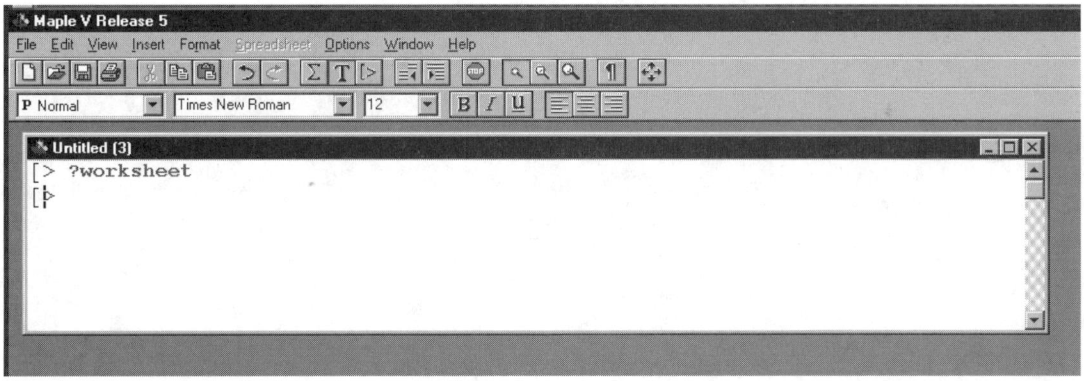

Figure 2.3. Entering Text

Practice the use of text by creating two text lines, using the method shown in Figure 2.3. Each time you press ↵, a prompt will appear:

STEP 4:
ENTERING
TEXT

I am text.↵   *Move the cursor left one space. Enter this line.*

I am text like the line above me.↵   *Move the cursor left one space. Enter this line.*

>   *The prompt appears each time you press ↵.*

To underline portions of the text, highlight the text with your mouse. Next, press the underline icon **U** while in text mode. Select F̱ormat for more formatting word-processing functions. Also, consult **?worksheet[documenting]**.

2.2.10 Comments

You may mix commentary and Maple input with the number-sign symbol (**#**). Maple ignores input following the **#**:

STEP 5: ENTERING MAPLE COMMENTS

Enter # to mix comments and command input.

```
> 1*2; # Use "*" for multiplication↵
```
Evaluate 1×2, and include a comment.

2

Maple produced output 2, but ignored the comment.

2.2.11 Inert Math

You can also convert any executable, **active** Maple input into **inert math**, a nonexecutable form of input that is shown in black. To do so, highlight the active input shown in red, and click on the leaf icon ⬛. Click the same icon to return the input to an active, executable state.

2.2.12 Editing

To perform editing functions, use the mouse to highlight portions of your worksheet. Then, select <u>E</u>dit or the Tool Bar icons for many editing operations. You can also delete text with the Del and Backspace keys.

PRACTICE!

9. Find Maple's on-line glossary inside the Help Browser.

10. Enter $\frac{1}{2}$ in both Maple Notation and Standard Math notation. (Hint: Try the forward-slash key to create the fraction.)

11. Ensure that Maple notation is the default input option.

12. Evaluate $1 + 2 + 3$ with Maple.

13. Evaluate $1 + 1$ and 2×2 on the same input line. Suppress the output of $1 + 1$.

14. Repeat Step 1. Add the comment **# I am a comment** on the input line.

2.3 EXECUTION GROUPS

This section introduces how Maple collects input, text, and output together in execution groups.

2.3.1 Paragraphs

Maple considers each line of text, input, and output as a **paragraph**:

- Add lines by selecting <u>I</u>nsert→<u>P</u>aragraph followed by either <u>B</u>efore or <u>A</u>fter.
- Delete lines with <u>E</u>dit→<u>D</u>eleteParagraph or the Del and Backspace keys.

To display the paragraph symbol (¶) on each line, select the ¶ icon or <u>V</u>iew→ Show<u>I</u>nvisibleCharacters. Other normally invisible characters will appear as well.

2.3.2 Creating Execution Groups

Execution groups collect paragraphs together. Execution groups can consist of single or multiple paragraphs. Most commonly, input lines are followed by output lines inside one execution group. Range brackets connect groups as shown in Figure 2.4:

- Select View→ShowGroupRanges to show or remove brackets.
- Press ↵ or the icon ▷ to create a new execution group.
- Select Insert→ExecutionGroup followed by BeforeCursor or AfterCursor to insert a new group before or after the cursor.

Range Bracket

```
>  1+1;
        2
```

Maple Prompt
Maple Input
Maple Output

Figure 2.4.   Execution Group

2.3.3 Joining Execution Groups

Execution groups can include multiple input and output lines. For instance, first create the following execution group:

STEP 6:
INCLUDING
MORE
PARAGRAPHS

```
I am text.↵                     Create a basic execution group. First, add a text line.

>  1+1;↵                                                     Enter input.

            2                          Maple includes output inside the group.
```

Inside the next execution group that appears, enter **1+2**:

```
>  1+2;↵                       Compute 1+2 inside the second execution group.

            3                          Maple includes output inside the group.
```

Follow these steps to join the execution groups:

- Place the cursor in the first execution group, which has the input **1+1**.
- Then, select the menus Edit→SplitorJoin→JoinExecutionGroups.

STEP 6:
(continued)
JOINING
EXECUTION
GROUP

```
I am text.                This execution group is joined from the previous two groups.

>  1+1;                              Press ↵ to rearrange the input and output.

            2                 Each input statement creates a separate output paragraph.

>  1+2;                      Maple evaluates input from left to right and top to bottom.

            3                 Each input statement creates a separate output paragraph.
```

- Now, press ⏎ to reorganize the input and output lines. Maple evaluates each input statement in sequence, from top to bottom:

STEP 6:
(continued)
JOINING
EXECUTION
GROUP

⌐ I am text.   *This execution group is joined from the previous two groups.*

> `1+1;`⏎   *Press ⏎ to rearrange the input and output.*

> `1+2;`   *Maple evaluates input from left to right and top to bottom.*

               2   *Each input statement creates a separate output paragraph.*

               3   *Each input statement creates a separate output paragraph.*

PRACTICE!

15. Select <u>V</u>iew→Show<u>I</u>nvisibleCharacters or the ¶ icon. What do you see? Now turn off the invisible-character display.

16. Create an execution group with three paragraphs of text and no Maple input.

17. Evaluate 1 + 1, 1 − 1, and 1 × 2 on separate paragraphs in the same execution group.

2.4 USING MAPLE

Maple provides powerful tools for solving problems. This section provides a brief overview of common commands and important Maple features that are discussed more thoroughly later in the text.

2.4.1 Expressions

Mathematical expressions like $y = 2x$ combine numbers and symbols with *operators*. You have already used some of the basic arithmetic operators: **+**, **-**, *****, and **/**. Maple denotes symbols, like variables x and y, as *names*. Chapter 3 reviews names and operators.

2.4.2 Case Sensitivity

Maple distinguishes between uppercase and lowercase letters: Maple is ***case sensitive***! For instance, never enter **a** when you mean **A**!

2.4.3 Functions

Maple functions have the syntax: ***func(arg1,arg2,...)***. Find help on any function called ***func*** by entering **?*func*** at the Maple prompt. For an example use of the help operator **?**, enter **?sqrt** for help on **sqrt**, Maple's square root function:

STEP 7:
INTRODUCING
FUNCTIONS

⌐   *Find help for a basic function.*

  `?sqrt`⏎   *Find help on* **sqrt**. *Maple pops up a window that discusses* **sqrt**.

Now, enter **sqrt(*expr*)** to find the square root of ***expr***:

STEP 8:
SQUARE ROOT
FUNCTION

Experiment with **sqrt**.

> **sqrt(4);**↵   *Find the square root of* 4.

        2   *Maple succeeded! For more fun, enter* **sqrt(x^2)**.

Chapter 6 introduces many functions. Also, review Appendix D after you have become more familiar with Maple.

2.4.4 Assignments

An ***assignment*** stores an expression for a value or formula inside a Maple variable name. Maple assignments have the syntax ***name*** **:=** ***expr***, where ***name*** stores ***expr***. Never use a lone equals sign (=) for assignments, and always add a colon (:) before the equals sign! Names resemble variables, symbols that act as placeholders for other values:

STEP 9:
INTRODUCING
ASSIGNMENTS

Use **:=** *for assignments. Never use just* **=**!

> **A := 1+1;**↵   *Compute* 1+1. *Then, store the value inside name A.*

        $A := 2$ *Maple reports your assignment.*

Maple now considers all future occurrences of A as the value 2. Thus, you can check the value of A by entering the name **A** as input:

STEP 10:
CHECKING
VALUES

Enter a variable name to check its value.

> **A;**↵   *What value is A assigned?*

        2   *Maple reports the value of* A.

Beware that opening a new worksheet may not erase all assignments. Instead, enter **restart** to begin a new Maple session that erases previous assignments. Chapter 4 delves deeper into the nature of Maple assignments.

PRACTICE!

> **18.** Assign x to the value 2. Assign X to the value 1.
>
> **19.** Check the values of x and X. Why should x and X report different output?
>
> **20.** Now, enter **restart**. Check the values of x and X. What happened?

2.4.5 Graphics

Equations may be visualized with ***plots***, which are graphs generated by Maple. For instance, plot the equation $y = f(x) = 2x + 3$ for $0 \leq x \leq 5$. To do so, enter an expression of the form **plot(*expr*, *ranges*, *options*)** such that you:

- Enter the expression $2x + 3$ as **2*x+3**. Never enter both sides of the equation, **y=2*x+3**, for plotting.
- Enter the interval of the independent variable $0 \le x \le 5$ as the range **x=0..5**.
- Display a title made up of a string with the option **title="plot title"**.

STEP 11: BASIC PLOTTING

Plot a two-dimensional equation.

```
> plot(2*x+3,x=0..5,title="Test Plot");↵
```
Plot $f(x) = 2x + 3$ along $0 \le x \le 5$.

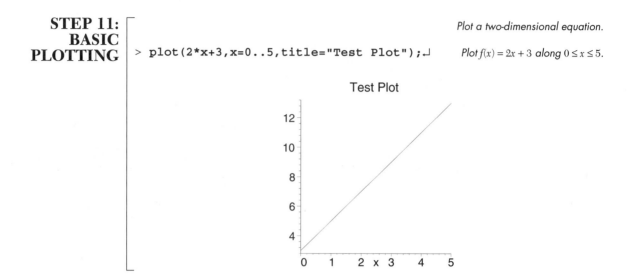

If a separate plot window appears, select the following menu options: Option→ PlotDisplay→Inline. Also, Maple VR4 requires backquote characters instead of double quotes, as in **title='Test Plot'** as discussed in Appendix H.

PRACTICE!

21. Assign y to the expression $2\sqrt{x}$.

22. Plot y for $0 \le x \le 100$. Title your plot "Hello, I am a plot."

2.4.6 Worksheet Management

Select File for worksheet operations, like opening and closing. Appendix C reviews how to save and print Maple worksheets. Beware that saving work in Maple worksheet "mws" format creates a file that only Maple understands. Never print files saved in "mws" format! See Appendix C for further details.

PRACTICE!

23. Save the open worksheet as **test1.mws**.

24. Open a new worksheet. Save it as **test2.mws**.

25. Print **test1.mws** to a PostScript file **test1.ps**. Can you load **test1.ps** into Maple? Can you directly print **test1.mws**?

2.5 APPLICATION: ZEBRA MUSSELS

This section demonstrates a brief example from the fields of environmental engineering and science that illustrates key Maple commands.

2.5.1 Background

Assume that the exponential-growth equation

$$P = P_0 e^{(rt)} \tag{2-1}$$

governs the zebra-mussel population in a given body of water. Parameter P_0 represents the initial size of the colony, which has a growth rate r over time period t.

2.5.2 Problem

Given a growth rate $r = 0.1$ (years^{-1}), what relative population growth P does the model in Eq. 2-1 predict in a span of ten years?

2.5.3 Methodology

Inside Maple, retype pertinent parameters and data:

**STEP 12:
RESTATE**

Label each parameter as Maple text for reference.

P = population and P0 = initial population
(units = critters/meter^2)↵

Enter text.

r = growth rate (1/year) and t = time (year)↵

Enter text.

In larger reports, consider using typeset equations and paragraph styles for a more professional look.

Next, state your known data and assign Maple variables to these values:

**STEP 13:
SEPARATE**

Assign known values.

> **r:=0.9;**↵

Assign the name r to the value 0.9.

$$r := .9$$

Maple reports your assignment.

Now, assign the model in Eq. 2-1. Using an assignment statement, place the unknown variable P on the left and the function on the right. Express the function e^{rt} as $\exp(rt)$:

**STEP 14:
MODEL**

Build your model, which is the equation that you will solve or evaluate.

> **P:=(P0)*(exp(r*t));**↵

Assign the name P to the equation $P_0\exp(rt)$.

Use parentheses to distinguish equation elements P0 and $\exp(rt)$. Also, do not forget the multiplication operator (*).

$$P := P0\mathbf{e}^{.9t}$$

The function $\exp(x)$ is also written as e^x, as discussed in Chapter 6. For now, just duplicate the input written here.

Since the problem has not provided an initial zebra-mussel count, divide the equation by P_0, and plot P/P_0 for the given time interval $0 \leq t \leq 10$ years:

STEP 15:
SOLVE

```
> plot(P/P0,t=0..10,title="Exponential Growth");
```

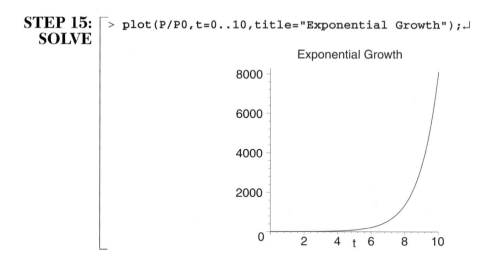

Finally, find the relative increase at ten years:

STEP 16:
REPORT

Answer the problem.

```
> t:=10: P/P0;
```
Assign t to the value 10, but suppress the output.

8103.083928

Maple's evaluation of the expression $\frac{P}{P_0}$.

2.5.4 Solution

After 10 years, the zebra-mussel population will have grown to about 8000 times the original population, according to the chosen model. The exponential function models rapid and compounding changes, as that of zebra-mussel reproduction. However, this model provides only a crude approximation. Numerous factors that were not represented in the model contribute to the growth and death of zebra mussels.

SUMMARY

This chapter has provided an overview of key Maple features. The most common Maple interface, GUI Maple, uses worksheets inside a main workspace for computations. The user enters Maple input to evaluate output. Execution groups collect input and output. Various forms of input include assignments and plots. Assignments store values inside variables. Find on-line help with the help operator **?**. When printing Maple files, never confuse Maple worksheet format with PostScript format.

KEY TERMS

active input
assignment
case sensitive
execution group
inert math

Maple input
Maple Notation
Maple output
paragraph
plot

Standard Math notation
text
worksheet

Problems

Write your answers to the problems inside Maple worksheets. Be neat, and beware of case-sensitive variable names! Use the following example format:

Problem 0.1

Solve for 1+1.

```
> 1+1;
```

$$2$$

1. Enter the following information on the top of your worksheet:

   HOMEWORK 1

   Name:

   Section:

   Date:

   Hint: Use four text lines inside an execution group.

2. What is Maple?
3. Specify three uses of Maple.
4. What is an execution group?
5. Indicate the menu selections to insert a section and a subsection.
6. How do active and inert input differ?
7. How do Maple input and output differ?
8. How do Standard Math and Maple Notation differ?
9. Find help on Maple "help" using the ? command.
10. Find help on Maple names.
11. Suppose that you save your worksheet to **hw1.mws** using the menu-selection sequence File→SaveAs. . . . Assume that you then exit Maple. How can you print the contents of **hw1.mws**?
12. Assign the name *B1* to the value 10.
13. Assign the name *B2* to the expression $1 + \frac{1}{2}$.
14. Evaluate $1 + 2$, $1 - 2$, 1×2, and $1 \div 2$ using Maple.
15. Start a fresh Maple session. Enter the following Maple input:

    ```
    [ > A:=2:
    ```

    Generate output from the following input:

    ```
    [ > A; a;
    ```

    Does Maple report the same values for *A* and *a*? Why or why not?

16. Assign *B3* to the expression $\dfrac{100}{10}$, but prevent Maple from showing the output. Next, display the value of *B3* in a new execution group.

17. Find help on the sine function. Next, compute $\sin\dfrac{\pi}{2}$. (Hint: You must represent π with `Pi`.)

18. Plot $y = x^2$ for $0 \le x \le 2$. Label your plot "Parabola."

19. Plot $y = mx + b$ for $m = 1$ and $b = -1$ over the range $-2 \le x \le 2$.

20. Produce execution groups in Maple that appear as the following groups. Make your execution groups look like what you see written below:

Problem 2.20a

```
> 1+1:
```

```
> 'Hello';
```

```
> EQN:= y=m*x+b:
```

```
> A:=10:
```

$$\textit{Hello}$$

Problem 2.20b

Hello, I am just text.

Now, try **boldface** and *italic* styles.

```
> # Hello, I am just a comment.
```

Problem 2.20c

Use the backslash (\) as a continuation character for Maple input:

```
> 1 + 2 +\
```

```
> 3 + 4;
```

$$10$$

Problem 2.20d

Here is an embedded inert equation: $\dfrac{a+b}{c}$. Hint: Investigate the Insert menu selections.

Here is the same equation, $\dfrac{a+b}{c}$, but now it's active input. Hint: Investigate the icons on the context bar.

$$\frac{a+b}{c}$$

Problem 2.20e

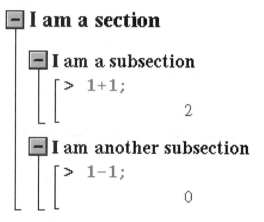

3

Maple Language

3.1 INTRODUCTION

Understanding how Maple interprets commands will greatly assist your work. This section introduces key features of the Maple language.

3.1.1 Maple Language

Maple commands constitute a ***language***. Whereas human languages combine words, punctuation, grammar, and meaning to communicate concepts, Maple's "words" include commands, functions, and other symbols formed from standard keyboard characters. Other symbols "punctuate" Maple commands. Other elements of language include *syntax* and *semantics*. In Maple, syntax governs the "grammar" of command entry. Semantics supplied by Maple's kernel give "meaning" for producing output.

3.1.2 Elements

The following items make up the written-language elements of Maple: *characters*, *tokens*, *token separators*, and *escape characters*.

3.1.3 Characters

Maple uses standard keyboard characters:

- Uppercase letters: A B C D E F G H I J K L M N O P Q R S T U V W X Y Z
- Lowercase letters: a b c d e f g h i j k l m n o p r s t u v w x y z
- Digits: 0 1 2 3 4 5 6 7 8 9
- Miscellaneous characters: @ # $ % ~ _ | ^ * + - = & , . ? ! : ; " ' ` / ( ) [ ] { } < > *space*

OBJECTIVES

After reading this chapter, you should be able to:

- Distinguish elements of the Maple language
- Classify Maple statements
- Illustrate common Maple operators
- Explain how to build expressions
- Describe Maple's variable-naming conventions

23

	230	231	232	233	234	235	236	237
0	2300	2310	2320	2330	2340	2350	2360	2370
1		2311	2321	2331	2341	2351	2361	2371
2	2302	2312	2322	2332	2342	2352	2362	2372
3	2303	2313	2323	2333	2343	2353	2363	2373
4	2304	2314	2324	2334	2344	2354	2364	2374
5	2305	2315	2325	2335	2345	2355	2365	2375
6	2306	2316	2326	2336	2346	2356	2366	2376
7	2307	2317	2327	2337	2347	2357	2367	2377
8	2308	2318	2328	2338	2348	2358	2368	2378
9	2309	2319	2329	2339	2349	2359	2369	2379
A	230A	231A	232A	233A	234A	235A	236A	237A
B	230B	231B	232B	233B	234B	235B	236B	
C	230C	231C	232C	233C	234C	235C	236C	
D	230D	231D	232D	233D	234D	235D	236D	
E	230E	231E	232E	233E	234E	235E	236E	
F	230F	231F	232F	233F	234F	235F	236F	

Unicode provides a standard for using 16 bits of space to represent 65,536 different characters. Though it is not currently implemented in Maple, imagine being able to type different languages, symbols, and pictures without changing fonts! Reproduced with permission of Unicode, Inc.

PROFESSIONAL SUCCESS: CHECK YOUR RESULTS!

Never blindly trust computers. Consider the following story: For one assignment, my students had to estimate a person's weight given a random sampling of height and weight data. Using statistical formulas, the students determined models to predict individual weights from the data. Unfortunately, some students did not check their work. Some reports estimated individual weights as averaging over a relatively uncommon 500 pounds. A few students even determined that some people weigh −80,000 pounds! Perhaps in another universe people commonly achieve such stupendous weights, but not here. Worse yet, these students left no explanation for these "interesting" results.

How can you avoid making such mistakes? Respect the adage, "garbage in, garbage out." Often, a misplaced number or character can yield rather bizarre answers. Also, perhaps, a model might break the assumptions required by the computer's imple-

mentation. Computer-software bugs present even more insidious problems. Input data and output might appear reasonable, but inside lurks an error. Protect yourself by trying these tips:

- ❏ Think about the numbers that your program spits out.
- ❏ Run multiple test cases.
- ❏ Try different software packages and compare results among them.
- ❏ Test your results with manual methods found in textbooks whenever possible.
- ❏ Ask yourself, "Do the answers make sense physically?"
- ❏ Investigate Maple's **?verify** library.

Remember that engineers and scientists bear the responsibility to produce safe, reliable solutions.

If you are unfamiliar with some of these character names, you should review Appendix A.

3.1.4 Tokens
Composed of characters, basic words and other symbols called *tokens* construct Maple commands. Maple's tokens include the following entities:

- *Reserved words*: reserved, unassignable command names. (See **?keyword**.)
- *Strings*: characters enclosed by double quotes (""). (See **?string**.)
- *Integers*: whole numbers that use the digits 0, 1, 2, 3, 4, 5, 6 , 7, 8, and 9. (See **?integer**.)
- *Punctuation*: symbols, like **;** and **( )**, that separate other tokens. (See Chapter 4.)
- *Operators*: symbols that perform mathematical tasks. (See Section 3.2.)
- *Names*: labels for functions, mathematical variables, and system variables. (See Section 3.3.)

3.1.5 Token Separators
Maple distinguishes language elements with token separators that include blank spaces, tabs, and new lines. Use as many token separators as you wish, but never break apart an element like the assignment operator (**:=**)!

3.1.6 Escape Characters
Consult **?help**, or **??**; **?comment**; **?backslash**, or **?**; and **?escape** (as in, **!***command*) for help on characters that perform special functions. For instance, entering **?***func* executes a search for help on *func* outside of the current worksheet.

3.1.7 Expressions

Expressions combine tokens. For instance, the equation $y = 2x$ states an expression that combines two names (x and y), two operators (= and *), and an integer (2) for a total of five tokens. Chapter 4 elaborates further on expression structure and building expressions from tokens.

3.1.8 Statements

Maple input is entered as ***statements***, which are Maple-language elements that resemble sentences and are composed of tokens and punctuation. Statements instruct Maple to perform tasks. Two common statement types include expression input and assignments:

[> ***expr;***   *Entering an expression instructs Maple to evaluate the expression.*

[> ***name := expr;***   *Assignments instruct Maple to store expressions as names.*

Other statements include programming constructs that employ many reserved words, as discussed in Appendix E. Overall, Maple classifies eight categories of statements: *expression, assignment, selection, repetition, reading, saving, quitting,* and *empty.* Investigate **?index[statement]** for more information about statement commands.

PRACTICE!

> 1. Identify the following pieces of input in terms of Maple-language elements:
>   1, +, **TEST**, **sin**, **and**, :, (), **"Test Plot"**.
> 2. Which portion of the input **1+1** is an expression? statement?
> 3. How does Maple classify **restart?**

3.2 OPERATORS

Mathematical symbols called ***operators*** perform assigned tasks, as shown in this section.

3.2.1 Arithmetic

Maple uses the common notation for arithmetic operations that Table 3-1 shows. Also, consult **?arithop** for more information on arithmetic operations. For instance, the expression 1 + 2 combines the integers 1 and 2 with the addition operator, the plus sign (+). Elements acted upon by operators are called ***operands***. For instance, try adding numbers together and dividing them:

STEP 17: ARITHMETIC OPERATORS

Practice using addition and division.

```
> restart;
```
Clear all previous assignments. (See Section 2.4.)

```
> 1 + 1/1 + 1/2 + 1/6 + 1/24;
```
Add fractions together. Remember to press ⏎ from now on!

$$\frac{65}{24}$$

Maple simplifies the result into a fractional form.

TABLE 3-1   Arithmetic Operators

OPERATION	SYMBOL	STANDARD MATH	MAPLE NOTATION
Exponentiation	^	$2^3 = 8$	2^3 2**3
Multiplication	*	$2 \times 3 = 6$	2*3
Division	/	$2 \div 3 = \frac{2}{3}$	2/3
Addition	+	$2 + 3 = 5$	2+3
Subtraction	–	$2 - 3 = -1$	2-3

3.2.2 Read Me!

Suppose you wish to multiply **a** by **b**. Never forget to specify operators! Never enter **ab**. Never enter **a(b)** or **(b)a** or **a(b)**. Never even think of entering **a times b**. However, *do* enter **a*b** or **b*a**. As discussed later, you can also surround an operand with parentheses, as in **(a)*b**, **a*(b)**, and **(a)*(b)**.

3.2.3 Miscellaneous Operators

Consult **?index[expression]** or **?operator** for a complete list of operators. Consult **?operators[binary]**, **?operators[unary]**, and **?operators [nullary]** for listings according to operator type. Consult **?define** for information on how to create customized operators.

PRACTICE!

4. In Maple Notation, determine the operators that the expression $-1 + 2^3$ employs.

5. Assign a to 1 and b to 2. Multiply a and b. Now, enter **ab**. Compare the two pieces of output.

6. Enter $4 \le 5$ and $5 \ge 4$ into Maple. Hint: Consult **?inequality**. Compare the two pieces of output.

3.2.4 Operator Precedence

Beware of **operator precedence**. Operator precedence dictates that certain operators always act upon expressions *before* other operators do. For example, multiplication and division precede addition and subtraction. Suppose you incorrectly enter the expression $\frac{1}{2+3}$ such that you ignore the rules of operator precedence:

STEP 18: TREAT OPERATORS WITH CARE!

```
> 1/2+3;
```

$$\frac{7}{2}$$

Deliberately generate wrong results.

Attempt to solve the problem $\frac{1}{2+3}$.

Why does Maple not produce $\frac{1}{5}$?

Surrounding **2 + 3** with parentheses enforces Maple's evaluation to produce $\frac{1}{5}$:

STEP 19: ENFORCE OPERATOR PRECEDENCE!

```
> 1/(2+3);
```

$$\frac{1}{5}$$

Now, generate correct results. Use parentheses to

solve the problem $\frac{1}{2+3}$.

Now you have the correct answer!

Always surround ambiguous expressions with parentheses, but never use square brackets (`[ ]`), curly braces (`{ }`), or angle brackets (`< >`) when you need parentheses! Consult `?operators[precedence]` and `?syntax` for more information.

3.2.5 Operator Associativity

Operator associativity resolves the treatment of operators that have equivalent precedence. Many operations are *left associative*, like subtraction (−), which means that they compute *left* to *right*.

For instance, consider the expression $1 - 2 - 3$. First, enter input without parentheses:

STEP 20:
OPERATOR
ASSOCIATIVITY

> `1-2-3;`

$$-4$$

Demonstrate how subtraction is left associative.

Subtract three numbers. Which order does Maple pick for the operations?

Maple automatically evaluates $(1 - 2) - 3 = -4$ by default.

Next, change the order of Maple's operations with by surrounding `2-3` with parentheses:

STEP 21:
OPERATOR
ASSOCIATIVITY

> `1-(2-3);`

$$2$$

Demonstrate how subtraction is left associative.

Subtract three numbers. Deliberately supply parentheses

Maple now evaluates $1 - (2 - 3) = 2$.

In fact, *non-associative* operators, such as exponentiation (`^`), require parentheses if the operators are used in conjunction with another operator. For instance, you must enter `2^(-2)` to express 2^{-2}.

PRACTICE!

> 7. Enter **restart**. What Maple input will produce the following output:
>
> $$\frac{a^2}{A + \dfrac{1}{a}}?$$
>
> 8. What happens if you enter `sin((a+b);`? What correction should you make?
> 9. Will `[1+3]/4` produce the same output as `(1+3)/4`? Why or why not?
> 10. Is `1^2^3` acceptable Maple input? Hint: Consult `?operators[precedence]`.

3.3 MAPLE NAMES

Equations, like $y = mx + b$, use letters as variables that represent parameters and uncertain quantities. Maple expressions are often constructed from such variables. This section reviews variable naming conventions.

3.3.1 Symbols

Keyboard characters form ***symbols***, which are words that build Maple's language. Maple symbols are constructed using lowercase letters (a-z), uppercase letters (A-Z), digits (0-9), and the underscore character (_). But, never use a digit as the first character of symbol!

You should also avoid using characters other than letters, digits, and the underscore inside a symbol. Consult **?type[symbol]** for further rules and information.

3.3.2 Names

Names are symbols with the additional property of *indexing* as discussed in later chapters. Available and assignable names resemble mathematical variables used for building and assigning expressions. Other names label functions and constants. When choosing names, follow rules for symbols and these additional rules:

- Remember that Maple is case sensitive!
- Avoid using the underscore (_) as the first character in a name.
- Create more complex symbols and names by surrounding any characters with backquotes (` `). See Section 3.3.5 for more details.

Examples of valid names include **A**, **A1**, **A11**, **A1A**, **A_1**, **a**, and **alpha**. Maple outputs a name that has no assigned value as just the name:

STEP 22:
NAMES

Practice using Maple names.

> `restart:`   *Restart your worksheet.*

> `AAA;`   *Check the value of name AAA.*

$$AAA$$ *Maple outputs just the name when the name has no assigned value.*

Beware that the older Maple VR4 considers strings and names as equivalent types as discussed in Appendix H. Consult **?name**, **?symbol**, **?type[name]**, and **?indexed** for a complete set of rules and more information.

3.3.3 Protected Names

Maple predefines certain names, called ***protected names***, for library functions, variables, and constants. You have already seen examples of protected names such as **sin**, **sqrt**, and **type**. Maple prevents protected names from assignments. How can you identify protection? Keep track of error messages:

STEP 23:
CHECK FOR
PROTECTED
NAMES

Check name protection with error messages.

> `D := 10;`   *Attempt to assign D to 10.*

`Error, attempting to assign to `D` which`   *Maple reports an error.*
`is protected`

Otherwise, you may check for protection with **type(*name*,protected)**:

STEP 24:
CHECK FOR
PROTECTED
NAMES

*Check name protection with **type**.*

> `type(D,protected);`   *Check if Maple protects D from assignment.*

$$true$$ *Maple confirms that D is protected.*

Also, try entering **?name** to see if Maple already uses **name** for a function or command name. Investigate **?protect**, **?unprotect**, and **?ininames** for further details.

3.3.4 Reserved Words

Maple does not consider reserved words as protected names. Instead, reserved words form many operators and belong to Maple's *statements*, which are discussed in the next chapter. However, you will receive similar error messages if you attempt to assign a reserved word to an expression:

Check reserved word protection with error messages.

> **STEP 25:**
> **CHECK FOR**
> **RESERVED**
> **WORDS**

```
> and := 10;
```

Attempt to assign and to 10.

```
reserved word 'and' unexpected
```

Maple reports an error.

Consult **?keyword** for a listing of Maple's reserved words that you cannot assign.

3.3.5 Backquotes

Back Quote

To create more complex and descriptive names, surround characters with backquotes, as in **'A'**. Backquotes help you create names that Maple would normally consider illegal, such as **'1A'** and **'Even I am a name!'**. Such names are also available for assignments:

Use backquotes (` `) to create complex names.

> **STEP 26:**
> **ASSIGN NAMES**
> **WITH**
> **BACKQUOTES**

```
> 'David I. Schwartz':='Civil Engineer';
```

Assign a "backquoted" name.

$$David\ I.\ Schwartz := Civil\ Engineer$$

Maple reports your assignment.

(And yes, I am indeed a Civil Engineer.)

Beware of cases when you surround a name with backquotes, and that name is not protected or reserved. Maple will automatically replace that name with the actual name not written with backquotes. For instance, compare the names **A** and **'A'**:

Backquotes do not change valid names.

> **STEP 27:**
> **CHECK NAMES**
> **WITH AND**
> **WITHOUT**
> **BACKQUOTES**

```
> 'A':=10;
```

Assign the name 'A' := 10.

$$A := 10$$

Maple shows that A has been assigned to 10.

```
> A;
```

Check the value of the name A entered without backquotes.

$$10$$

Maple automatically replaced 'A' with the equivalent name A.

You can also use backquotes to assign some reserved words, but, in general, you should stick to unprotected and unreserved names. Note also that Maple VR4 considers backquoted names as strings—current versions of Maple do not.

PRACTICE!

11. Which of the following is a valid Maple name: **1** and/or **'1'**?
    Hint: Try **type(*expr*,name)**.
12. What input will generate *Success := Practice + Patience* as output?
13. Are the Maple names *Ira* and *ira* equivalent? Why or why not?
14. Does Maple protect A (**Alpha**) and B (**Beta**)?

3.4 APPLICATION: ENGINEERING ECONOMICS

This section introduces Maple assignments, naming, and arithmetic operations with an engineering-economics example.

3.4.1 Background

Engineers must often choose alternative plans based on economic decisions. In this section, you will calculate an item's *annual worth* (AW), which is a "leveled" annual payment that represents the item's yearly income and cost. AW converts single payments, like P (the present purchase price) and SV (the future salvage value), into an equivalent annual amount. Assuming a yearly interest rate i over an item's life cycle n, annual worth is calculated as

$$AW = (P)(A/P, i, n) + (SV)(A/F, i, n) + A, \tag{3-1}$$

where

$$(A/P, i, n) = \frac{(i)(1+i)^n}{(1+i)^n - 1} \tag{3-2}$$

and

$$(A/F, i, n) = \frac{i}{(1+i)^n - 1}. \tag{3-3}$$

- The factor $(A/P, i, n)$ converts a present value P into an annual cash flow A.
- The factor $(A/F, i, n)$ converts a future value F into an annual cash flow A.
- The lone A in Eq. 3-1 indicates operating costs that do not need conversion into annual amounts.

3.4.2 Problem

Determine the annual worth of a machine that has a purchase price of $72,000, an annual maintenance and labor cost of $1000, and a salvage value of $14,000, given an interest rate of 12% over a 10-year life cycle.

3.4.3 Methodology

First, distinguish the cash-flow values between negative cost and positive income:

STEP 28:
RESTATE

Label each parameter as Maple text for reference.

P (initial price) = −72000 and A (annual cost) = −1000
(these are cash "outflows")

SV (salvage value) = +14000 (this value is a cash "inflow")

i (interest rate) = 12%, n (life cycle) = 10 years

Arrange the steps in your solution to build the model in Eqs. 3-1, 3-2, and 3-3 without any preassigned values:

STEP 29:
MODEL

Build your model, the equation that you will evaluate.

```
> restart:
```
Restart Maple.

```
> AgivenP:=(i*(1+i)^n)/((1+i)^n-1):
```
Assign (A/P,i,n). Suppress the output.

```
> AgivenF:=(i)/((1+i)^n-1):
```
Assign (A/P,i,n). Suppress the output.

```
> AW:=(P)*AgivenP + (SV)*AgivenF + A;
```
Assign AW to (P)(A/P,i,n) + (SV)(A/F,i,n) + A.

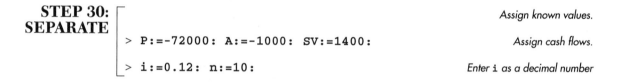

$$AW \; := \; \frac{Pi(1+i)^n}{(1+i)^n - 1} + \frac{SVi}{(1+i)^n - 1} + A$$

Maple reports the assignment.

Now, assign the cash-flow values:

STEP 30:
SEPARATE

Assign known values.

```
> P:=-72000: A:=-1000: SV:=1400:
```
Assign cash flows.

```
> i:=0.12: n:=10:
```
Enter i as a decimal number

You can now evaluate the annual worth simply by entering the variable name:

STEP 31:
SOLVE AND
REPORT

Solve the problem and report your solution.

```
> AW;
```
Evaluate the annual worth.

$$-13663.08199$$

Maple evaluated AW using the assigned values.

In the previous step, Maple automatically substitutes assigned values into your equation for *AW* when you enter **AW**. The next chapter discusses this process, which is called *full evaluation*, in more detail.

3.4.4 Solution

The annual worth of the machine is –$13,663.08. Look at **?finance** for built-in Maple functions that implement Step 29.

SUMMARY

In this chapter, features of the Maple language have been introduced. Keyboard characters form the operators, commands, functions, numbers, and other elements used in Maple. These elements form expressions and statements, which make up a majority of Maple input. Statements are commands that Maple evaluates. Two important elements, operators and names, help build expressions. Be wary of operator precedence. Use parentheses when operator precedence is unclear. Also, avoid assigning protected names and reserved words to anything.

KEY TERMS

expressions
integers
language
names
operands

operator associativity
operator precedence
operators
protected names
punctuation

reserved words
statements
strings
symbols
tokens

Problems

Note: You may wish to enter **restart:** at the beginning of each problem to avoid conflicting assignments with other problems.

1. Name four elements of the Maple command language.
2. Explain the difference between a mathematical expression and a Maple expression that you enter as a statement.
3. How do Maple names and symbols differ?
4. Assume that you discover the expression $[x(y + z)]$ inside another textbook. Enter this expression in Maple as input using Maple Notation. Hint: Should you avoid square brackets?
5. Demonstrate Maple input that will produce the following output. Hint: You may wish to frequently enter **restart** before each input:

3.5a A	3.5g $x + \dfrac{y}{z}$
3.5b $A + 1$	3.5h $\dfrac{x}{z} + y$
3.5c $A + \dfrac{1}{a}$	3.5i $A := x + 1$
3.5d A^2	3.5j $A \le B$
3.5e $A^3 + \dfrac{1}{2}$	3.5k $A = B$
3.5f $\dfrac{x+y}{z}$	3.5l $\sqrt{\sin(x)}$

6. Evaluate the following expressions using Maple. Hints: Be careful with operator precedence and associativity. Do not worry if Maple produces a fractional result:

3.6a $1+2+3$	3.6g $\left(\dfrac{1}{2}\right)\left(-\dfrac{3}{4}\right)$
3.6b $\dfrac{1}{2}+3$	3.6h $2\left(\dfrac{3}{1+4}\right)$
3.6c $1-2-3$	3.6i 2^3
3.6d $1-(2-3)$	3.6j $2^{(-1)}$
3.6e $1\times2\times3$	3.6k $2^{(2-4)}$
3.6f $2\div3$	3.6l $2^{\frac{-1}{5+\frac{4}{3}}}$

7. If you invert the factor $(A/F, i, n)$ will you determine the factor

$$(F/A, i, n) = \frac{(1+i)^n - 1}{i}?$$

Why or why not? Demonstrate with Maple. (Hint: Consult Section 3.4.)

8. Ceramics mix metallic and non-metallic compounds and have found wide-ranging use in branches of technology. A type of ceramic called *spinel* has the chemical compound $MgAl_2O_4$. Express the spinel compound using Maple names for each individual element. Hints: Use Maple input. For names with an index, use square brackets. For instance, enter **B[1]** to express B_1. See also **?name**.

9. Assume that an elastic bar is axially loaded with a force P, as shown in Figure 3.1.

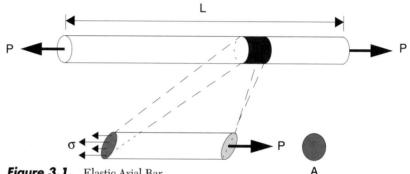

Figure 3.1. Elastic Axial Bar

Define the engineering strain ε as a body's change of length Δ divided by the original length L. Also, assume that the engineering stress σ on the bar uniformly divides the load P by the original area A before deformation. Thus,

$$\varepsilon = \frac{\Delta}{L} \quad \text{and} \quad \sigma = \frac{P}{A}.$$

Assume a linear relationship $\sigma = E\varepsilon$ between stress and strain, and solve these problems:

9a. Assign the stress σ to the expression $E\varepsilon$. Hint: Refer to Appendix A for names of Greek letters. E is called Young's Modulus.

9b. Assuming fundamental units of force and length, what units does stress have? What units does strain have? What units does Young's Modulus have? Hint: Consider the formulas for ε and σ.

9c. Plot stress versus strain for Young's Modulus $E = 10$. Hint: Plot the expression 10ε for $0 \le \varepsilon \le 1$.

9d. Substitute the expression for stress $\frac{P}{A}$ and that for strain $\varepsilon = \frac{\Delta}{L}$ into the relationship $\sigma = E\varepsilon$. (You can do this task by hand, but type the results as text in Maple.) You should determine that $P/A = E\Delta/L$.

9e. Assign the name EQN to the entire expression determined in the previous problem. Your assignment should have the form **EQN:=expr1=expr2**. (Hint: Include the equals sign! This expression is called an *equation*.)

9f. Solve for P using Maple. (Hints: Investigate **?solve**. Your input should be of the form **solve(EQN, something)**. Your output should be $\frac{E\Delta A}{L}$.)

9g. Hooke's Law for a spring states that $P = K\Delta$. Relate this equation to your results in the previous step. You should be able to show a formula for K in terms of E, A, and L. Compare and contrast the equations.

4

Expressions and Assignments

4.1 EXPRESSIONS

In the previous chapter, many elements of the Maple language were introduced. In this chapter, these elements are combined into expressions. This section further explains expressions.

4.1.1 Expression Elements

Maple-language elements provide building blocks for expressions. In turn, expressions help construct mathematical formulas. For instance, consider the mathematical expression $\sqrt{1 + \frac{1}{10}}$. The Maple expression statement **sqrt(1+1/10);** uses the function name **sqrt** along with operators (**+** and **/**) that connect the integers **1** and **10**. Parentheses (**()**) and the statement separator (**;**) punctuate this expression. Consult **?syntax** and **?index[expression]** for more information.

4.1.2 Expression Trees

Consider the decomposition of the expression $\sqrt{1 + \frac{1}{10}}$, as shown in Figure 4.1. Maple divides expressions into ***expression trees***, like the one shown in Figure 4.1. Operators and functions form nodes where expressions branch into subexpressions for each operation and function. Syntax rules, like operator precedence, govern the decomposition.

OBJECTIVES

After reading this chapter, you should be able to:

- Describe how to form expressions
- Decompose expressions into expression trees
- Assign names to expressions
- Unassign previously assigned names
- Describe automatic-simplification and full-evaluation rules

Microprocessor-based electronic control units (ECUs) monitor data from sensors and help physical devices react to changes. For instance, an ECU stored inside an automobile could warn a driver about a forgotten key left in the ignition. Devices such as the HP-TS5430, shown here, help design and test ECUs. Courtesy of Hewlett-Packard Company

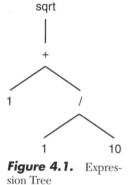

Figure 4.1. Expression Tree

4.1.3 Expression Palette

Besides traditional keyboard entry, you can also enter expressions using the palettes. To use the expression palette shown in Figure 4.2:

- First, select <u>V</u>iew→<u>P</u>alettes→<u>E</u>xpressionPalettes.
- Next, place your cursor in an execution group.
- Then, click on the icon that shows the expression-type that you wish to enter.

Maple will automatically type the selected expression for you. Depending on your current input mode, Maple will leave placeholders for subexpressions, such as names and values:

- Maple Notation: **%?**. Delete all **%?** placeholders and type in your desired subexpressions.
- Standard Math: ?. Type while a ? placeholder is highlighted. Press ↵ when finished typing.

Figure 4.2. Expression Palette

Practice using the expression palette with Maple Notation:

STEP 32:
EXPRESSION
PALETTE

Select <u>V</u>iew→<u>P</u>alettes→<u>E</u>xpressionPalette.

`> sqrt(%?);`   *Click on the $\sqrt{a}$ icon. Maple automatically types the input you see here.*

Delete the characters %?.   *Each placeholder is represented as %?.*

Type the number 2.   *You can also just directly type the number 2 as input.*

Press ↵ after you see the input `sqrt(2);`.   *You can also go back and edit your input as you normally would.*

$$\sqrt{2}$$ *Maple reports the output.*

Note that you can use the Tab key to jump between placeholders. For more information, consult **?palette**.

PRACTICE!

1. Which of the following Maple inputs is an expression: **x=10**, **x**, **10**, **sqrt(10+x/(10-x))**? Hint: Consult **?equation**.
2. Is the input **x:=10** an expression?

4.2 ASSIGNMENT STATEMENTS

Assigning names to long expressions lessens the amount of typing that must be done and improves the clarity of tasks. This section demonstrates rules and tips for assigning names to expressions.

4.2.1 Assigning Names

Maple's general assignment statement **name:=expression** stores **expression** inside **name**. After an assignment is entered, Maple replaces each instance of **name** with **expression**. For example, assign the name A to the value 1:*

STEP 33:
ASSIGNMENT

Practice assigning expressions to names.

`> A := 1;`   *Assign the name A to the value 1.*

$$A := 1$$ *Maple evaluates your assignment.*

Note that you should never enter assignments in reverse order (e.g., **1:=A**)! When used for assignments, Maple names are sometimes called **variables**, which are quantities that vary in value. Maple provides different kinds of variables, as discussed in the next chapter. Consult **?:=** and **?assign** for more rules of syntax.

4.2.2 Checking Names

After Step 33 is performed, Maple treats all future instances of A as 1. Recall that expressions form valid Maple statements. Therefore, you can check **name**'s current value simply by entering **name**:

*I call the assignment **name := expr**, "assign *name* to *expr*," to stay consistent with the terminology used in *Maple V: Learning Guide* (see Bibliography). Others might prefer to say, "assign *expr* to *name*," which is common when speaking of programming. Either approach will suffice for Maple.

STEP 34: CHECKING ASSIGNMENTS

> *Practice checking your assignment statements.*

```
> A;
```
Be sure first to have entered `A:=1`*. Check the value of the name* A.

$$1$$

The expression 1 *is stored inside* A.

Until you reassign or remove the value of *A*, Maple uses *only* the assigned value 1 for *A*:

STEP 35: MAPLE REMEMBERS ASSIGNMENTS

> *Maple replaces assigned names with assigned values.*

```
> A+2;
```
Form an expression using the name A.

$$3$$

Maple replaced A *with the value* 1.

Consult **?assigned**, **?anames**, and **?unames** for more information on checking assignments.

4.2.3 Assign and Equal Are Different!

Expressions built with the equals sign (=) are *equations*, not assignments! Equations are a specific type of expression, as discussed in Chapter 5. So, what happens if you enter equals (=) instead of the assign operator (:=)?

STEP 36: EQUATIONS ARE NOT ASSIGNMENTS!

> *Equations will not assign expressions.*

```
> restart;
```
Clear all current assignments.

```
> test = 1;
```
The input `test=1` *is an expression, not an assignment.*

$$test = 1$$

Maple reports the expression.

```
> test;
```
Check the value of test.

$$test$$

Maple reports the expression.

Assign *test* by entering **test:=1** instead!

" ◄	Double Quote
' ◄	Forward Quote

4.2.4 Unassigning Names

Once assigned, a name remains assigned until the name is assigned to another value, or the name is cleared. **Unassigning** removes any previously assigned expression stored in a name. Unassign **name** by surrounding **name** with forward quotes, as in **name := 'name'**:

STEP 37: ASSIGN A NAME

> *Store an expression inside a name.*

```
> A:=1;
```
Assign the name A *to the value* 1.

$$A := 1$$

Maple evaluates the assignment.

<table>
<tr><td>**STEP 38:**
UNASSIGN
A NAME</td><td>`> A:='A';`

$A := A$</td><td>*Use forward quotes to remove an assigned expression from a name.*

Unassign the name A.

Unassigning A *removed the stored expression.*</td></tr>
</table>

<table>
<tr><td>**STEP 39:**
CHECK
A NAME</td><td>`> A;`

A</td><td>*Check the current value of a name.*

Is A *assigned to any value?*

No: Unassigning A *cleared its value.*</td></tr>
</table>

Consult **?unassign** and **?evaln** for alternative approaches to unassigning variables.

4.2.5 Maple Quotes
Quotes in Maple are confusing. Worksheets and help windows show quotes in different styles:

- Forward quotes: ', ', '
- Backquotes: `, `
- Double quotes: ", ","

Consult **?quotes** to review the differences between the respective uses of these types of quotes.

PRACTICE!

3. Explain the difference between the input statements `J=72` and `J:=72`.
4. Assign the name *J* to the expression 72. Check the value of *J*.
5. Now, unassign *J*. Check the value of *J*. Was the value cleared?

4.3 ASSIGNMENTS AND WORKSHEETS

Assigned names may conflict with other assignments on different worksheets during the same Maple session. This section presents methods for efficient worksheet management.

4.3.1 Restart
The **restart** command resets Maple worksheets and removes all assignments and loaded library packages:

<table>
<tr><td>**STEP 40:**
ASSIGN
A NAME</td><td>`> A:=1;`

$A := 1$</td><td>*Store an expression inside a name.*

Assign the name A *to the value* 1.

Maple evaluates the assignment.</td></tr>
</table>

STEP 41: RESTART

> restart;

> A;

   A

Enter `restart` *to restart Maple sessions without exiting.*

Restart Maple. All assignments are erased.

Check the value of A.

All assignments were erased.

PROFESSIONAL SUCCESS: MANAGING ASSIGNMENTS

How Maple "remembers" assignments is confusing. Worksheets show only input and output without an indication of when computations were entered. So, keep track of statement order! The following example demonstrates the danger if you do forget.

Initiate a small Maple session. Create four empty execution groups. Next, *type* these input lines without entering the statements:

```
[> A := 1:    #1

[> A := 'A': #2

[> B := A:    #3

[> B;         #4
```

What input order will assign *B* to the value *1*? Enter statements in the order #2, #3, #1, and #4. Such situations might arise when you forget your statement entry order. Since Maple stores the most recent assignment, unexpected results often arise when one does not keep track of this order.

If Maple reports bizarre results, check for missing assignments or unassignments. If you still lose track of assignments, try these tips:

- ❏ Select Edit→Execute→Worksheet to enter all input statements from top to bottom.
- ❏ Enter **anames()** to see a list of all currently assigned variables.
- ❏ Frequently check the current values of your names.
- ❏ Unassign names before assigning new expressions.
- ❏ Look for case-sensitive names and missing operators.
- ❏ Use parallel worksheets.
- ❏ Delete everything and enter **restart**, only as a last resort, of course.

4.3.2 Kernel Modes

During a new session, opening new worksheets does not necessarily restart your Maple session! Two kernel modes determine how worksheets share name assignments:

- *Shared-kernel mode*: Worksheets share all assignments, regardless of where the statements are entered. Entering **restart** in any worksheet erases all assignments from all worksheets.
- *Parallel-kernel mode*: Worksheets operate independently and do not share assignments with other worksheets. In this mode, **restart** only affects the worksheet in which **restart** was entered.

Consult **?configuring** for more details.

4.3.3 Dittos

Maple employs *nullary operators* for **dittos**: %, %%, and %%%. Dittos reissue previous expressions:

STEP 42:
DITTO

Shortcuts for reissuing expressions.

> `A:=hello:` *Assign A to hello and suppress the output.*

> `%;` *Reissue the most recently entered expression.*

hello *Dittos are replaced by the most recently entered expression.*

Beware that Maple VR4 employs the double quote (`"`) instead of the percent sign (`%`) as a ditto. Consult `?ditto` and `?operators[nullary]` for more information.

PRACTICE!

6. Determine your system's default kernel mode.
7. Run Maple in parallel-kernel mode. Open two worksheets. Enter the statement `A:=1` in one worksheet. Check the value of A in both worksheets.
8. What output would you expect from the following Maple input statements?
   `[> A:=3: B:=2: C:=1: %%%;`

4.4 EVALUATING EXPRESSIONS

Maple maintains exact, symbolic expressions whenever possible. Towards this goal, Maple uses built-in rules for simplifying and evaluating expressions, as discussed in this section.

4.4.1 Automatic Simplification

Simplification attempts to reduce expressions to simpler forms and often requires ingenuity by the user. For instance, the fraction $\frac{1}{2}$ is simpler than $\frac{2}{4}$. Maple employs **automatic simplification** rules for reducing expressions that contain basic operations:

STEP 43:
AUTOMATIC
SIMPLIFICATION

Maple removes and combines common terms.

> `x:='x':` *Ensure that x is unassigned. Enter a sequence of expressions.*

> `x+x, x-x, x*x, x/x;` *Sequences separate expressions with commas.*

$2x, 0, x^2, 1$ *Maple automatically simplified each expression in the sequence.*

Chapter 7 reviews Maple's expression-manipulation techniques. Also, consult `?assume` for information on functions that enhance Maple's simplification capabilities.

PRACTICE!

9. Does Maple automatically simplify expressions such as $\sin(x + x)$?
10. Enter $\frac{2(x+y)}{4(x+y)}$ such that Maple performs automatic simplification.
11. Does Maple simplify $\sqrt{x^2}$ to x? Why or why not? How might you use **assume** to generate x from $\sqrt{x}$?

4.4.2 Full Evaluation

Managing Maple assignments is tricky. Each time you enter a statement, Maple performs **full evaluation**. Full evaluation first converts expressions into trees that replace all assigned names with their respective values. Maple also attempts to perform all possible automatic simplifications. Then, starting from the bottom, Maple performs mathematical operations for each subexpression until the top of the tree is reached. Finally, Maple reports the fully evaluated result. But, remember, only assignments can change a name's assigned value in Maple's memory.

Consider the example of a sequence of Maple inputs and outputs shown in Table 4-1. The "Expression" columns indicate how Maple stores each subexpression in memory after the input statements are entered. Now, trace the session:

TABLE 4-1 Full Evaluation   Section 4.

			EXPRESSION		
ORDER	INPUT STATEMENTS	OUTPUT	m	x	y
①	`> restart: y;`	y	m	x	y
②	`> y := m*x;`	$y := mx$	m	x	mx
③	`> m:=2: x:=3: y;`	-6	-2	3	mx
④	`> m:=2: x:='x': y;`	$2x$	2	x	mx
⑤	`> m:='m': x:='x': y;`	mx	m	x	mx

- Input ① erases all values and restores variables to their names only.
- Input ② assigns y to the expression mx.
- Input ③ changes values of m and x. Maple's full evaluation produces a y value that uses values for m and x. But, Maple still thinks of y as mx.
- Input ④ resets x and changes m. Now, y has a value based on the new values of m and x.
- Input ⑤ clears both x and m. The expression for y remains mx.

Maple fully evaluates new values of y for inputs ② through ⑤, but the assignment for y never changes after input ②. Why? The name y remains assigned to the expression mx throughout future inputs until you assign another expression, unassign y, or restart your worksheet.

4.4.3 Execution Groups

Maple evaluates input inside an execution group from left to right, and then, from top to bottom. So, the top input line is evaluated from left to right. The next input line is evaluated from left to right, and so forth. Note that pressing ↵ anywhere inside an execution group enters the *entire* group as input, starting at the top.

4.4.4 Unevaluation

Forward quotes surrounding an expression, such as **'expr'**, "delay" evaluation. When you enter **'expr'**, Maple first strips the input of the forward quotes (**' '**). Next, Maple attempts automatic simplification on **expr**. Finally, Maple reports the results of possible simplification on the expression **expr** without any evaluation. This process is called **unevaluation**, also known as delaying evaluation. For instance, try delaying the evaluation of **sqrt(4)**:

STEP 44:
DELAY
EVALUATION

Use forward quotes to delay the evaluation of an expression.

> `A:='sqrt(4)';`   *Delay the evaluation of $\sqrt{4}$.*

$$A := \sqrt{4}$$ *Maple stripped* `sqrt(4)` *of its quotes and left the unevaluted*

expression $\sqrt{4}$ as output. Note that Maple cannot automatically simplify $\sqrt{4}$.

> `A;`   *Now, evaluate $\sqrt{4}$.*

2   *Without quotes, Maple can freely evaluate the expression.*

Now do you see why entering ***name:='name'*** unassigns a name? Maple first strips ***'name'*** of the forward quotes, and in turn, leaves ***name:=name***. Hence, ***name*** is assigned to itself using the literal symbol for ***name*** and not any value. Consult **?uneval** and **?eval** for more information.

PRACTICE!

> **12.** Predict the output from the following input statements and then test your prediction with Maple:
>
> [> `restart: A:=1: B; B:=A: B; A:=2: B; # input 1`
>
> [> `restart: B:=A: B; A:=1: B; A:=2: B; # input 2`
>
> **13.** How does Maple compute $\frac{2^{2^2}}{4}$? What answer do you obtain?
>
> **14.** Does Maple simplify the input **'1+2'**? Hint: Consult **?uneval**.

4.5 APPLICATION: CIRCUIT ANALYSIS

This section demonstrates Maple's full evaluation rules with an example of electrical-engineering.

4.5.1 Background

Consider a circuit composed of resistors and a voltage source that generates electrical current, as shown in Figure 4.3. For instance, a battery creates a voltage "drop," an energy potential that initiates and maintains current flow. This electrical current then

Figure 4.3.   Electrical Circuit

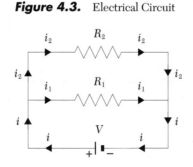

powers electrical devices that "resist" the current, such as light bulbs. Ohm's law relates a circuit's voltage V, the current i, and resistance R in the following manner:

$$V = iR. \tag{4-1}$$

When different branches of wire divide current, the sum of currents entering a branch equals the sum of currents leaving that branch. (Think of current as water flowing through a pipe.) Thus, from the circuit in Figure 4.2, you can determine $i = i_1 + i_2$. In general, the voltage across each resistor remains constant. Therefore,

$$i = i_1 + i_2 = \frac{V}{R_1} + \frac{V}{R_2} = \frac{V}{R_{eq}}. \tag{4-2}$$

You can determine the equivalent resistance R_{eq} from the equation

$$\frac{1}{R_{eq}} = \frac{1}{R_1} + \frac{1}{R_2}. \tag{4-3}$$

Equation 4-3 represents the formula for parallel resistor configurations like that in Figure 4.2. Now, you can express Ohm's Law in terms of R_{eq}:

$$V = iR_{eq}. \tag{4-4}$$

4.5.2 Problem

Given the circuit shown in Figure 4.2 with current $i = 10$ amps, determine the necessary voltage given these values of resistance in units of Ohms (Ω):

1. $R_1 = 5\,\Omega$ and $R_2 = 10\,\Omega$
2. $R_1 = 12\,\Omega$ and $R_2 = 15\,\Omega$

How does raising individual resistance affect the required voltage to maintain the same current?

4.5.3 Methodology

Because the value of the current will not change for this example, you can assign i without affecting later assignments:

STEP 45:
RESTATE AND
SEPARATE

Assign known values.

```
> restart:
```
Clear all previous assignments.

```
> i:=10;
```
Assign the current $i = 10$.

$$i := 10$$
Variable i is assigned to the value 10.

Now, assign the model for Ohm's law. Maple uses the assigned value of i due to full evaluation:

STEP 46:
MODEL OHM'S
LAW

Build your model, the equation that you will solve or evaluate.

Assign V to $iReq$.

```
> V:=i*Req;
```

$$V := 10Req$$
Ohm's law for $i = 10$ amps.

Assign a formula for equivalent resistance:

STEP 47:
MODEL
RESISTANCE

Build your model, the equation that you will solve or evaluate.

```
> Req := (1/R1 + 1/R2)^(-1);
```

Use the formula for parallel resistors.

$$Req := \dfrac{1}{\dfrac{1}{R1} + \dfrac{1}{R2}}$$

Maple does not automatically simplify the output.

Although the analysis does not require further simplification, you could rearrange the *Req* expression with the function **simplify(expr)**, as discussed in Chapter 7.

Now, solve both cases by assigning resistance values. Maple automatically evaluates and simplifies the expressions for V:

STEP 48:
SOLVE AND
REPORT CASE1

Solve Case 1.

```
> R1:=5: R2:=10: V;
```

Assign resistor values and evaluate voltage.

$$\frac{100}{3}$$

Maple performed full evaluation to solve for V.

STEP 49:
SOLVE AND
REPORT CASE2

Solve Case 2.

```
> R1:=12: R2:=15: V;
```

Assign resistor values and evaluate voltage.

$$\frac{200}{3}$$

Maple performed full evaluation to solve for V.

Why does Maple produce fractional answers? As long as you use integers with exact operations, Maple produces exact results whenever possible.

4.5.4 Solution

Raising the resistance at the same current increases the voltage demand.

SUMMARY

This chapter has reviewed methods for assigning and evaluating expressions. Maple's language elements, like operators and names, make up expressions. Once constructed, expressions can be assigned to names for later evaluation. Expressions are automatically simplified whenever possible, usually by rules of arithmetic. Maple fully evaluates an expression by substituting assigned values into each subexpression. But, full evaluation does not change the stored expression once the expression is assigned.

KEY TERMS

automatic simplification
dittos
expression trees
full evaluation

parallel-kernel mode
shared-kernel mode
simplification

unassigning
unevaluation
variables

Problems

1. Explain how Maple elements make up expressions. Give an example of an expression that employs addition and division with integers.
2. Draw an expression tree for the expression $\sin(a + b)$. (Hint: Do this by hand!)
3. Explain the difference between shared- and parallel-kernel modes.
4. Can you assign the name A to the value 1 with the input statement `1:=A;`? Why or why not? Demonstrate with Maple. Perform the following tasks:

    4a. Assign the name A to the value of 1.

    4b. Assign the name a to the value of 2.

    4c. Check the values of both names A and a.

    4d. Unassign the name A.

    4e. Unassign the name a.

5. Enter the following input statements:

    ```
    [> restart: y=mx+b: m=1: b=2: x=3: y;
    ```

    Why does Maple not produce the output of 5? Correct the input statements so that Maple does. Enter your corrected input.

6. Produce the Maple output *'I am a name that includes backquotes'* using a Maple name as input. (Hint: Consult `?name`.)
7. Assign a to the value 10. Assign b to a. Now, change the value of a to 20. Is the current value of b 10 or 20? Explain why. Demonstrate your answer with Maple.
8. Fill in the missing information for Table 4-2. (Hints: Refer to Table 4-1. Note that the Order column indicates the order in which you enter the input statements.)

TABLE 4-2   Full Evaluation (Problem 4.8)

ORDER	INPUT STATEMENTS	OUTPUT	EXPRESSION x	y
①	`> x:='x'; y:='y';`			
②	`> x:=10;`			
③	`> y:=x+5;`			
④	`> x:=20: y;`			
⑤	`> x:='x': y;`			

9. Assign C to the value 123. Next, assign c to the same value. Are the values of C and c the same? Why or why not? Demonstrate your results and conclusions with Maple.
10. You can compute the power of an electrical current as $P = i^2 R_{eq}$. What power does the circuit shown in Figure 4.3 require? Use $R_1 = 15\ \Omega$ and $R_2 = 10\ \Omega$. (Hints: Refer to Section 4.5. Solve for R_{eq}.)
11. Resistors connected in series are connected along the same current path, as shown in Figure 4.4. The equivalent resistance of resistors in series is $R_{eq} = R_1 + R_2 + \dots$.

$$R_1 \qquad\qquad R_2$$

Figure 4.4.   Resistors in Series

Assume a series configuration for both resistors in Figure 4.2 and solve the problem in Section 4.5.

12.   Many ingredients, such as cement, water, sand, and coarse aggregate (rocks), compose standard structural concrete. Assuming the proper vibration to remove entrapped air, you can approximate the total volume of concrete for a pour using the following densities: cement ρ_c = 195 pcf (pound-mass per cubic foot), water ρ_w = 62.4 pcf, and aggregate (includes rocks and sand) ρ_a = 165 pcf. Suppose that you can mix a batch of concrete that contains 250 lbm (pound-mass) of gravel, 150 lbm of sand, 100 lbm of cement, and 50 lbm of water. How many batches of concrete do you need to fill a rectangular wall with dimensions 20 ft × 5 ft × 1 ft? Assume no volume loss due to rebar reinforcement. (Hint: Both gravel and sand make up aggregate, so add their weights together.)

12a.   Restart Maple.

12b.   Assign the densities. For instance, `rho[w]:=62.4*l6m/ft^3`. (Hint: See Appendix A and `?name`.)

12c.   Calculate the volume of each component: Volume = Density (lbm/ft³) × Mass (lbm).

12d.   Calculate the total volume in one batch. (Hint: Sum the volumes in the previous step.)

12e.   Calculate the required volume of concrete, i.e., the volume of the wall.

12f.   Calculate the number of batches: Batches = Volume of wall (ft³) ÷ Volume of Batch $\left(\dfrac{\text{ft}^3}{\text{batch}}\right)$.

5

Maple Types

5.1 EXPRESSION TYPES

Different models employ different forms of data. Maple supplies a wealth of data types, which are introduced in this chapter.

5.1.1 Type Definition

According to `?type[definition]`, Maple defines *types* as anything recognized by the **type** function. Circular reasoning aside, Maple types correspond to language elements and expressions constructed from those elements, like *integers*, *names*, and *functions*. Maple also sometimes refers to types as "objects." Consult `?type` for a complete list of Maple types.

5.1.2 Type Classifications

All Maple expressions have types. Using types, Maple classifies expressions in two manners:

- **Surface Type**: the uppermost, principal element in an expression tree. For instance, the surface type of $a + b$ is "+". Consult `?type[surface]` for more information.
- **Structured Type**: a type built from individual types in an expression. For instance, the structured type of $a + b$ is "*name + name*". Consult `?type[structured]` for further details.

5.1.3 Checking Types

Expression types may be checked with **type(*expr*, *type*)**. Maple reports *true* when *expr* has *type*:

OBJECTIVES

After reading this chapter, you should be able to:

- Define surface and structured types
- Practice using different types of numbers
- Distinguish between local, global, and environment variables
- Use pre-defined Maple constants
- Classify data types used by Maple expressions

Physical systems have inherent uncertainty; behaviors and properties elude exact prediction. Besides statistics, other techniques, like interval analysis, help incorporate numerical uncertainty in equations. Interval-valued sets replace traditional numerical quantities and predict behavior "spaces," as shown in the accompanying Maple plot of an uncertain structural system. Courtesy of myself, David I. Schwartz

STEP 50:
CHECK
EXPRESSION
SURFACE TYPES

> `restart;`

> `type(x^2,`‵^‵`);`

                        true

Check surface types.

Start with a fresh worksheet.

Is the surface type of x^2 exponentiation? Surround operators with backquotes (‵ ‵).

Yes, x^2 has the surface type of exponentiation (^).

STEP 51:
CHECK
EXPRESSION
STRUCTURED
TYPES

> `type(x^2,name^integer);`

                        true

Check structured types.

Does the expression structure of x^2 contain $name^{integer}$?

Yes, x^2 has the structured type $name^{integer}$.

You may enter **op(*expr*)** and **whattype(*expr*)** to display surface types. Enter **op(0,*expr*)** to display the main operands of the surface type. Also, consult **?indets**, **?type[anything]**, **?type[type]**, and **?hastype** for more details.

PRACTICE!

13. Determine the surface and structured expression types for $\sin(x + y)$.

14. Enter **whattype(1+2)**. Why is the expression type not "+"?

5.2 REAL NUMBERS

Most forms of engineering and science measure numerical quantities. Thankfully, Maple enumerates numerous numerical number types, which are reviewed by this section.

5.2.1 Integers

As introduced in Section 3.1, integers are exact, whole numbers written as a series of digits with no decimal point. *Natural integers* are only positive. *Signed integers* have positive or negative signs. For example, 72 and 1216 are integers, whereas 438.0, 0.01, and $\sqrt{2}$ are not integers. Maple prefers integers because integer operations produce exact results:

STEP 52: INTEGERS

Demonstrate integer arithmetic.

```
> 1+10+100
```
Add integers together. Do not use decimal points.

$$111$$

Maple retains exact values whenever possible.

Consult `?integer` and `?type[integer]` for more information.

5.2.2 Rational Numbers

Maple defines **fractions** as numbers of the form $\frac{signed\ integer}{natural\ integer}$:

STEP 53: FRACTIONS

Demonstrate fraction arithmetic.

```
> 2/(-3);
```
Divide two integers.

$$\frac{-2}{3}$$

Maple converts the number to fractional form.

Rational numbers include both integers and fractions. The word "rational" arises from the notion of a ratio. Rational numbers preserve exactness in Maple expressions. Maple automatically simplifies rational numbers by removing common factors:

STEP 54: RATIONAL NUMBERS

Demonstrate rational arithmetic.

```
> 1/3 + 1/3 + 1/3 - 1;
```
Add rational numbers together.

$$0$$

Maple simplified the expression.

Also, consult `?fraction`, `?type[fraction]` and `?type[rational]` for more information.

PRACTICE!

15. Does Maple simplify the expression $\frac{72}{42}$?
16. Will entering `1./3.+1./3.+1./3.` produce an integer output of 1? Why or why not?

5.2.3 Floating-Point Numbers

Numerical analysis relies on ***floating-point numbers*** or just *floats*. Floats are base-10 or *decimal* numbers like 10., 10.0, and 0.01. Maple considers numbers input with decimal points (.) as floats. As discussed in **?float**, Maple supplies a variety of methods for entering floats:

- *integer.integer*: e.g., **100.1**.
- *.integer*: e.g., **.01**.
- *integer.*: e.g., **100.**.
- *integer.integerEinteger*: e.g., **1.0E2** and **1E2** yield $1 \times 10^2 = 100$.
- *integer.integereinteger*: e.g., **1.0e2** and **1e2** yield $1 \times 10^2 = 100$.
- **Float(*integer_m, integer_e*)**: e.g., **Float(2,3)** yields $2 \times 10^3 = 2000$.

Note that many syntaxes use scientific notation $m \times 10^e$, given mantissa m and exponent e. Also, you can interchange the symbols **E** and **e** when entering floats. Consult **?type[float]** and **?type[numeric]** for further details.

5.2.4 Floating-Point Arithmetic

Arithmetic operations that contain floats produce floats:

**STEP 55:
FLOATING-
POINT
NUMBERS**

Demonstrate decimal numbers and arithmetic.

```
> Float(-1,2) - 20. - 3.0 - 0.4 - 5E-2 - 6.0E-3 - 7e-4;
```

$$-123.4567$$

The floats above demonstrate the variety of forms.

Maple automatically converts integers to floats when types are mixed:

**STEP 56:
MIXING FLOATS
WITH INTEGERS**

Demonstrate mixed types.

Add the float 0.5 to the rational number $\frac{1}{2}$.

```
> 0.5 + 1/2;
```

$$1.000000000$$

Mixed floats and rational numbers produce floats.

The environment variable **Digits** determines the number of mantissa digits used for computations, as discussed in Section 5.4. Also, investigate **?evalf** and **?round** for more information.

PRACTICE!

17. Express 123.0 in Maple floating-point notation with three different syntaxes.

18. Why does entering **123*10^(-1)** yield a rational number? Change the input to produce a floating-point answer.

5.2.5 Irrational Numbers

Irrational numbers cannot be expressed as a ratio of two integers. When expressed as floats, irrational numbers have nonrepeating decimals with no determined bounds.

Some examples of irrational numbers include $\sqrt{2}$, π, $\sin\left(\frac{\pi}{3}\right)$, and the exponential constant e. See Sections 2.5, 5.4.3, and 6.4.5 for example irrational numbers.

For instance, Maple will refuse to compute a floating-point value of the exact irrational input **sqrt(2)** in order to maintain exactness:

STEP 57: **DISPLAY** **IRRATIONAL** **NUMBERS**		*Maple preserves irrational numbers to maintain exactness.*
	`> sqrt(2);`	*Attempt to evaluate $\sqrt{2}$.*
	$\sqrt{2}$	*Maple cannot further reduce the irrational value $\sqrt{2}$.*

To evaluate a floating-point approximation of **sqrt(2)**, enter **sqrt(2.0)**:

STEP 58: **COMPUTE** **IRRATIONAL** **NUMBERS**		*Use floats or consult the **evalf** function.*
	`> sqrt(2.0);`	*Evaluate a numerical approximation of $\sqrt{2}$.*
	1.414213562	*The float 2.0 forces a rounded-off floating-point evaluation.*

You can also enter **evalf(expr)** to force a floating-point computation, as discussed in Chapter 9 and **?evalf**.

PRACTICE!

> **19.** Classify the following expressions as rational or irrational: $\sin 0$, 10.1, $\sqrt{2}$, e.
> **20.** Compute $4^{\frac{1}{3}}$ in both exact and floating-point forms.

5.3 IMAGINARY NUMBERS

Can you take the square root of a negative number? Technically, no, but some physical quantities are negative due to sign conventions. To resolve this dilemma, ***imaginary numbers*** were conveniently invented! Complex numbers, or numbers that contain imaginary numbers, often arise in mathematical analysis, so yes, you should learn the material in this section.

5.3.1 Definition

The imaginary number i is defined as follows:

$$i = \sqrt{-1}. \tag{5-1}$$

Therefore, $i^2 = -1$. For example, $\sqrt{-2} = \sqrt{2}i$. Numbers containing i are called ***complex***. Complex numbers, like $a + bi$, contain a *real* component a and an *imaginary* component b. Consult **?complex** and **?type[complex]** for more information.

5.3.2 Arithmetic

Enter **I** when you need the imaginary number $i = \sqrt{-1}$, as discussed by **?I**. Maple attempts to evaluate both real and imaginary components of complex numbers expressed with **I**. Try an example of complex arithmetic:

STEP 59: COMPLEX NUMBERS

Demonstrate arithmetic with real and imaginary numbers.

> (1+2*I)+(2+I);

Add two complex numbers. Never enter i.

$$3 + 3I$$

1 + 2 = 3 and 2i + i = 3i.

Consult **?I** for more information on the use of i in Maple. Maple implements **I** as an *alias*. Aliases rename expressions, as discussed by **?alias** and Problem 5.16. See also **?Re**, **?Im**, and **?evalc** for more information on functions for complex numbers.

PRACTICE!

21. Do the inputs **sqrt(-1)**, **(-1)^(1/2)**, and **I** produce different outputs?

22. Enter the expression $\sqrt{-2}$ into Maple.

23. Evaluate $(1 + 2i)(-1 - i)$.

5.4 INITIALLY KNOWN NAMES

Maple protects many function names for built-in library functions. Consult **?inifcn** and **?index[function]** for a complete list. Maple predefines other names as well; these names are listed in **?ininames** and are demonstrated in this section.

5.4.1 Variables

Recall that assignable names are variables, terms that can store different expressions. Maple employs three kinds of variables:

- **Global Variables**: assignable names known to all Maple functions and procedures. Virtually every name you assign at the prompt is global. (Consult **?global** or **?procedure** for more information.)
- **Local Variables**: names that exist only within library functions and customized procedures. Local variable values do not change global behavior. (Consult **?local** or **?procedure** for more information.)
- **Environment Variables**: predefined constants that affect how certain Maple functions perform. These variables can affect both local and global behavior. (Consult **?envvar** for more information.)

Investigate Appendix E for further explanation and implementation of variables.

5.4.2 Environment Variables

Digits, a common environment variable, determines the maximum number of digits used and reported in floating-point calculations and output. The default value of 10 limits numerical evaluation to 10 digits used when evaluating floats:

STEP 60: CHECKING DIGITS

*Check the environment variable **Digits**.*

> Digits;

*Display **Digits**'s current value.*

$$10$$

Assuming no previous altering, 10 is the default value.

STEP 61:
CHANGING
DIGITS

> `Digits:=4:`

Change the environment variable `Digits`.

Assign a new value of 4.

> `10.0/3;`

Divide 10.0 *by* 3. *Maple will produce a float.*

$$3.333$$

Maple reports only four digits.

STEP 62:
RESET DIGITS

> `Digits:=10:`

Restore `Digits`*'s original value.*

Reset to the old value of 10.

Many functions, like **solve** (see Chapter 9), provide other environment variables that customize behavior. These variables usually start with an underscore (_). You may also wish to use **evalf(*expr*, *n*)** instead of changing **Digits**, as discussed in **?evalf** and Chapter 9.

5.4.3 Constants

Numbers, such as integers, fractions, and floats, are numerical constants. Maple also contains predefined *symbolic constants* that may be listed by entering the global variable **constants**:

STEP 63:
LIST OF
SYMBOLIC
CONSTANTS

> `constants;`

Show Maple's built-in constants.

This variable stores symbolic constants.

$$false, \gamma, \infty, true, Catalan, FAIL, \pi$$

Each item here is a built-in constant.

Typically, Maple only displays the symbols of symbolic constants, such as the symbolic constant **Pi**:

STEP 64:
DISPLAY
SYMBOLIC
CONSTANT PI

> `Pi;`

Enter `Pi` *when you need* π = 3.1415....

Display π.

$$\pi$$

Maple displays `Pi` *symbolically.*

To display a numerical value of a symbolic constant, like π, force Maple's evaluation with **evalf(*expr*)** ("evaluate float") function. For instance, evaluate the numerical value of π:

STEP 65:
EVALUATE
NUMERICAL PI

> `evalf(Pi);`

Enter `Pi` *when you need* π = 3.1415....

Evaluate the floating-point value of π.

$$3.141592654$$

Maple displays `Pi` *as a float.*

Remember that Maple is case sensitive!

STEP 66:
THIS NAME
IS NOT THE
NUMERICAL PI!

> pi;

Beware of the difference between `Pi` *and* `pi`!

Try evaluating `pi`, *though* `pi` *will not yield a numerical value.*

π

So far, `pi` *seems ok.*

> evalf(pi);

Try evaluating `pi`, *though the attempt will fail.*

π

Never use `pi` *when you need a numerical value.*

Also, consult **?constant** and **?type[constant]** for more information.

5.4.4 Greek Characters
Maple automatically converts Greek letters into their correct font:

STEP 67:
GREEK
LETTERS

Maple recognizes the Greek alphabet.

> alpha,beta,gamma,delta;

Enter some Greek letters using Maple Notation.

$\alpha, \beta, \gamma, \delta$

Maple automatically converts each name.

Also, try the symbol palette shown in Figure 5.1 by selecting <u>V</u>iew→<u>P</u>alettes→ Symbol Palette. Just click on the appropriate letter. See Appendix A for a complete listing of Greek symbols and names. Beware that Maple uses many uppercase Greek letters for functions, so beware of protection!

PRACTICE!

> **24.** Evaluate π to five digits.
> **25.** Produce these symbolic constants by entering their Maple names:
>
> $$false, \gamma, \infty, true, Catalan, FAIL, \pi.$$
>
> **26.** Enter the symbol $-\infty$ in Maple Notation.
> **27.** Assign the name β to the value 1.
> **28.** Assign the name **Beta** to the value 1. Explain the output.

Figure 5.1. Symbol Palette

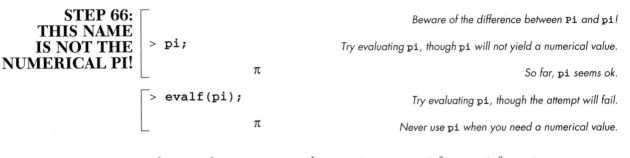

5.5 MISCELLANEOUS TYPES

Maple expressions include more than numbers and constants. This section scratches the "surface," so to speak, of more Maple types.

5.5.1 Boolean

Expressions that contain relational operators (=, >, >=, <, <=, <>) or logical operators (**and**, **or**, **not**) are called **Boolean**. Boolean expressions evaluate to *true*, *false*, or *FAIL* using rules of logic. For instance, **type(123,integer)** evaluates to the boolean value *true*. Use **evalb(*expr*)** to evaluate the logical, or Boolean, truth of *expr*:

STEP 68: BOOLEAN VALUES

> A:=1: evalb(A>2);

Evaluate the truth of an expression.

Is A greater than 2?

      false

No, A is not greater than 2.

Remember that **evalb** will not assign expressions or produce values other than *true*, *false*, or *FAIL*! See **?boolean**, **?evalb**, **?type[boolean]**, and **?logic** for more information.

5.5.2 Strings

Strings provide text labels. You can also assign names to strings:

STEP 69: STRINGS

Strings are not names, but names can be assigned to strings!

> STR:="Hi Dave!": type(STR,string); *Surround strings with double quotes ("").*

      true

The name STR was indeed assigned.

Consult **?string**, **?type[string]**, and the worksheet **?example[strings]** for more details. Also, see **?dot** and **?cat** for string operations.

5.5.3 Equations

Equations employ the syntax **expr1 = expr2**, but using the equals sign (=) does not assign **expr1** to **expr2**! Use equations for comparison and solution (see **?solve**), not for assignment:

STEP 70:
ASSIGN
EQUATIONS

Assign a name to an equation.

> `EQN:= y=m*x+b; type(EQN,equation);`   *Assign the name EQN to an equation.*

$$y = mx + b$$ *EQN was assigned to the expression $y = mx + b$.*

$$true$$ *Yes, EQN is an equation.*

> `EQN;`   *Show the value of EQN.*

$$y = mx + b$$ *Yes, EQN really has the value $y = mx + b$.*

> `y;`   *Show the value of y.*

$$y$$ *The equals sign does not assign.*

Note that entire equations still constitute expressions, as evidenced by the **type** function. Also, consult **?equation**, **?type[equation]**, and Chapters 9 and 10 for more information.

5.5.4 Relations

Consult Table 5-1 and **?relation** for descriptions of relational operators. ***Relations*** have the syntax ***expr1 rel expr2*** and contain either **=, <, <=,** or **<>** as ***rel*** inside an expression. What about **>** and **>=**? Maple automatically reverses "greater than" inequalities into "less than" form.

STEP 71:
RELATIONS

Check equality and inequality expressions.

> `REL:= 1>0; type(REL,relation);`   *Assign the name REL to a relation.*

$$REL := 0 < 1$$ *Maple automatically converts ">" into "<" form.*

$$true$$ *Yes, REL is a relation.*

Note that an equation is a special form of a relation. Consult **?operators[binary]** and **?inequality** for more information.

5.5.5 Ranges

As introduced in Section 2.4, ***low..high*** is entered to represent an interval, or range, of numbers between ***low*** and ***high***:

TABLE 5-1   Relational Operators

OPERATOR	STANDARD MATH	MAPLE NOTATION	EXAMPLE
Equal to	$=$	**=**	**1=1**
Not Equal to	$\neq$	**<>**	**1<>2**
Greater Than	$>$	**>**	**2>1**
Greater Than or Equal to	$\geq$	**>=**	**2>=2**
Less Than	$<$	**<**	**1<2**
Less Than or Equal to	$\leq$	**<=**	**2<=2**

STEP 72:
RANGES

> R:=1..2: type(R,range);

Express a range of numbers between an upper and lower bound.

Assign the interval of numbers between 1 and 2.

true

Yes, R was assigned to the range.

You will commonly find ranges in plotting and sequence commands. Also, consult **?range**, **?plot[range]**, and **?type[range]** for more information.

5.5.6 Sequences

Expressions separated by commas (,) such as ***expr1, expr2, ...,*** are called ***sequences***. Sequences help store related expressions in a specific order:

STEP 73:
SEQUENCES

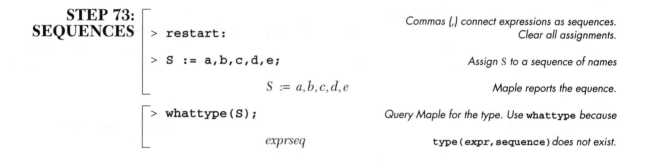

> restart:

Commas (,) connect expressions as sequences.
Clear all assignments.

> S := a,b,c,d,e;

Assign S to a sequence of names

$$S := a,b,c,d,e$$

Maple reports the equence.

> whattype(S);

Query Maple for the type. Use **whattype** *because*

exprseq

type(*expr*, sequence) *does not exist.*

Also, consult **?exprseq**; **?seq**; **?$**, or **?dollar**; **?map**; and **?op** for more information.

5.5.7 Lists

Sequences surrounded by square brackets (**[]**) form ***lists***. Lists collect a sequence of expressions. Also, sequences and lists may repeat expressions:

STEP 74:
LISTS

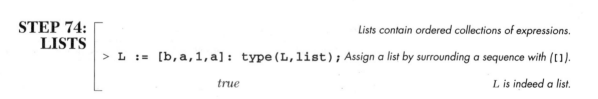

Lists contain ordered collections of expressions.

> L := [b,a,1,a]: type(L,list); *Assign a list by surrounding a sequence with ([]).*

true

L is indeed a list.

Consult **?list**, **?type[list]**, **?op**, and **?map** for more information.

5.5.8 Sets

Sets contain nonordered collections of *unique* items. Curly braces (**{}**) indicate sets:

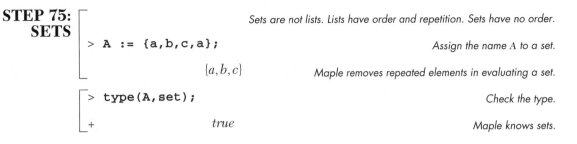

STEP 75: SETS

> `A := {a,b,c,a};`   *Sets are not lists. Lists have order and repetition. Sets have no order.*

Assign the name A to a set.

$$\{a,b,c\}$$ *Maple removes repeated elements in evaluating a set.*

> `type(A,set);`   *Check the type.*

+   *true*   *Maple knows sets.*

Consult `?set`, `?type[set]`, and `?intersect` or `?union` for set operations.

5.5.9 Selection

Square brackets (`[]`) assist with indexing and extracting elements from sequences, lists, and sets. Maple counts each expression from left to right starting from 1. Given a sequence input `S`, entering the expression `S[i..j]` extracts the ith to jth expressions from `S`. You can enter just `S[i]` to select only the ith element:

STEP 76: SELECTION

Extract elements from a sequence S. See Step 73.

> `S;`   *What value was S assigned to?*

$$a,b,c,d,e$$ *S is this sequence:* $S_1 = a, S_2 = b, S_3 = c, S_4 = d, S_5 = e.$

> `S[1..3]; S[5];`   *Extract the first through third elements. Then, extract the fifth element.*

$$a,b,c$$ *Elements 1, 2, and 3 from S.*

$$e$$ *Maple found the fifth element of S.*

5.5.10 Indexing

According to `?name`, you can also index a name with a subscript. Just enter **name [subscript]**:

STEP 77: INDEXING

Provide indices to names. Recall that names are symbols that can be indexed.

> `x:='x':`   *Unassign x.*

> `x[1],x[2],x[3];`   *Provide indices for x.*

$$x_1, x_2, x_3$$ *If x were a sequence, Maple would report the first, second, and third entries inside x.*

Consult `?selection`, `?indexed`, `?type[indexed]`, and `?op` for more details.

5.5.11 Functions

Functions have the form of **name(exprseq)**. They are discussed in Chapter 6.

5.5.12 Many More Types!

Consult Appendix E and `?type` for information on many other useful types.

PRACTICE!

29. Can you create the output $\dfrac{I\ love}{using\ Maple!}$ with strings?

30. What does the input statement `'i^2' $ 'i'=0..3` indicate and produce?

31. Produce the sequence of integers 0, 1, 8, 27. Assign S to the result.

32. Show the first and second elements of S.

33. Create a list that contains only the previously assigned name S. Assign SL to that list.

34. Create a set that contains only the previously assigned name S. Assign SS to that set.

35. Does Maple consider SL and SS to be identical? Hint: Enter `evalb(SL=SS)`.

5.6 APPLICATION: INTERVAL ANALYSIS

This section demonstrates interval analysis to further explore the variety of Maple types that you can apply to engineering and science problems.

5.6.1 Background

Interval analysis (IA) provides an analytical approach that incorporates uncertainty in mathematical models. As opposed to traditional statistical methods with probability distributions, IA directly enhances equations with *intervals*, which are bounded sets of numbers. IA converts a precise, or "crisp," quantity x into an uncertain interval quantity x^I such that

$$x^I = [\underline{x}, \bar{x}] = \{\tilde{x} \mid \underline{x} \le \tilde{x} \le \bar{x}\}, \tag{5-2}$$

where the lower bound $\underline{x}$ and the upper bound $\bar{x}$ enclose all possible values of $\tilde{x}$ inside x^I. For instance, assuming that a value $L = 10$ has 10% uncertainty yields the interval

$$L^I = [100 - (0.1)(100),\ 100 + (0.1)(100)] = [90, 110]. \tag{5-3}$$

When analytical approaches for intervals are adapted, two rules of interval arithmetic help derive arithmetic operations:

1. *Independence*: Assume that values contained inside intervals are independent of other values.
2. *Extremes*: Produce lowest and highest possible bounds assuming independent values.

Consult Table 5-2 for common rules of interval arithmetic.

TABLE 5-2 Interval Arithmetic

OPERATION		RULE	
Addition	$x^I + y^I$	$[\underline{x} + \underline{y},\ \bar{x} + \bar{y}]$	(5-4)
Subtraction	$x^I - y^I$	$[\underline{x} - \bar{y},\ \bar{x} - \underline{y}]$	(5-5)
Multiplication	$x^I y^I$	$[\min(\underline{x}\underline{y}, \underline{x}\bar{y}, \bar{x}\underline{y}, \bar{x}\bar{y}),\ \max(\underline{x}\underline{y}, \underline{x}\bar{y}, \bar{x}\underline{y}, \bar{x}\bar{y})]$	(5-6)
Division	x^I/y^I	$[\min(\underline{x}/\underline{y}, \underline{x}/\bar{y}, \bar{x}/\underline{y}, \bar{x}/\bar{y}),\ \max(\underline{x}/\underline{y}, \underline{x}/\bar{y}, \bar{x}/\underline{y}, \bar{x}/\bar{y})],\ 0 \notin y^I$	(5-7)

5.6.2 Problem

Apply interval methods to the model $ax = b$. Assume that $a = 2$ and $b = 4$, both with 25% uncertainty, and solve for x^I. Then, compare your results by using Maple's built-in interval-arithmetic routines, which are stored in the **evalr** library.

5.6.3 Methodology

First, state and assign pertinent variables:

STEP 78: RESTATE AND SEPARATE

	Initialize problem and system variables.
> `restart:`	*Restart your Maple session.*
> `Digits:=4:`	*Use and report only four digits for all computations.*
> `p:=25.0:`	*Assign a percent uncertainty of $p = 25\%$.*
> `a:=2: b:=4:`	*Assign "crisp," noninterval values.*

Convert the values into interval quantities. Use the formulas

$$\underline{x} = x - \frac{xp}{100} \tag{5-8}$$

and

$$\bar{x} = x + \frac{xp}{100} \tag{5-9}$$

for the percent uncertainty p:

STEP 79: MODEL

	Convert crisp values into intervals.
> `al:=a-a*p/100: au:=a+a*p/100:`	*Assign lower and upper values of a.*
> `bl:=b-b*p/100: bu:=b+b*p/100:`	*Assign lower and upper values of b.*

From Eq. 5-7 in Table 5-2, divide all of the end points from both intervals and store the results in a sequence:

STEP 80: SOLVE AND REPORT

	Perform interval division.
> `DivSeq:= bl/al,bl/au,bu/al,bu/au;`	*Assign the sequence of all possible answers.*
2.000, 1.200, 3.333, 2.000	*You still need to produce an interval enclosure.*

Ease your labor with the **min(*Seq*)** and **max(*Seq*)** functions, which find minimum and maximum values of sequences:

STEP 81:
SOLVE AND
REPORT

Form the interval.

```
> xI:=[min(DivSeq),max(DivSeq)];
```
Select the minimum and maximum values.

$$xI := [1.200, 3.333]$$

x^I forms an interval of $1.2 \leq x \leq 3.333$.

However, what happens if you backsubstitute your results? That is, compute $a^I x^I$ and compare the result to the initial interval value b^I. To double check your work, now try Maple's built-in IA command **evalr(*expr*)**, or "evaluate range." Use an interval data type with the syntax of **INTERVAL(*range*)**:

STEP 82:
USE EVALUATE-
RANGE
FUNCTION

*Use Maple's **evalr** command to double check your answers.*

```
> readlib(evalr):
```
*Load the **evalr** command into Maple's memory. (Consult Appendix D.)*

```
> aI:=INTERVAL(al..au);
```
Assign a^I to $[\underline{a}, \bar{a}]$.

```
> bI:=INTERVAL(bl..bu);
```
Assign b^I to $[\underline{b}, \bar{b}]$.

$$aI := \text{INTERVAL}(1.500..2.500)$$

$a^I = [1.5, 2.5]$.

$$bI := \text{INTERVAL}(3.000..5.000)$$

$b^I = [3,5]$.

STEP 83:
CHECK YOUR
WORK

*Use Maple's **evalr** command to double check your answers.*

```
> xI:=evalr(bI/aI);
```
Perform interval division.

$$xI := \text{INTERVAL}(1.200..3.334)$$

Maple produces essentially the same result from Step 81.

STEP 84:
BACK-
SUBSTITUTE

*Use Maple's **evalr** command to double check your answers.*

```
> aIxI:=evalr(aI*xI);
```
Check if $a^I x^I = b^I$.

$$aIxI := \text{INTERVAL}(1.800..8.335)$$

This interval contains b^I, but is too large.

5.6.4 Solution

Interval division on $[1.5, 2.5]/[3,5]$ yields $x^I = [1.2, 3.333]$, whereas Maple's **evalr** function produces a slightly wider interval to account for round-off error on 3.333.... Backsubstituting produces too large of an interval because interval arithmetic operations are nonassociative! You can only go one way with most IA operations. Nevertheless, IA does guarantee outer bounds and provides a useful tool for solving problems with multiple uncertainties.

PROFESSIONAL SUCCESS: UNITS

Never let software foster laziness! Many programs allow numerical input without unit labels. However, engineering and science quantities measure *units*, which are properties associated with a physical system. Always write down your units, especially to help those who check your work. Your instructors and managers will thank you. Consider these tips when using Maple:

❏   Pick unit names:

Reserve certain names for unit labels. Protect your units with **protect(*name*)**:

> **restart: protect(m): protect(ft):**   *Prevent unit names from being assigned.*

> **ft := 1;**   *Try to assign anyway.*

Error, attempting to assign to 'ft' which is protected   *Nope!*

❏   Label your input:

For example, interpret the quantity "one foot" as *one* × *foot*. Now, multiply expressions by unit labels:

> **Side:=10.0*ft: Area := Side^2;**   *Compute Area in terms of feet (ft).*

$$Area := 100\,ft^2$$ *Maple now shows units!*

❏   Convert your units:

Let Maple ease your work. For example, the function **convert** will convert U.S. units into metric units:

> **Digits := 3:**   *Set a reasonable number of digits with which to show results.*

> **Area2 :=convert(Area,metric);**   *Convert your area into square meters.*

$$Area2 := 9.30m^2$$ *Maple reports your results in metric units.*

Consult **?convert[metric]**, **?convert[degrees]**, and **?convert[decimal]** for other great conversion tricks.

SUMMARY

This chapter has introduced many Maple types. Maple usually classifies expressions by the surface type, which is the uppermost element in an expression tree. Common numerical types consist of integers, fractions, ratios, floats, and irrational numbers. In general, Maple prefers to maintain an exact form of numbers when possible. Maple's global, local, and environment variables also help determine how Maple evaluates expressions. Other types include many built-in values, such as defined constants, strings, equations, ranges, sequences, lists, sets, and functions. These types help construct a variety of expressions, many of which are demonstrated throughout this text.

KEY TERMS

Boolean

complex

environment variables

equations

floating-point numbers

fractions

global variables

imaginary numbers

irrational numbers

lists

local variables

rational numbers

relations

sequences

sets

structured type

surface type

symbolic constants

types

Problems

1. What is a Maple data type?
2. Explain the difference between surface and structured types.
3. Identify the surface and structured type of the expression $a + bc$.
4. Explain the difference between real and imaginary numbers.
5. Explain the difference between rational and irrational numbers.
6. Explain the differences between sequences, lists, and sets.
7. Evaluate the following expressions using Maple. You must demonstrate both exact and floating-point (decimal) results for all output. (Hints: Be careful with operator precedence and associativity. To find decimal results, either enter floats in the input, or use **evalf(expr)**.)

7a. $1 + \dfrac{1}{2} + \dfrac{1}{3}$	7f. i^2
7b. $1 + 0.51$	7g. $\dfrac{2i + 3}{4i}$
7c. $1 + \sqrt{2}$	7h. $\sqrt{-10}$
7d. $\dfrac{1}{3} + \sqrt{0.1}$	7i. $e^2 + 3$
7e. 2π	7j. $e^{\sin\left(\frac{\pi}{3}\right)}$

8. Is the number zero (0) an integer? Prove your answer with Maple.
9. Evaluate $\sqrt{-\pi}$ both exactly and approximately.
10. Maple's **Digits** variable can often produce surprising results. Consider the following session:

```
> restart:
> 2*1.05;
        2.10
> Digits:=2:
> 2*1.05;
        2.2
```

Demonstrate the same Maple session. Why do you think that Maple produced an answer of 2.2 after **Digits** was set to **2**?

11. Why does entering **evalb(exp(1)=e)** produce the answer *false?*
12. The volume of a sphere is $V = \dfrac{4}{3}\pi r^3$, where r is the radius of the sphere. Do the following tasks:

   12a. Given $r = 3$ cm, compute V. Be sure to specify units in your assignments!

   12b. Find the floating-point value of your answer to Problem 5.12a.

   12c. Convert your result to inches. 1 in = 2.54 cm. (Hint: Maple won't permit **in** as a name. Why? Use **inch**.)

13.   Given the data in Table 5-3, do the following tasks:

TABLE 5-3   Data Points

INDEX	1	2	3	4	5
x	2	−4	3	1	0
y	−1	5	2	6	1

13a.   Assign X to the sequence of x values. (Hint: Do not use a list or set type!)

13b.   Assign Y to the sequence of y values.

13c.   Generate a list of data pairs. Each pair of data must have a list structure in the form of $[x_i, y_i]$ as well. Assign the variable DP to your result. (Hint: Enter `DP:=[[2, -1], [-4, 5],....`)

13d.   Extract the y value from DP's third value, DP_3. (Hint: Use the selection operator `[]` twice.)

14.   Demonstrate that $(A \cup B)^c = A^c \cap B^c$, which is one of DeMorgan's Laws, with Maple. Use two sets $A = \{a, b, c\}$ and $B = \{a, d\}$, along with a *Universe of Discourse* $U = \{a, b, c, d, e\}$. (A complement of a set S, S^c, is the difference between U and S. Hint: See `?minus`.)

15.   Electrical engineers often distinguish imaginary numbers by using the letter j in order to prevent confusion with the symbol for current, i. Change Maple's default alias `I` to `j`. (Hint: Investigate `?alias`.) Next, demonstrate your new alias by evaluating $\sqrt{-1}$ with `evalc`.

16.   Assume that part of a circuit you are analyzing contains a *resistor R* (resistance is measured in Ω, or Ohms) and a *capacitor C* (capacitance is measured in F, or farads) connected together in a series, as shown in Figure 5.2:

Figure 5.2.   Resistor and Capacitor in Series

(Capacitors store electrical charge. Section 4.5 reviews resistors.) *Impedance* measures the effect that elements such as capacitors and resistors have on electrical current. You can calculate this configuration's impedance Z (measured in Ohms) with the formula

$$Z = R - \frac{j}{\omega C},$$

where ω (rad/s) represents the angular frequency of the voltage source. The symbol j represents an imaginary number, as discussed in Problem 5.15. Given $\omega = 400$ rad/s, $R = 5$ Ω, and $C = 1 \times 10^{-9}$ F:

16a.   Evaluate Z using Maple's default imaginary number, the variable I.

16b.   Evaluate Z using an alias j, as described in Problem 5.16.

17.   Use Maple to evaluate $[1,2] - [1,2]$ with interval arithmetic:

17a.   Apply the rules in Table 5-2 using Maple. (This answer will *not* be zero!)

17b.   Use Maple's `evalr` function. (This answer will be zero.)

17c.   Why should interval arithmetic yield a different answer than the answer to part b? (Hint: The answer is not "because `evalr` is defined that way!" See Chapter 4.)

6

Functions

6.1 MAPLE FUNCTIONS

Maple provides a incredible wealth of functions for many mathematical models. This section reviews important aspects of Maple functions. Inspect `?inifcn` and `?index[function]` for information on a multitude of Maple library functions. Also, consult Appendix D for methods on finding, loading, and viewing functions.

6.1.1 Notation

Maple functions have the syntax **name(exprseq)**. As discussed in previous sections, the **name** labels the function. Consider the expression sequence **exprseq** as **expr1, expr2, ...**, where each **expr** is called either an **argument** or a **parameter**. Arguments and parameters serve as function *inputs*, which are quantities upon which functions act. For instance, entering `sqrt(4)` produces the square root of the argument 4. Functions, like `plot(x^2,x=1..2)`, require multiple arguments, whereas some functions, like `anames()`, can accept zero arguments. Consult `?function` and `?type [function]` for further discussion.

6.1.2 Nested Functions

Functions are yet another Maple type that form expressions. You can enter functions into one another as **nested functions**, which are functions that employ functions as arguments. Why bother with nesting? Well, you can either enter expressions the long way, as in Step 85:

OBJECTIVES

After reading this chapter, you should be able to:

- Understand the structure of Maple functions
- Find Maple functions
- Simulate functions with assignments
- Use functions for polynomials, trigonometry, logarithms, and more
- Develop customized Maple functions using functional notation

Niagara Falls provides one of the greatest sources of hydroelectric power in the world. Water from the Great Lakes in North America drains into the Niagara River and eventually flows over the famous Niagara Falls. During peak visitor hours, about 168,000 cubic meters (6 million cubic feet) of water flows past the crest line per minute. At other times, the United States and Canada siphon off water at intakes before the falls to generate 4.4 million kilowatts (5 million horsepower). Courtesy of Michael Lamanna

STEP 85:
TEDIOUS
METHOD

Functions are not nested.

```
> restart;
```
Clear all assignments.

```
> A:=Pi/6: B:=sin(A): sqrt(B);
```
This method is time consuming.

$$\frac{1}{2}\sqrt{2}$$

Maple evaluated `sqrt(sin(Pi/6))`.

Or, you can more efficiently nest functions as *func(func(expr))*:

STEP 86:
NESTED
FUNCTIONS

Supply functions as arguments to other functions to ease labor.

```
> sqrt(sin(Pi/6));
```
Functions are expressions. Enter `sin(Pi/6)` *as an argument of* `sqrt`.

$$\frac{1}{2}\sqrt{2}$$

Both methods produce the same results.

Maple permits nesting of functions to many levels as in *func(func(func(...)))*.

PROFESSIONAL SUCCESS: UNDERSTANDING FUNCTIONS

Introductory courses in engineering and science provide tools for later study. However, tools, like mathematics, seem to fixate on apparently unimportant theories and concepts. Many students often complain, "Why are we learning *this*? How on earth will *this* ever help us?" Knowing how underlying theories reflect physical principles helps to motivate study. Consider, for instance, a *function*, which is a one-to-one correspondence between a domain and range. Have you ever wondered why we really need functions? Functions provide realistic physical models, as demonstrated in the following example.

Consider the experiment shown in Figure 6.1. A weight w hangs from an unstretched spring and is slowly released. The final displacement u is then measured and plotted. Different weights yield different displacements, as shown in Figure 6.2. Numerous experiments eventually develop a pattern, which is a line drawn through the individual points.

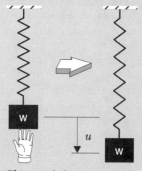

Figure 6.1. Experiment

Because w is chosen for arbitrary values, w is called an *independent variable* and is plotted on the horizontal axis. Independent variables are not measured during the experiment. The displacement u *depends* on the choice of w. Experimentally measured variables are called *dependent variables* and are plotted on the vertical axis.

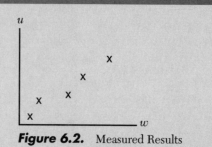

Figure 6.2. Measured Results

Each weight causes a unique displacement. Thus, u is a *function* of w. In mathematical terms, $u = f(w)$. From Figure 6.3, the relationship appears to be linear. The slope of the line may be expressed as $\frac{1}{k}$, where k is the stiffness of the spring. Thus, $u = \frac{w}{k}$, or just $w = ku$.

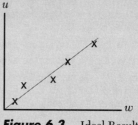

Figure 6.3. Ideal Results

Why choose a function? Consider the fake model shown in Figure 6.4. This model predicts that one weight can yield *different* displacements! Remember the vertical-line test for functions? This fake relationship fails that test. Rules for defining functions are crucial for building accurate and realistic models!

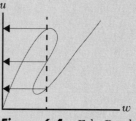

Figure 6.4. Fake Results

Now, consider other mathematical theories. Very often, mathematical definitions and theories grow from desires to solve certain problems. Though the reasons might seem obscure, have faith that many of your early studies truly have importance!

6.1.3 Operators

You may combine and manipulate functions as you would with other expressions. In general, operators should be entered *after* the right parenthesis ("**)**") that terminates a function. For instance, enter **sin(x)^2** to square sin x, where x is a mathematical expression:

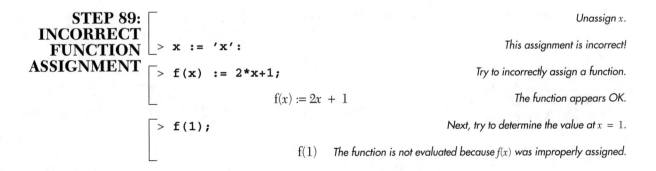

STEP 87:
RAISING
FUNCTIONS
TO POWERS

Enter operators after the right parenthesis (") ").

> **sin(Pi/4)^2;**

Determine $\sin^2\left(\dfrac{\pi}{4}\right) = \left(\sin\dfrac{\pi}{4}\right)^2$.

$$\dfrac{1}{2}$$

$\sin^2\left(\dfrac{\pi}{4}\right) = \dfrac{1}{2}\sqrt{2}$; *thus,* $\left(\dfrac{1}{2}\sqrt{2}\right) = \left(\dfrac{1}{4}\right)(2) = \dfrac{1}{2}$.

To evaluate $\sin^2 x$, never enter **sin^2(x)** or **sin(x^2)**! Also, remember that Maple still attempts full evaluation and automatic simplification on expressions that are composed of functions.

6.1.4 Assignments

Use assignments to simulate functions by entering the statement **name:=expr**. Maple then replaces each instance of **name** with **expr**:

STEP 88:
SIMULATED-
FUNCTION
ASSIGNMENT

Assign expressions to names to simulate functions.

> **y := 2*x+1;**

Assign the variable y to the expression $2x + 1$.

> **x:=1: y;**

Assign x to 1. Now, evaluate the value of y.

$$y := 2x + 1$$

So far, so good...

$$3$$

Yes, the correct answer is 3. Maple replaced x with 1.

The name y here simulates the function $f(x)$.

However, never enter $f(x) = mx + b$ as **f(x):=m*x+b** to express $f(x)$:

STEP 89:
INCORRECT
FUNCTION
ASSIGNMENT

Unassign x.

> **x := 'x':**

This assignment is incorrect!

> **f(x) := 2*x+1;**

Try to incorrectly assign a function.

$$f(x) := 2x + 1$$

The function appears OK.

> **f(1);**

Next, try to determine the value at $x = 1$.

$$f(1)$$ *The function is not evaluated because $f(x)$ was improperly assigned.*

Section 6.6 discusses how to enter functional notation that allows **f(x)** as valid input.

PRACTICE!

1. Enter the expression $\sin^2\theta + \cos^2\theta$ using Maple Notation.
2. Try the function **simplify(expr)** to reduce the expression in the previous problem.
3. Simulate the equation $f(t) = \sin t$ with the name y and an assignment.

6.2 POLYNOMIALS

Polynomials, which are incredibly common functions, often approximate intricate models. This section demonstrates many functions for operating and manipulating polynomials. For information on many polynomial functions, consult Mathematics... Algebra...Polynomials... in Maple's Help Browser.

6.2.1 Definition

Polynomials contain sums of terms with integer exponents, where each *term* represents virtually any name or constant:

$$(term)^0 + (term)^1 + (term)^2 + \ldots + (term)^n \tag{6-1}$$

Not all terms and powers must be present in a polynomial:

STEP 90: POLYNOMIAL TYPES

Test for polynomials.

```
> x:='x':y:='y':
```
Clear any x and y assignments.

```
> type(x^2+y+30,polynom);
```
Enter a polynomial.

$$true$$

$x^2 + y + 30$ *is indeed a polynomial.*

Consult **?polynom**, **?content**, **?ratpoly**, **?type[polynom]**, and **?type[monomial]** for more information.

6.2.2 Polynomial Arithmetic

Maple operators and functions may be used on polynomials. Beware that sometimes Maple will not simplify the result. First, assign two polynomials with which to play:

STEP 91: ASSIGN POLYNOMIALS

Do not forget to unassign x, if necessary!

```
> P1 := x^2+3*x+2;
```
Assign P1 to a polynomial.

$$P1 := x^2 + 3x + 2$$

*Did you remember your operators * and +?*

```
> P2 := x+4;
```
Assign P2 to a polynomial.

$$P2 := x + 4$$

*Did you remember your operators * and +?*

Now, perform polynomial arithmetic operations:

STEP 92:
POLYNOMIAL
ADDITION

> P1+P2;

$$x^2 + 4x + 6$$

Perform arithmetic operations on polynomials.

Add and subtract polynomials.

Maple automatically simplifies common terms.

STEP 93:
POLYNOMIAL
MULTIPLICA-
TION

> P1*P2;

$$(x^2 + 3x + 2)(x + 4)$$

Perform arithmetic operations on polynomials.

Multiply and divide polynomials.

Chapter 7 discusses how to simplify these results.

6.2.3 Factoring

As discussed in **?factor**, enter **factor(*polynom*)** to split a polynomial into factors. Recall that factors are the smallest divisible expressions whose product yields the polynomial:

STEP 94:
FACTOR
POLYNOMIALS

> factor(P1);factor(P2);

$$(x + 2)(x + 1)$$

$$(x + 4)$$

Split polynomials into factors.

Factor P1 and P2.

$(x + 2)(x + 1) = x^2 + 3x + 2 = P1$

$(x + 4)$ *is the only factor of* $x + 4$.

Maple simply returns the polynomial as the sole factor when no factorization is possible. Enter **ifactor(*integer*)** to factor integers.

6.2.4 Expanding

In Step 93, Maple did not distribute the product $(x^2 + 3x + 2)(x + 4)$. To multiply out the factors $x^2 + 3x + 2$ and $x + 4$, enter **expand(*expr*)**:

STEP 95:
EXPAND
POLYNOMIALS

> expand(P1*P2);

$$x^3 + 7x^2 + 14x + 8$$

Multiply out polynomials and factors.

expand performs all possible multiplication and addition operations.

$(x^2 + 3x + 2)(x + 4) = x^3 + 7x^2 + 14x + 8$

Actually, **expand(*expr*)** distributes products over sums. In the next chapter, **expand** is used for more general expressions.

PRACTICE!

> **4.** Determine whether the following statements produce a polynomial:
>
>   `[> a:='a': x:=sin(a): poly:=x^2+2;`
>
> **5.** Unassign x. Now, assign A to $x^2 - 1$. Assign B to $x^2 + 3x + 2$.
> **6.** Evaluate $A^2 + AB$. Assign $C1$ to the result.
> **7.** Evaluate $\dfrac{A}{B}$. Assign $C2$ to the result.
> **8.** Enter **expand** and/or **factor** to simplify $C1$ and $C2$.

6.2.5 Polynomial Division

Given two expressions a and b, you can divide a by b by specifying $a \div b$ or a/b. Dividing a by b produces a *quotient q* and a *remainder r* such that

$$a = bq + r. \tag{6-2}$$

For instance, $5 \div 4$ yields $5 = 4(1) + 1$. Given expressions **a** and **b** in Maple, enter either **quo(a,b,term,'r')** or **rem(a,b,term,'q')** to divide **a** by **b**:

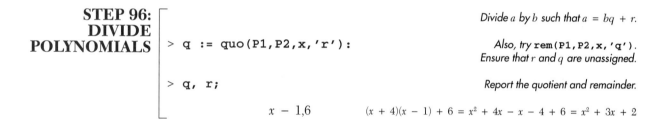

STEP 96: DIVIDE POLYNOMIALS

Divide a by b such that $a = bq + r$.

```
> q := quo(P1,P2,x,'r'):
```
Also, try **rem(P1,P2,x,'q')**.
Ensure that r and q are unassigned.

```
> q, r;
```
Report the quotient and remainder.

$$x - 1, 6 \qquad\qquad (x + 4)(x - 1) + 6 = x^2 + 4x - x - 4 + 6 = x^2 + 3x + 2$$

Supply **'r'** or **'q'** arguments to **quo** or **rem**, respectively, to automatically assign a remainder **r** or quotient **q** value. Also, consult **?divide**, **?gcd**, **?lcm**, **?evala**, and **?irem** or **?iquo** for more details.

6.2.6 Root Finding

Factorable polynomials have **roots** that equate polynomials to zero when the roots are substituted back into the polynomial. For instance, $x^2 + 3x + 2$ factors into $(x + 2)(x + 1)$ with roots $x = -2$ and $x = -1$. Either root will cause $x^2 + 3x + 2$ to become zero. Other polynomials, like $x^2 + 2x + 1$, have repeated factors, as in the example $(x + 1)(x + 1)$. This polynomial has a repeated root -1 that appears twice. Thus, the root -1 has a *multiplicity* of 2.

Maple reports polynomial roots as a list of pairs in the form $[[r_1, m_1], [r_2, m_2], \dots , [r_n, m_n]]$. Each $[r_i, m_i]$ pair is the ith root r with multiplicity m. For instance, find the roots of the polynomial $P1 = x^2 + 3x + 2$:

STEP 97:
ROOTS

Find the roots of a polynomial.

```
> x:='x':
```
Unassign x.
```
> factor(x^2+3*x+2);
```
Find the factors of P1.

$$(x + 2)(x + 1)$$

From Step 94: $(x + 2)(x + 1) = x^2 + 3x + 2 = P1$.

```
> roots(x^2+3*x+2);
```
Find the roots of P1.

$$[[-2, 1], [-1, 1]]$$

P1 has two roots, –2 and –1.

–2 factors P1 only once. –1 factors P1 only once.

Compared with the results of **factor**, you can verify that **roots** found each root of $x^2 + 3x + 2$. Also, consult **?root**, **?realroot**, and **?Roots**.

PRACTICE!

9. Evaluate the quotient q and remainder r in Step 96 with **rem**.

10. Confirm that your quotient and remainder are valid. Hint: Use **expand**.

11. What are the roots of $x^3 - 3x - 2$? Do any roots repeat? If so, how many times?

6.3 TRIGONOMETRY

Many equations rely on trigonometry to transform physical models into different coordinate systems. After all, nature knows no axes! Trigonometry helps model a variety of problems throughout all branches of engineering and science. This section introduces basic trigonometric functions in Maple.

6.3.1 Angles

Many programs require angles to be entered in terms of ***radians***. Use the conversion

$$2\pi \text{ radians} = 360° \tag{6-3}$$

or the command **convert(*angle*,radians)**:

STEP 98: ANGLE
CONVERSION
TO RADIANS

Convert degrees to radians.

```
> convert(45*degrees,radians);
```
Enter 45° as 45 degrees.*

$$\frac{1}{4}\pi$$

Maple evaluates radians in terms of π when possible.

Remember to always specify π as **Pi** when entering angles in terms of radians! Consult **?convert[degrees]** and **?convert[radians]** for more information.

6.3.2 Trigonometric Functions

Table 6-1 summarizes common trigonometric functions. Consult **?trig** for a full listing that includes information on hyperbolic functions. Inverse trigonometric functions are described in **?invtrig**.

TABLE 6-1   Trigonometric Functions

FUNCTION	STANDARD MATH	MAPLE NOTATION	DESCRIPTION
sine	$\sin\theta$	`sin(theta)`	
cosine	$\cos\theta$	`cos(theta)`	
tangent	$\tan\theta = \dfrac{\sin\theta}{\cos\theta}$	`tan(theta)`	
cosecant	$\csc\theta = \dfrac{1}{\sin\theta}$	`csc(theta)`	
secant	$\sec\theta = \dfrac{1}{\cos\theta}$	`sec(theta)`	Inverse trigonometric functions start with **arc**: Standard Math: $\sin^{-1}\frac{y}{r} = \arcsin\frac{y}{r} = \theta$ Maple Notation: `arcsin(y/r)`
cotangent	$\cot\theta = \dfrac{1}{\tan\theta}$	`cot(theta)`	

PRACTICE!

12. Convert 120° to radians. Convert the result back to degrees.

13. Find the secant of 30°.

14. Find the tangent of $\dfrac{\pi}{2}$.

15. Assume that the sine of an angle is 0.35. What is the angle in degrees?

6.4 POWERS AND ROOTS

This section reviews functions that are associated with powers and roots.

6.4.1 Exponentiation

Recall that the exponentiation operators **^** and ****** operators raise an expression to a power:

STEP 99: EXPONENTIA-TION

```
> 123.*10^(-2);
```

$$1.230000000$$

Raise expressions to powers.

Simulate scientific notation.

Also, try entering `123.0E-2`.

6.4.2 Roots

You have already used **sqrt(x)** for $\sqrt{x}$. In general, you can also find the nth root of x

$$\sqrt[n]{x} = x^{\frac{1}{n}} \tag{6-4}$$

with fractional powers:

STEP 100: ROOTS WITH FRACTIONAL POWERS

```
> A:=8^(1/3);
```

$$A := 8^{\frac{1}{3}}$$

Find roots of expressions.

Find the cube root of 8.

This expression is the cube root of 8.

Except in special cases, such as floating-point evaluations, often Maple cannot simplify expressions as demonstrated in Step 100. To force simplification, enter `simplify(expr)`. See Chapter 9 for more details:

STEP 101:
SIMPLIFY
ROOTS WITH
FRACTIONAL
POWERS

> `simplify(A);`

2

Find roots of expressions.
Often, you might need to simplify the resulting output.
You may also enter `evalf(A)` *to produce a float.*

You may also enter `root(x, n)` to directly find a root:

STEP 102:
ROOTS WITH
root FUNCTION

> `root(8,3);`

2

Find roots of expressions.
Find the cube root of 8.
$2^3 = 8.$

Beware that when using **root**, Maple finds the *principal root*, as defined by the formula

$$\text{root}(x, n) = e^{\left(\frac{\ln x}{n}\right)}. \tag{6-5}$$

See Sections 6.4.4 and 6.4.5 for explanations of ln and e. In general, principal roots yield complex results:

STEP 103:
COMPLEX
ROOTS

> `simplify((-1)^(1/3));`

$\frac{1}{2} + \frac{1}{2} I \sqrt{3}$

Generate imaginary numbers when finding roots.
Find the cube root of −1.
What happened to the real root, −1? $(-1)^3 = -1!$

6.4.3 Real Roots

To find real number roots, enter `surd(expr, root)`, which is the function for finding *non-principal roots*. When n is odd, then

$$\text{surd}(x, n) = \begin{cases} x^{1/n} & x \geq 0 \\ -(-x)^{1/n} & x < 0 \end{cases} \tag{6-6}$$

These equations can generate real roots. For instance, find the real root for $(-1)^{1/3}$:

STEP 104: REAL ROOTS

> `surd(-1,3);`

Generate real roots when possible.

Find the cube root of -1 as $(-1)^{1/3}$.

Produce a "real" result if possible.

$$-1$$

Now, Maple found $(-1)^{1/3} = -1$.

When no real root exists, **surd** returns a complex root.

Investigate **?assume** for information on applying properties that can assist exponentiation operations on variables. For instance, entering **assume(x>=0)** tells Maple that x is positive. Also, consult **?sqrt** and **?realroot** for related functions.

6.4.4 Logarithms

Consult Table 6-2 for a review of logarithms. ***Natural logarithms***, $\ln x$, employ the irrational base $e = 2.71828\ldots$. Logarithms of a general base b can be converted to ln form using the formula

$$\log_b y = \frac{\ln y}{\ln b}. \tag{6-7}$$

Maple usually expresses logarithms in terms of ln using the conversion in Eq. 6-7.

TABLE 6-2 Logarithms

FUNCTION	STANDARD MATH		MAPLE NOTATION
Logarithm of Base b	$b^x = y$	$\log_b y = x$	`log[b](y)`
Base-10 Logarithm	$10^x = y$	$\log_{10} y = x$	`log[10](y)` `readlib(log10): log10(y)`
Natural Logarithm	$e^x = y$	$\log_e y = \ln y = x$	`ln(y)` `log(y)`

STEP 105: LOGARITHMS

> `A:=log[10](100);`

> `simplify(A);`

$$A := \frac{\ln(100)}{\ln(10)}$$

$$2$$

Find a base-10 log.

Evaluate $\log_{10} 100 = x$, where $10^x = 100$.

Also, try `evalf` *for floating-point values.*

`log` *functions tend to produce answers in terms of* ln.

$10^2 = 100$

Consult **?log** and **?ilog** for more details.

6.4.5 Exponential Function

Enter the ***exponential function*** $\exp x$, where $\exp x = e^x$, to raise the constant e to a power:

STEP 106:
EXPONENTIAL
FUNCTION

> `exp(x), exp(2), exp(x)*exp(y);`

$$e^x, e^2, e^x e^y$$

Practice entering e^x as exp(x).

Enter the sequence e^x, e^2, $e^x e^y$.

Maple outputs e as e. But, never enter "e" as input!

Maple outputs **exp(expr)** as **e**^{expr}. However, never enter "e" or "E" for the constant e! Also, never confuse the exponentiation operator represented by the caret (^) with the exponential function **exp**!

PRACTICE!

16. Evaluate $\sqrt[3]{-8}$. Find all real and complex roots.
17. Find x such that $7^x = 163$. Show your answer as a float. Check the answer that Maple produces.
18. Evaluate the exponential constant to five decimal places.
19. Find $\ln(\exp(x))$. How are ln and exp related?

6.5 MISCELLANEOUS

Table 6-3 reviews common mathematical operations and functions that you might encounter throughout your education and career in engineering and science. ***Procedural Maple functions***, like manipulation, evaluation, solving, plotting, and programming, are reviewed elsewhere in this text.

PRACTICE!

20. Evaluate |–18|, |0|, and |18|.
21. Add the real and imaginary components of e^{ix}.
22. Generate the sequence 1, 2, 4, 8 with **seq** or **$**. Assign S to the result.
23. Add each element of S. Hint: Consult **?sum**.
24. Multiply each element of S. Hint: Consult **?product**.

6.6 FUNCTIONAL NOTATION

Entering assignments in the form of **y:=m*x+b** provides only a shortcut. This section discusses how entering functions in ***functional notation*** in the form of **f(x)** is more natural than using simulated functions.

6.6.1 Definition

Enter the operator **->** to create your own functions that use functional notation in the form of **name(args)**. Assign the function **name** with the syntax **name:=args->expr**:

- **name** defines the function name. Avoid using protected names.
- **args** are function arguments. Use parentheses when there are multiple variables as in **f:=(x,y)->x+y**.
- **expr** is the actual expression of the function in terms of **args**.

Consult **?->** or **?operators[functional]** and **?operators[example]** for more information. Consult **?student[makeproc]** for an alternative syntax.

TABLE 6-3   Miscellaneous Functions and Operations

FUNCTIONS	STANDARD MATH	MAPLE NOTATION	RELATED FUNCTIONS AND HELP
Absolute Value	$|x|$	`abs(x)`	`?abs, ?sign,` `?signum, ?csgn`

Boolean	$x \wedge y$
	 $x \vee y$
	 Is $x \neq y$?
		`x and y`
		 `x or y`
		 `evalb(x <> y)`
			`?boolean, ?equation,` `?evalb, ?logic`

Complex	$\Re(x) + \Im(x)$ e^{ix}	`Re(x) + Im(x)` `evalc(exp(I*x))`	`?argument, ?conjugate,` `?csgn, ?evalc, ?polar`
Factorial	$x!$	`x!` `factorial(x)`	`?binomial, ?combinat,` `?combstruct,` `?factorial, ?group`
Floats	$\sqrt{2} = 1.414...$	`evalf(sqrt(2))`	`?evalf, ?float, ?fsolve,` `?numapprox, ?trunc`
Integer	$72 = (2)^2(3)^2$	`ifactor(72)`	`?arith, ?ifactor,` `?integer,` `?trunc`
Inverse	f^{-1}	`f@@(-1)`	`?@, ?@@, ?invfunc,` `readlib(invfunc)`
List	$[x_1, x_2]$ $[f(x_1), f(x_2)]$	`[x[1], x[2]]` `map(f,[x[1],x[2]])`	`?list, ?member,` `?select, ?sort`
Piecewise	$f(x) = \begin{cases} e^x & 0 < x \\ 0 & \text{otherwise} \end{cases}$	`piecewise(0<x,exp(x))`	`?piecewise`
Product	$\displaystyle\prod_{i=1}^{n} x_1$	`product(x[i],i=1..n)`	`?mul, ?product`
Sequence	x_1, x_2, x_3	`seq(x[i],i=1..3)` `x[i] $ i=1..3)`	`?seq, ?sequence, ?$`
Series	$\cos x = 1 - \dfrac{1}{2} x^2$ $+ O(x^4)$	`series(cos(x),x=0,4)`	`?Order, ?powseries,` `?series, ?taylor`
Set	$x \cap y$ $x \cup y$	`x intersect y` `x union y`	`?intersect, ?minus,` `?set, ?union`
Summation	$\displaystyle\sum_{i=1}^{n} x_i$	`sum(x[i],i=1..n)`	`?add, ?sum`

6.6.2 Creating Functions in Functional Notation

For instance, create a function $f(x) = x^2$:

STEP 107: **FUNCTIONAL** **NOTATION WITH** **ONE VARIABLE**	`> f := x -> x^2;` $f := x \rightarrow x^2$	*Define a function as $f(x)$.* *Assign $f(x) = x^2$.* *Maple now considers f as the functional form $f(x)$.*
STEP 108: **SHOW VALUES** **WITH** **FUNCTIONAL** **NOTATION**	`> f(0),f(1),f(2),f(3);` $0, 1, 4, 9$	*Use $f(x)$ notation in expressions.* *Use $f(x)$ to find four distinct values of x.* *Do not assign x to any expression. Use $f(x)$.*

Investigate **?unapply** for information on converting an expression assignment into functional notation.

PRACTICE!

25. Create a function dis$(x) = x^3 + x^2 + x + 1$ using functional notation.
26. Find the value of dis(x) at $x = -1$ and $x = 1$.
27. Plot dis(x) on the interval $-1 \le 0 \le 1$.
28. Create a function $f(x, y, z) = x + y + z$ using functional notation.

6.7 APPLICATION: WEIRS

This section introduces aspects of hydraulics and fluid flow that apply various Maple functions.

6.7.1 Background

Open-channel flow refers to fluid flow that is partially exposed to the atmosphere. Common examples include water flowing though rivers, canals, and sewers. Often, such flows need control to limit their height without completely blocking the flow. As shown in Figure 6.5, weirs resemble dams that permit overflow.

Sharp-crest weirs have flat, sharp surfaces like that of the triangular, or V-notch, weir illustrated in Figure 6.5. Besides limiting flow, triangular weirs can also aid the calculation of flow-rate measurements, especially when rates greatly vary. The formula for the flow Q (m³/s) over a triangular weir is

$$Q = C_d \left(\frac{8}{15}\right) \tan\left(\frac{\theta}{2}\right) \sqrt{2g} h^{2.5}. \tag{6-6}$$

Q depends on the experimentally derived *discharge coefficient* C_d, the notch angle θ, and the flow height h (m). Use the gravitational constant $g = 9.81 \text{m/s}^2$.

6.7.2 Problem

Given a triangular weir with a notch angle of 60° and a flow height $h = 2.3$ m, determine the flow rate over the weir.

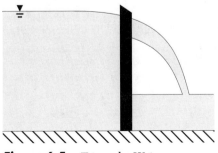
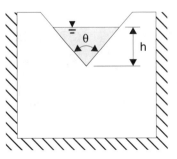

Figure 6.5.   Triangular Weir

6.7.3 Methodology

First, state and assign pertinent variables:

**STEP 109:
INITIALIZE
MAPLE**

Initialize system variables.

```
> restart:
```
Restart your Maple session.

```
> Digits:=3:
```
Use three digits in your calculations.

**STEP 110:
RESTATE AND
SEPARATE**

Initialize problem variables.

```
> g:=9.8*m/s^2:
```
Assign the gravitational constant.

```
> h:=2.3*m:
```
Assign the flow height.

```
> theta:=convert(60*degrees,radians):
```
Assign the notch angle, but use radians!

For a "prettier" solution, use an indexed name to represent the coefficient C_d:

**STEP 111:
RESTATE AND
SEPARATE**

Initialize problem variables.

```
> C[d]:=0.59;
```
Express C_d as an indexed name to format the subscript d.

$$C_d := 0.59$$
Now your output looks like typeset mathematics.

Now, express the entire formula for the flow rate Q:

**STEP 112:
MODEL**

Assign the model for flow rate.

```
> Q:=C[d]*(8/15)*tan(theta/2)*sqrt(2*g)*h^(5/2);
```
Model the flow rate Q.

$$3.78\sqrt{3}\sqrt{\frac{m}{s^2}}\, m^{\frac{5}{2}}$$
Remember that Maple prefers exact values.

Try to convince Maple to express Q in a more useful form:

**STEP 113:
SOLVE AND
REPORT**

Show your results.

```
> simplify(Q);
```
Attempt to reduce the numbers and units by simplification.

$$6.54\sqrt{\frac{m}{s^2}}\, m^{\frac{5}{2}}$$
Maple will not automatically reduce roots of variables.

Maple will not reduce roots of expressions that *might* be negative. However, the variables m and s must represent positive units! You can try to use either **simplify (expr, symbolic)** (see Chapter 7) or **assume (relations)** to restrict variable properties:

STEP 114:
SOLVE AND
REPORT

Further reduce your results.

> **assume (m>0, s>0);**   *Tell Maple to assume that both m and s are positive.*

> **simplify (Q);**   *Now, try to reduce Q with positive unit variables.*

$$6.54 \, \frac{m\mathord{\sim}^3}{s\mathord{\sim}}$$ *It worked!*

A trailing tilde (~) on a name indicates that the variable carries an assumption.

6.7.4 Solution

The flow rate Q over the triangular weir is approximately 6.54 m/s³.

SUMMARY

This chapter has introduced many mathematical functions. Common functions include polynomials. Polynomial arithmetic directly follows from arithmetic between numbers. However, when multiplying and dividing, you might need to expand results. Other operations, such as root finding and factoring, have been demonstrated in this chapter. When using trigonometric functions, you should enter angles in terms of radians. When finding roots, you should use **root** and **surd** to find all roots. Also, never confuse exponentiation (**^**) with **exp**! Maple provides a functional-notation operator (**->**) to assign customized functions in the form $f(x)$.

KEY TERMS

argument	natural logarithms	procedural Maple functions
exponential function	nested functions	radians
functional notation	parameter	roots
Maple functions	polynomials	

Problems

1. What is a function? How do you express functions in Maple? Demonstrate with an example.
2. Given $f(x) = 2x^3$, evaluate $f(-1), f(0),$ and $f(1)$ using Maple.
3. For Problems 6.3a through 6.3d, let $P = x^2 + 6x + 7$ and $Q = x + 1$.
   a. Evaluate $P + Q$ and $P - Q$.
   b. Evaluate $PQ, P^2Q,$ and $\frac{P}{Q}$. Distribute (multiply out) all products and sums.
   c. Divide P by Q using both **rem** and **quo**. Display the quotient and remainder as output in both cases. (Hint: For instance, enter **rem(P, Q, x, 'q')** for **rem**.)
   d. Confirm your results in Problem 6.3c. (Hint: Use both **evalb** and **expand**.)
4. Factor the polynomial $x^4 - 2x^2 + 1$. How many different roots does the polynomial contain? How many times does each root factorize the polynomial? (Hint: Try **factor** and **roots**.)
5. Evaluate $\sqrt[3]{-72}$. For both real and complex roots in exact irrational form. (Hints: Use **simplify** to clarify results. Note that Maple will show fractional exponents.)
6. Can you take the natural logarithm of a negative number? Demonstrate your answer with a plot of $\ln(x)$ on $-1 \le x \le 1$.

7. Evaluate the following expressions:

---

a. $\sin^2(x)$

b. $\sin\left(\dfrac{\pi}{4}\right)$

c. $\sin^2\left(\dfrac{\pi}{4}\right)$

d. $\sqrt{\sin(17)}$ (produce both exact and decimal results)

e. $\tan(45°)$

f. $\log_{10} 100$

g. $\ln 5.216$

h. $2.4^{-1.2}$

i. $\dfrac{1}{e}$ (produce both exact and decimal results)

j. πe^2 (produce both exact and decimal results)

---

8. Create a function that finds a trapezoid's area

$$\text{trap}(b_1, b_2, h) = h \times \left(\frac{b_1 + b_2}{2}\right)$$

by using functional notation. Also, evaluate trap(1, 2, 3).

9. Given a triangular weir with a notch angle of $75°$ and flow height $h = 1.9$ m, determine the flow rate over the weir. (Hint: Refer to Section 6.7.)

10. Snow blowing over a large unblocked distance called *fetch* contributes to accumulating snow drifts. Given the relationship between snow transport capacity $\dfrac{Q_t}{Q_{inf}}$ and fetch F(m),

$$\frac{Q_t}{Q_{inf}} = \left(1 - 0.14^{\frac{F}{3000}}\right).$$

Solve for F assuming that $\dfrac{Q_t}{Q_{inf}} = 0.8$. (Hints: Rearrange the equation with logarithms on both sides. Also, consider entering **assume(F>0)**). Does transport capacity increase or decrease as fetch increases? (Hint: Use a plot.)

11. A *tautology* is a logical proof, or a sequence of statements that demonstrates the truth or falsehood of a given statement. For instance, the logical statement "p implies q," often expressed as $p \to q$, has a logical equivalence to the expression $(\neg p) \vee q$ ("not p or q").

    a. Investigate Maple's logic library package. (Hint: Consult Table 6-3, Appendix D, **?logic**, and **?with**.)

    b. Demonstrate the tautology that the statement *true* ∧ *false* is false. (Hints: Consult **?tautology** inside the logic library package. Use the binary operator **&and** to represent the operator ∧.)

    c. Complete the following table by using **tautology**, assuming true (T) and false (F) values for p and q. (Hint: A few answers have been provided. For instance, try **tautology(true &implies false)**.)

    TABLE 6-4   Tautology

p	q	p → q	(¬p) ∨ q
T	T		T
T	F	F	
F	T		
F	F		T

    d. Logically equivalent statements yield the same tautologies. Are the statements $p \to q$ and $(\neg p) \vee q$ logically equivalent based on your results in Table 6-4?

12. Review the material discussed on page 68. Devise an experiment that measures forces for given spring displacements. Identify the dependent and independent variables. Explain your experimental configuration, and supply appropriate directions and descriptions.

7

Manipulating Expressions

7.1 INTRODUCTION

Expressions have many equivalent forms. Accordingly, Maple might not always generate the answers that you expect. This chapter introduces ***expression manipulation***, which is the term that describes methods that change an expression into equivalent forms. You have already used procedural functions that manipulate expressions, such as **simplify**, **factor**, and **expand**. Consult Mathematics...Algebra... in the Help Browser for information on a variety of procedural functions.

OBJECTIVES

After reading this chapter, you should be able to:

- Manipulate Maple expressions
- Convert expressions into other forms
- Simplify and reduce expressions into smaller forms
- Expand expressions into larger forms
- Sort and extract expressions

Automotive engineers strive to produce efficient, affordable, and reliable vehicles. The DIATA (Direct Injection Aluminum Through-Bolt Assembly) engine powers Ford's Hybrid Electric Vehicle called the P2000. With this engine, the five-passenger P2000 vehicle can achieve over 60 miles per gallon (mpg) with performance and comfort comparable to that of conventional cars. Courtesy of Ford Motor Company

---

PROFESSIONAL SUCCESS: WRITE "WELL," NOT "GOOD"!

Strive for clarity! Treat your writing as you would your calculations. Study these writing tips that are adapted from a popular file floating around the Internet:

- ❏ Prepositions are not words to end sentences with.
- ❏ Avoid clichés like the plague. Besides, they are old hat.
- ❏ Pronouns confuse readers. They are uncertain, so avoid them, unlike this.
- ❏ Don't use contractions that aren't necessary.
- ❏ It was, perhaps, decided that sentences, like this, might possibly avoid responsibility.
- ❏ Avoid ampersands & abbreviations, etc.
- ❏ Parenthetical remarks (however relevant) are not necessary.
- ❏ Profanity sucks.
- ❏ "Alternative" is the best alternative between the alternatives, "alternative" and "alternate".
- ❏ Be more or less specific.
- ❏ Exaggeration is a billion times better than understatement.
- ❏ One-word sentences? Eliminate!
- ❏ On the other hand, excessively long sentences detract from readability and clarity by not only providing a barrage of detailed concepts, but by boring the reader as well, hence obfuscating pertinent ideas originally intended for incisive communication.
- ❏ The passive voice is to be avoided.
- ❏ Rhetorical questions? Who needs them?
- ❏ *Its you're roll too reed four* homophones. *Sew than, due ewe sea there affects hear?*
- ❏ Eschew sesquipedalianism.

7.2 CONVERSION

Recall that expressions have a *type*, which is the dominant Maple language-element of an expression. Review **?type** and Chapter 5 for more information. This section reviews the ***conversion*** of expressions into other types. **convert(*expr, form*)** casts, or converts, expressions into other types. Other chapters demonstrate the use of **convert** for unit and angle conversions. Now, try converting a function:

STEP 115:
CONVERT
EXPRESSIONS

Change an expression's type into another type.

> `restart:`   *Clear all assignments.*

> `convert(exp(I*x),trig);`   *Convert e^{ix} into sin's and cos's.*

$$\cos(x) + I\sin(x)$$ *Yes, this expression is equivalent to e^{ix}.*

The **convert** function also helps swap between set and list types:

STEP 116:
CONVERT
EXPRESSIONS

Change an expression's type into another type.

> `convert({a,b,c},list);`   *Convert the set $\{a,b,c\}$ into a list.*

$$[a,b,c]$$ *Square brackets indicate a list.*

Consult **?convert** for the available types. You can also enter **?convert[*type*]** for help on converting to *type*.

PRACTICE!

1. Maple uses RootOf as a place holder for roots of expressions. Enter **RootOf(x^2+1=0)**. Now, convert the entire expression into Maple's **radical** form.
2. Convert the integer 438 into a float.

7.3 SIMPLIFICATION

Simplification usually implies the reduction of an expression into a more condensed, simpler form. Regardless of Maple's automatic simplification capabilities, Maple often needs additional coaxing to simplify expressions further. This section demonstrates functions for simplifying expressions.

7.3.1 Simplify

Generally, you should first attempt to use the **simplify** function when you want to simplify an expression. In general, enter **simplify(*expr*)** to simplify *expr*:

STEP 117:
SIMPLIFICATION

Simplify expressions.

```
> A:=(x+1)/(x^2-1);
```

$$A := \frac{x+1}{x^2-1}$$

Simplify $\dfrac{x+1}{x^2-1} = \dfrac{x+1}{(x+1)(x-1)}$.

Automatic simplification cannot find the common factor.

```
> simplify(A);
```

$$\frac{1}{x-1}$$

Simplify $\dfrac{x+1}{x^2-1}$.

simplify *removed the common factor.*

However, not all simplifications produce the *smallest-looking* expressions:

STEP 118:
SIMPLEST ≠
SMALLEST!

Built-in rules might cause larger expressions.

```
> simplify(sin(x)^2);
```

$$1 - \cos(x)^2$$

Simplify $\sin^2 x$.

Maple prefers cosine to sine.

In fact, not all simplification statements actually work:

STEP 119:
SIMPLIFICATION
MIGHT FAIL!

simplify *sometimes fails.*

```
> simplify(sin(2*x)/cos(2*x));
```

$$\frac{\sin(2x)}{\cos(2x)}$$

Does Maple produce $\tan 2x$?

Maple does not think that $\tan 2x$ is simpler!

You can also try **simplify(*expr*,*form*)**, where *form* includes the labels **symbolic**, **trig**, **power**, **ln**, and **exp**:

STEP 120:
SIMPLIFICATION
WITH SUPPLIED
FORMS

Modify **simplify**'s *behavior.*

```
> sqrt(x^2);
```

$$\sqrt{x^2}$$

Find $\sqrt{x^2}$.

Maple refuses to simplify because x might be negative.

```
> simplify(sqrt(x^2),symbolic);
```

$$x$$

Require Maple only to consider the symbolic nature of x.

Now Maple can find that $\sqrt{x^2} = x$.

Enter **?simplify[*form*]** for help on individual forms.

7.3.2 Combine

When your expressions involve sums, products, and powers, enter **combine(*expr*)** to simplify *expr*. The **combine** function's built-in transformation rules help reduce the size of an expression:

STEP 121:
COMBINING
EXPRESSIONS

Simplify expressions with sums, products, and powers.

```
> combine(sin(x)*cos(y)-cos(x)*sin(y));
```
Does Maple know this trigonometric identity?

$$\sin(x - y)$$

Yes, Maple can transform many identities.

Maple might also report $-\sin(-x + y)$.

Enter **combine(*expr, form*)** for specific transformations, where ***form*** is a name or list of names:

STEP 122:
COMBINING
EXPRESSIONS
USING SPECI-
FIED TRANS-
FORMATIONS

*Enhance **combine**'s rules.*

```
> A:=(x^a)*(x^b): combine(A);
```
Attempt to reduce $(x^a)(x^b)$.

$$x^a x^b$$

combine(A) *does not suffice.*

```
> combine(A,power);
```
Simplify $(x^a)(x^b)$ by combining the powers.

$$x^{(a+b)}$$

*Supplying the **power** rule helps **combine**.*

Investigate **?combine** for its possible transformations and forms. Also, consult **?combine[*form*]** for rules concerning each ***form***.

7.3.3 Normal

Recall from Section 5.2 that *rational numbers* express numbers as integer ratios. Similarly, ***rational functions*** are ratios of polynomials. The function **normal** seeks rational functions in ***factored normal form***, which is a ratio in the form of $\frac{numerator}{denominator}$, without common factors. For instance, you can eliminate common factors with **normal(*expr*)**:

STEP 123:
RATIONAL
EXPRESSIONS

*Enter **normal** to remove common factors.*

```
> normal((x+1)/(x^2-1));
```
Remove the common factor $x + 1$.

$$\frac{1}{x - 1}$$

*Try **simplify** as well.*

In general, use **normal** for expressions that are in terms of sums and products. See **?normal** for more information.

7.3.4 Radicals

A ***radical expression***, or just *radical*, in Maple has the syntax **expr^(*fraction*)**. See also **?type[radical]**. Maple provides many functions for simplifying and converting radicals. For instance, try **rationalize** in order to remove radicals from an expression's denominator:

STEP 124:
RADICAL
EXPRESSIONS

Experiment with modifying a radical expression.

```
> A:=1/(1+2^(1/3));
```

Assign A to an expression that contains the radical $2^{\frac{1}{3}}$.

$$A := \frac{1}{1+2^{\left(\frac{1}{3}\right)}}$$

Maple automatically keeps the radical in the denominator.

```
> rationalize(A);
```

Remove radicals from the denominator.

$$\frac{1}{3} - \frac{1}{3}\,2^{\left(\frac{1}{3}\right)} + \frac{1}{3}\,2^{\left(\frac{2}{3}\right)}$$

All radicals now appear in the numerator.

Consult **?radsimp**, **?radnormal**, **?rationalize**, **?simplify[radical]**, **?combine[radical]**, and **?convert[radical]** for more information.

7.3.5 Square Roots

Square roots are radicals that have the exponent 1/2, such as $x^{\frac{1}{2}} = \sqrt{x}$. See also **?type[sqrt]**. Many simplification and conversion functions for radicals also handle square roots. For instance, try reducing a square root with **simplify(*expr*,sqrt)**:

STEP 125:
SQUARE ROOT
EXPRESSIONS

Experiment with modifying a square root expression.

```
> A:=12^(1/2);
```

Assign A to $\sqrt{x^2}$.

$$A := \sqrt{12}$$

Maple does not automatically simplify this expression.

```
> simplify(A,sqrt);
```

Simplify the square root expression.

$$2\sqrt{3}$$

Maple expressed $\sqrt{12}$ as $\sqrt{4}\,\sqrt{3}$ and reduced the expression.

Try, also, the square root function **sqrt** that embodies many of the same simplifications. For more information, investigate the same functions in Section 7.3.4 as well as **?simplify[sqrt]**, **?convert[sqrfree]**, and **?convert[RootOf]**.

PRACTICE!

3. Convert $\sin x$ into an expression involving e^x. Simplify the resulting expression such that the original expression reappears.

4. Demonstrate the trigonometric identity $\sin^2 x + \cos^2 x = 1$. Try both **combine** and **simplify**.

5. Does **combine** reduce the expression $\sin x \sin y$? Why or why not?

6. Simplify the expression $x(x + 1) - x^2$.

7. Express $x + \frac{y}{x}$ in factored normal form.

8. Simplify the expression

$$\frac{x^2 - 1}{\sqrt{x+1}}$$

by eliminating the radical in the denominator.

7.4 EXPANSION

Expression *expansion* usually reverses the effects of **combine** and **factor**. Recall how you used **expand** to distribute polynomial factors in Section 6.2. In general, enter **expand(expr)** to distribute products of sums inside expressions:

STEP 126:
EXPANDING
EXPRESSIONS

*Enter **expand** to multiply out products of sums.*

```
> expand((x+1)*(x-1));
```
expand multiplies factored polynomials.

$$x^2 - 1$$
*Sometimes **expand** actually simplifies an expression.*

The **expand** function also understands many other functions:

STEP 127:
EXPANDING
EXPRESSIONS

*Enter **expand** for condensed expressions.*

```
> expand(cos(x-y));
```
expand will often generate identities used to simplify expressions.

$$\cos(x)\cos(y) + \sin(x)\sin(y)$$
*Enter **combine** to reverse this expansion.*

Investigate **normal(expr,expanded)** for rational functions and expressions. Consult **?expandon**, **?expandoff**, and **?factor** for more information.

PRACTICE!

9. How does Maple evaluate **expand(factor(x^2+3*x+2))**?
10. Simplify the resulting expression of **combine(sin(x)*sin(y))**.
11. Expand the expression
$$\frac{x+2}{(x+3)^3}.$$
Try both **expand** and **normal** to do so.

7.5 EXTRACTION AND SORTING

Structural manipulations of expressions include component separation, term rearrangement, and operand extraction, as introduced in this section.

7.5.1 Rational Functions

Enter **numer** and **denom** to extract the numerator and denominator, respectively, of a rational function or expression:

STEP 128:
EXTRACT
NUMERATOR
AND
DENOMINATOR

Extract the numerator and denominator

```
> A:=(a+b)/(c+d);
```
Assign a rational expression.

$$A := \frac{a+b}{c+d}$$
Maple displays your fraction.

```
> numer(A), denom(A);
```
Extract the numerator and denominator of A.

$$a + b, c + d$$
Maple produces the numerator and denominator.

7.5.2 Polynomials

Enter `collect(expr,term)` to rearrange coefficients around `term`:

STEP 129:
COLLECTING
LIKE TERMS

Rearrange a polynomial around specific terms.

`> P:=x*y-(x^2+1)*y;`   *Assign P to a polynomial.*

$$P := xy - (x^2 + 1)y$$ *This is the uncollected polynomial.*

`> P2:=collect(P,y);`   *Rearrange coefficients of P around y.*

$$P2 := (x - x^2 - 1)y$$ `collect` *rearranged all coefficients about y.*

Now, enter `sort(expr)` to sort the coefficients in order of powers:

STEP 130:
SORT TERMS

Rearrange polynomial terms in order of decreasing powers.

`> sort(P2);`   *Sort the coefficients and terms of P2.*

$$(-x^2 + x - 1)y$$ *Maple sorts the terms from highest to lowest power.*

You can also rearrange lists and sequences with `sort`. Investigate related commands inside Mathematics…Algebra…Polynomials… and in **?coeff**, **?lcoeff**, **?degree**, and **?split**.

7.5.3 Operands

Recall how expression trees connect subexpressions composed of Maple's language elements. The operand function **op** extracts these elements from an expression tree:

- `op(expr)` shows all operands contained in the expression's surface type.
- `op(0,expr)` determines the expression's surface type.
- `op(i,expr)` extracts the ith operand from `expr`'s surface type.

Now, experiment finding operands using a simple expression:

STEP 131:
OPERANDS

Extract operands from an expression.

`> a:='a':b:='b': expr:=a+b:`   *Assign expr to $a + b$.*

`> op(expr);`   *Show an expression's surface-type operands.*

$$a, b$$ *$a + b$ has two operands: a and b.*

`> op(0,expr);`   *Evaluate the expression's surface type.*

$$+$$ *Addition (+) connects the two operands a and b.*

Also, consult **?nops**, **?subsop**, **?applyop**, and **?map**.

7.5.4 LHS and RHS

Many types of expressions, such as equations, inequalities, and ranges, employ the syntax **LHS** *operator* **RHS**, where:

- LHS represents the left-hand side of the expression.
- RHS represents the right-hand side of the expression.

For instance, in the equation $y = mx + b$, LHS = y and RHS = $mx + b$. The relational operator, equals sign (=), connects both sides of the equation. You can extract the LHS and RHS of **expr** with **lhs(expr)** and **rhs(expr)**, respectively:

STEP 132:
LHS AND RHS

	Separate left and right operands of an equation.
`> restart:`	*Clear all variable assignments.*
`> EQN:=y=m*x+b;`	*Assign EQN to the equation $y = mx + b$.*
$EQN := y = mx + b$	*The variable EQN stores the entire equation $y = mx + b$.*
`> lhs(EQN);`	*Extract the LHS of EQN.*
y	*The LHS of EQN is not the name EQN.*
`> rhs(EQN);`	*Extract the RHS of EQN.*
$mx + b$	*The RHS of EQN is not the name y.*

PRACTICE!

12. Fully expand the polynomial in the Practice Problem 11 on page 89.
13. Arrange the polynomial $xy - (x^2 + 1)y$ about x. Now, sort the new polynomial.
14. Assign A to $1 + \sin(x + y)$. Determine the surface type and operands of A.
15. Assign *Spring* to the equation $p = ku$. Next, show the value assigned to *Spring*.
16. Enter **lhs(2>1)** and **rhs(2>1)**. Why does Maple reverse the relation $2 > 1$?

7.6 APPLICATION: TORSIONAL ANALYSIS

This section demonstrates Maple's expression-manipulation functions with a structural-mechanics example.

7.6.1 Background

Consider an I-beam (pronounced "eye" beam) that is loaded transversely with a uniform *torque*, which is a bending moment that twists the member, as illustrated in Figure 7.1. As expected, the member rotates about the z-axis at an angle ϕ. Most noncircular structural members, like this I-beam, also *warp* when twisted. That is, the cross section does not remain plane along the z-axis. (You can simulate this warping effect by twisting a soft rectangular object like an eraser or a long cardboard box.)

When determining how the member resists the applied torque, you can calculate the angle of twist ϕ with the formula

$$\phi = C_1 + C_2 z + C_3 \cosh \frac{z}{a} + C_4 \sinh \frac{z}{a} - \frac{a^2 m z^2}{2EC_w}, \qquad (7\text{-}1)$$

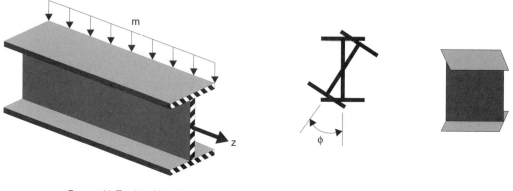

I-Beam with Torsional Load   Twisted Cross Section   Warped Section

Figure 7.1. Warping Torsion

where the coefficients a, C_1, C_2, C_3, C_4, C_w, and E represent structural parameters and boundary conditions. Equation 7-1 is derived from the differential equation

$$\frac{1}{a^2}\frac{d^2\phi}{dz^2} - \frac{d^4\phi}{dz^4} = -\frac{m}{EC_w}, \tag{7-2}$$

which uses the structural parameters C_w and E along with the derivatives $d^2\phi/dz^2$ and $d^4\phi/dz^4$. (See Chapter 11 for an introduction to calculus and differential equations in Maple.)

7.6.2 Problem

When Maple solves Eq. 7-2, Maple's result does not look like Eq. 7-1. Manipulate Maple's result such that you produce an equation that resembles Eq. 7-1.

7.6.3 Methodology

First, blindly accept the input and output in the following steps to establish that Maple really does not provide Eq. 7-1 as the solution of Eq. 7-2. After you take a few calculus courses, these equations will not seem so bad.

STEP 133:
INITIALIZE
MAPLE

Initialize system variables.

```
> restart:
```
Restart your Maple session.

STEP 134:
RESTATE

Initialize problem variables.

```
> DE:=(1/a^2)*diff(phi(z),z$2)-diff(phi(z),z$4)=
(-m)/(E*C[w]);
```

```
> phi1:=dsolve(DE,phi(z));
```
Don't worry for now. Just replicate what you see.

$$DE := \frac{\frac{\partial^2}{\partial z^2}\phi(z)}{a^2} - \left(\frac{\partial^4}{\partial z^4}\phi(z)\right) = -\frac{m}{EC_w}$$
This monstrosity is a differential equation.

$$\phi 1 := \phi(z) = -\frac{1}{2}\frac{a^2mz^2}{EC_w} + \_C1 + \_C2z + \_C3\mathbf{e}^{\left(\frac{z}{a}\right)} + \_C4\mathbf{e}^{\left(\frac{-z}{a}\right)}$$
*Here is
Maple's solution.*

Now, use structural-manipulation functions to express $\phi 1$ in terms of hyperbolic functions. Neglect $\phi(z)$, the LHS portion, and convert only the RHS of $\phi 1$:

STEP 135:
CONVERT

Convert the expression for $\phi 1$ into an equivalent form.

```
> phi2:=convert(rhs(phi1),trig);
```
Hyperbolic sine and cosine functions resemble the traditional trigonometric sine and cosine functions.

$$\phi 2 := -\frac{1}{2}\frac{a^2 m z^2}{EC_w} + \_C1 + \_C2z + \_C3\left(\cosh\left(\frac{z}{a}\right)+\sinh\left(\frac{z}{a}\right)\right) + \_C4\left(\cosh\left(\frac{z}{a}\right)\right) - \sinh\left(\frac{z}{a}\right)$$

Throughout this example, Maple might organize your output terms differently, but will still produce equivalent equations. Now, reorganize $\phi 2$ by using **collect** for each function:

STEP 136:
COLLECT

Reorganize subexpressions in an expression.

```
> phi3:=collect(phi2,cosh);
```
Collect terms in $\phi 3$ corresponding to **cosh**.

```
> phi4:=collect(phi3,sinh);
```
Collect terms in $\phi 4$ corresponding to **sinh**.

$$\phi 3 := (\_C3 + \_C4)\cosh\left(\frac{z}{a}\right) - \frac{1}{2}\frac{a^2 m z^2}{EC_w} + \_C1 + \_C2z + \_C3\sinh\left(\frac{z}{a}\right) - \_C4\sinh\left(\frac{z}{a}\right)$$

$$\phi 4 := (\_C3 - \_C4)\sinh\left(\frac{z}{a}\right) + (\_C3 + \_C4)\cosh\left(\frac{z}{a}\right) - \frac{1}{2}\frac{a^2 m z^2}{EC_w} + \_C1 + \_C2z$$

7.6.4 Solution

The equation for $\phi 4$ is essentially the same as Eq. 7-1. If you prefer, peek ahead into Chapter 9 for the function **subs**:

STEP 137:
SUBSTITUTE

Swap Maple's choices of expression names for your own..

```
> phi:=subs({_C1=C1,_C2=C2,(_C3+_C4)=C3,(_C3-_C4)=C4},phi4);
```

$$\phi := C3\cosh\left(\frac{z}{a}\right) + C4\sinh\left(\frac{z}{a}\right) - \frac{1}{2}\frac{a^2 m z^2}{EC_w} + C1 + C2z$$

You might also wish to rearrange terms further with **sort**.

SUMMARY

This chapter has introduced techniques for manipulating expressions. In general, first try to simplify an expression with **simplify**. Also, you may enhance **simplify**'s abilities with options. Other methods of expression manipulation include converting, combining, expanding, and sorting. Converting expressions with **convert** changes an expression's surface type. Use **combine** when aiming for the smallest expression size. Reverse the effects of combine with **expand**. Functions, like **sort** and **collect**, help to reorganize an expression. Extract operands with **op**, **lhs**, and **rhs**.

KEY TERMS

conversion

expansion

expression manipulation

factored normal form

LHS

radical expression

rational functions

RHS

simplification

structural manipulations

Problems

1. Explain the difference between conversion and simplification.
2. Under what conditions should you attempt to use the **normal** function?
3. Confirm the following identities using Maple:

a. $\sin^2 x + \cos^2 x = 1$

b. $1 + \tan^2 x = \sec^2 x$

c. $1 + \cot^2 x = \csc^2 x$

d. $\sin(x + y) = \sin x \cos y + \cos x \sin y$

e. $\cos(x + y) = \cos x \cos y - \sin x \sin y$

f. $\tan(x + y) = \dfrac{\tan x + \tan y}{1 - \tan x \tan y}$

g. $\sin 2x = 2 \sin x \cos x$

h. $\cos 2x = 2\cos^2 x - 1$

i. $\cos 2x = \cos^2 x - \sin^2 x$

j. $\sin^2 x = \dfrac{1 - \cos 2x}{2}$

k. $\cos^2 x = \dfrac{1 + \cos 2x}{2}$

l. $\sin x + \sin y = 2\sin\left(\dfrac{x + y}{2}\right)\cos\left(\dfrac{x - y}{2}\right)$

m. $\cos x + \cos y = 2\cos\left(\dfrac{x + y}{2}\right)\cos\left(\dfrac{x - y}{2}\right)$

n. $\sin x \sin y = -\dfrac{1}{2}\left(\cos(x + y) - \cos(x - y)\right)$

o. $\cos x \cos y = \dfrac{1}{2}\left(\cos(x + y) + \cos(x - y)\right)$

p. $\sin x \cos y = \dfrac{1}{2}\left(\sin(x + y) + \sin(x - y)\right)$

q. $x^a x^b = x^{(a+b)}$

r. $\dfrac{x^a}{x^b} = x^{(a-b)}$

s. $(x^a)^b = x^{(ab)}$ (assume real values)

t. $(xy)^a = x^a y^a$ (assume real values)

u. $\log_b xy = \log_b x + \log_b y$

v. $\log_b \dfrac{x}{y} = \log_b x - \log_b y$

w. $\log_b x^a = a \log_b x$

x. $\sinh x = \dfrac{e^x - e^{-x}}{2}$

y. $\cosh x = \dfrac{e^x + e^{-x}}{2}$

z. $\tanh x = \dfrac{e^x - e^{-x}}{e^x + e^{-x}}$

aa. $\cosh^2 x - \sinh^2 x = 1$

ab. $\cosh 2x = \cosh^2 x + \sinh^2 x$

ac. $e^{ix} = \cos x + i \sin x$

ad. $\sin x = \dfrac{e^{ix} - e^{-ix}}{2i}$

ae. $\cos x = \dfrac{e^{ix} + e^{-ix}}{2}$

af. $\tan x = -i\left(\dfrac{e^{ix} - e^{-ix}}{e^{ix} + e^{-ix}}\right)$

4. Express sin2x/cos2x in terms of the tangent function tan2x using Maple. (Hints: Simplification will not work. Try conversion instead.)
5. The equation $e^{i\pi} + 1 = 0$ combines five of mathematics' most famous symbols. Confirm this relationship using Maple.
6. Confirm that $(x + y)^3 = x^3 + 3x^2 y + 3xy^2 + y^3$.
7. Confirm that $x^3 - y^3 = (x - y)(x^2 + xy + y^2)$.

8. Express $\dfrac{1}{1-\sqrt{5}}$ such that no radical appears in the denominator.

9. Given the following portion of a Maple session, determine the expression to which A is assigned:

```
> op(A);

> op(0,A);

        ax², x, 2

    +
```

Indicate the first, second, and third operands by using the **op** function.

10. A force applied to a body creates *stress*, which is a force distribution applied on a surface. Stress has the units of force per unit area. For any surface, stress can be resolved into tangential (*shear*) or perpendicular (*normal*) components. However, rotating the perspective—that is, the coordinate system that defines the body's orientation—can produce a configuration that produces only normal stresses, as shown in Figure 7.2:

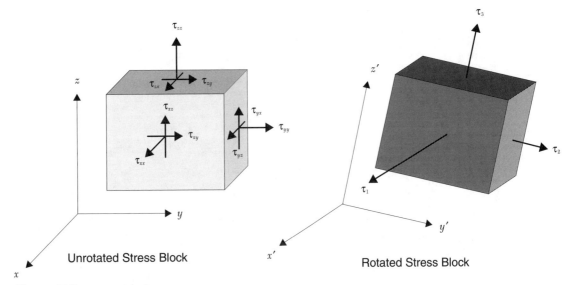

Figure 7.2. Stress Block

Whereas each surface of the unrotated block in Cartesian (x, y, z) coordinates yields two shear-stress components and one normal-stress component per face, a certain rotated axis can produce only normal stresses, called *principal stresses* and represented by τ_1, τ_2, and τ_3. You can find principal stresses from the formula

$$\tau^3 - A\tau^2 + B\tau - C = 0 , \qquad (7\text{-}3)$$

where

$$A = \tau_{xx} + \tau_{yy} + \tau_{zz} , \qquad (7\text{-}4)$$

$$B = \tau_{xx}\tau_{yy} + \tau_{yy}\tau_{zz} + \tau_{zz}\tau_{xx} - \tau_{xy}^2 - \tau_{yz}^2 - \tau_{zx}^2 , \qquad (7\text{-}5)$$

and

$$C = \tau_{xx}\tau_{yy}\tau_{zz} + 2\tau_{xy}\tau_{yz}\tau_{zx} - \tau_{xy}^2\tau_{zz} - \tau_{yz}^2\tau_{xx} - \tau_{zx}^2\tau_{yy} . \qquad (7\text{-}6)$$

Assume that a body has internal stresses $\tau_{xx} = 100$ kPa, $\tau_{yy} = 100$ kPa, $\tau_{zz} = 25$ kPa, $\tau_{xy} = \tau_{yx} = 10$ kPa, $\tau_{yz} = \tau_{zy} = 0$ kPa, and $\tau_{xz} = \tau_{zx} = 0$ kPa.

10a. Assign variables to the values for each stress. (Hint: See Appendix A for Greek letters.)

10b. Evaluate the constants A, B, and C.

10c. Note that all shear stresses associated with the z-axis are zero. You can immediately determine τ_3. (Big hint: It's τ_{zz}.)

10d. Solve for the three principal stresses using Maple's polynomial-division capabilities. (Hints: You know one root already: $\tau = \tau_{zz} = 25$ kPa. So now you need to divide $\tau^3 - A\tau^2 + B\tau - C = 0$ by the factor $\tau - 25$.)

8

Graphics

8.1 INTRODUCTION

Formulas model physical processes, and in turn, the graphical representations of models help you visualize qualitative physical behaviors. Maple graphics primarily include *plots*, which are graphs of points, expressions, and equations. Previous chapters introduced basic plotting. This chapter delves further into Maple's graphical tools.

8.1.1 Tutorials and Sources
Maple's plotting capabilities are very comprehensive, and Maple provides various ways to access information about these tools:

- Help: Worksheet Interface...Working with Plots...
- Menus: Worksheet Interface...Reference... Menus...2D Plots or...3D Plots
- Examples: "**General Symbolics**" and "**Mathematical Visualization**" inside `?examples[index]`
- Functions and Packages: Graphics...

8.1.2 Library Packages
Consult `?DEtools`, `?plottools`, `?plots`, `?stats`, `?geometry`, and `?geom3d` for information on a large variety of graphics-function libraries. Appendix D explains how to load library packages using the `with(package)` function.

OBJECTIVES

After reading this chapter, you should be able to:

- Locate plotting functions and packages
- Manipulate and customize plots
- Plot two-dimensional expressions
- Plot multiple expressions on the same graph
- Plot three-dimensional expressions
- Become familiar with miscellaneous plotting tools

North America has vast reserves of natural gas, the cleanliest burning fossil fuel. People, organizations, and industries use natural gas for many purposes, such as heating and generating power. Over 1.3 million miles of underground pipes deliver natural gas throughout the United States. ANR Pipeline Company is one the nation's largest providers of natural gas transportation and storage service. ANR operates approximately 10,600 miles out of the 200,000 miles of larger diameter-interstate pipeline. Courtesy of ANR Pipeline Company, subsidiary of The Coastal Corporation

8.1.3 Categories

Generic functions for plotting images include:

- **plot**: Create two-dimensional plots using command-line instructions. (See Sections 8.2 and 8.3.)
- **smartplot**: Create plots using the GUI. (See Appendix G.)
- **display**: Display plots stored as assigned names. (See Section 8.3.)
- **animate**: Animate plots of functions and equations. (See Section 8.5.)
- **draw**: Show images created using the **geometry** library package. (See Section 8.5.)

Many plotting functions also support three-dimensional plots. To call these functions, append the label **3d** to the function name, as in **plot** becoming **plot3d**. To import external graphical images, select Edit→InsertOLEObject . . . (not available with Unix).

8.1.4 Manipulating Graphics

To manipulate a graphical Maple object, such as a plot, select the image by pointing the mouse on it and clicking once with the left mouse button. A box surrounding the image will appear, as shown in Figure 8.1. You can now edit the selected object by performing the following tasks:

- Resizing: Select and drag the black squares, called handles, that surround the highlighted plot. Unix users might have to press the redraw icon R to redraw after resizing.

- <u>Editing</u>: Select <u>E</u>dit or press the right mouse button to cut, paste, and copy.
- <u>Customizing Plots</u>: Consult **?plot[options]** and **?plot3D[options]** for information on the command options that most functions will accept. Also, use menus, icons, and the right mouse button to customize plots.
- <u>Saving and Printing</u>: Selecting <u>O</u>ptions→<u>P</u>lotDisplay→<u>I</u>nline prints plots inside your worksheets. Consult Appendix C for more discussion.

PRACTICE!

1. Plot the function x that is shown in Figure 8.1.
2. Select the plot by using the left mouse button.
3. Resize the plot to about half the original size.
4. Cut the plot and insert it inside a new execution group.

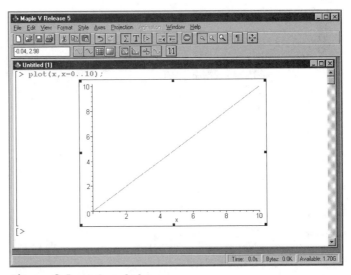

Figure 8.1. Selected Plot

8.2 TWO-DIMENSIONAL PLOTS

This section reviews further aspects of two-dimensional, or **2D**, plotting with **plot**.

8.2.1 Syntax
The **plot** function has the general syntax **plot(f,h,v,o)**, where

- **f** = an expression such as a name or function
- **h** = a horizontal range expressed as **name=low..high**
- **v** = a vertical range expressed as **name=low..high**
- **o** = options expressed as the sequence **opt1=value,opt2=value,...**

For instance, enter **plot(sin(x),x=0..Pi,title="Sine Plot")** to display a graph of sin x along $0 \leq x \leq \pi$ with the title Sine Plot printed on top.

8.2.2 Plotting Functions

The following statements produce the same plot of $y = f(x) = \sin x + 1$ using different forms of syntax:

**STEP 138:
EXAMPLES OF
PLOTTING
FUNCTIONS**

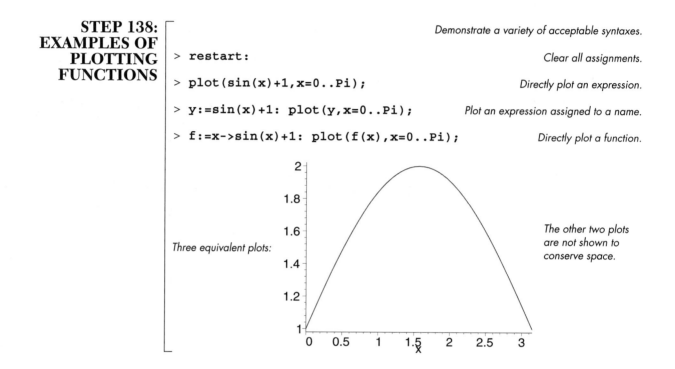

Demonstrate a variety of acceptable syntaxes.

```
> restart:
```
Clear all assignments.

```
> plot(sin(x)+1,x=0..Pi);
```
Directly plot an expression.

```
> y:=sin(x)+1: plot(y,x=0..Pi);
```
Plot an expression assigned to a name.

```
> f:=x->sin(x)+1: plot(f(x),x=0..Pi);
```
Directly plot a function.

Three equivalent plots:

*The other two plots
are not shown to
conserve space.*

Never specify an entire equation in **plot**! Except for **restart**, the following example is incorrect:

**STEP 139:
NEVER DO THIS!**

Never plot equations with **plot**.

```
> restart:
```
Clear all assignments.

```
> plot(y=sin(x)+1,x=0..Pi);
```
Attempt to plot an equation.

```
Plotting error, empty plot
```
plot *does not accept equations!*

Use *implicit plots*, as discussed in Section 8.5.4, if you wish to plot entire equations. Consult **?plot[function]** for further rules, syntax, and shortcuts.

8.2.3 Ranges

Maple plots values of *f* for a given *h*:

- The ***horizontal axis*** corresponds to the *independent variable* bounded by *h*.
- The ***vertical axis*** corresponds to the *dependent variable* evaluated as values of *f*. Supply a vertical-axis range *v* when plots seem too compressed or chopped.

Try Practice Problem 8.9 for a good example of constricting a plot with a vertical range. You can also specify infinite ranges with the symbolic constants **-infinity** and **infinity**. Consult **?plot[range]** and **?plot[infinity]** for more information.

8.2.4 Options

The following example demonstrates command-line plot options that are reviewed in **?plot[options]**:

STEP 140: COMMAND-LINE PLOT OPTIONS

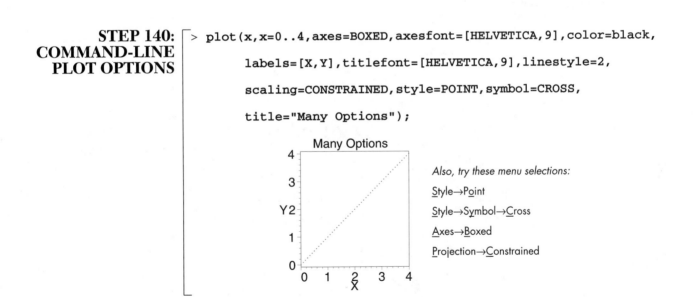

```
> plot(x,x=0..4,axes=BOXED,axesfont=[HELVETICA,9],color=black,
       labels=[X,Y],titlefont=[HELVETICA,9],linestyle=2,
       scaling=CONSTRAINED,style=POINT,symbol=CROSS,
       title="Many Options");
```

Also, try these menu selections:

Style→Point

Style→Symbol→Cross

Axes→Boxed

Projection→Constrained

By default, **plot** chooses different axis scales. Press the icon ⊞ or enter the **CONSTRAINED** option to force equal axis scales. Assign plot options with **setoptions** to avoid tedious customizing. Also, consult **?plot[color]**, **?plot[coords]**, and **?plot[style]** for more information.

PRACTICE!

5. Plot the function $x = y^2 - 1$. Which variable is independent? Which is dependent?

6. Plot the expression $\frac{1}{x}$. Hint: Consider setting "**discont**" as a **plot** option, since this curve is discontinuous.

7. Assign $f(x) = x \sin x$ using functional notation. Plot $f(x)$.

8. Plot the function $f(x) = e^{-x^2}$ for $-\infty \le x \le \infty$.

9. Create this plot:

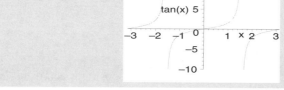

8.3 PLOTTING MULTIPLE EXPRESSIONS

Discover qualitative differences in models by plotting functions together. This section demonstrates different techniques for plotting multiple functions on the same graph.

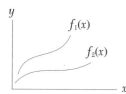

Figure 8.2.
Multiple Plots

8.3.1 Multiple Plots

Multiple plots contain graphs of different expressions in the general form of $y = f_1(x)$, $y = f_2(x), \ldots$, as shown in Figure 8.2. In this example, each function $f_i(x)$ has the same independent variable x and is graphed with the same vertical axis y.

Enter **plot({f1,f2,...},h,v,opts)** for multiple function plots. For instance, suppose you wish to plot both $y = \sin x$ and $y = x - \frac{x^3}{3!} + \frac{x^5}{5!}$ on the same graph. (Recall that $n!$ denotes a factorial: See **?!** and Table 6-3.) Try the following steps to create a multiple plot of these two functions:

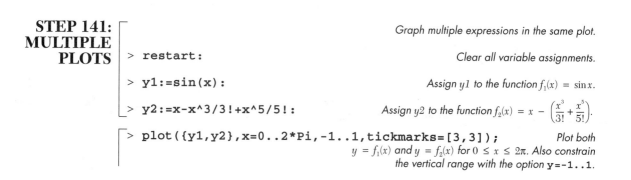

STEP 141:
MULTIPLE
PLOTS

> `restart:`   *Clear all variable assignments.*

> `y1:=sin(x):`   *Assign y1 to the function $f_1(x) = \sin x$.*

> `y2:=x-x^3/3!+x^5/5!:`   *Assign y2 to the function $f_2(x) = x - \left(\frac{x^3}{3!} + \frac{x^5}{5!}\right)$.*

> `plot({y1,y2},x=0..2*Pi,-1..1,tickmarks=[3,3]);`   *Plot both $y = f_1(x)$ and $y = f_2(x)$ for $0 \le x \le 2\pi$. Also constrain the vertical range with the option* `y=-1..1`.

Graph multiple expressions in the same plot.

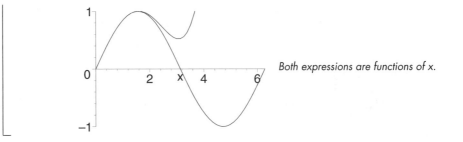

Both expressions are functions of x.

You should specify **[f1,f2,...]** and **opt=[opt1,opt2,...]** to apply different options to respective expressions. Also, consult **?plot[multiple]** for more details.

8.3.2 Superimposing Plots

Maple stores plots as **plot structures**, which are data that determine all plot characteristics. You can output a plot structure by assigning a name when calling **plot**. Using the assignments *y1* and *y2* in Step 141 from the previous section, try the following steps:

STEP 142: PLOT STRUCTURES

Show how Maple stores plot information.

```
> P1:=plot(y1,x=0..2*P:,y=-1..1);
```

Assign the name P1 to a plot structure.

A REALLY BIG Maple plot structure appears and is omitted to conserve space.

Next time, terminate the input with a colon to suppress the output!

Next, load the **plots** library package:

STEP 143: LOAD plots LIBRARY PACKAGE

plots contains the display function.

```
> with(plots);
```

Load the plots library package.

You will see many functions also omitted to conserve space.

Next time, use a colon to suppress the output!

Once you load the package, you can use every function contained in **plots** until you restart or end your session. Next, display the plot by entering **display(P,opts)**:

STEP 144: DISPLAY SINGLE PLOT

Display a plot using a plot structure.

```
> display(P1);
```

Evaluate the plot structure P1. Also, try entering just P1.

Maple displays a sine plot that is omitted to conserve space.

Maple automatically displays graphs from plot structures.

Now, redo Step 141 by using plot structures and the **display** function. Since you have already assigned *P1* to sin *x*, now assign *P2*:

STEP 145:
PLOT
STRUCTURES

Show how Maple stores plot information.

> `P2:=plot(y2,x=0..2*P:,y=-1..1):`   *Assign the name P2 to another plot structure.*

Display multiple plots with **display({P1,P2,...},opts)** where **P1,P2,...** represent plot structures:

STEP 146:
DISPLAY
MULTIPLE
PLOTS

Display multiple plots on the same graph.

> `display({P1,P2},tickmarks=[3,3]);`   *Display both functions in one plot.*

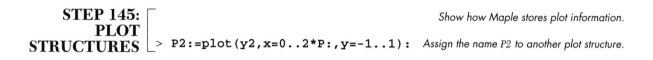

For more information, consult **?plot[structure]** and **?plot[display]**.

PRACTICE!

10.   Plot both $f_1(x) = x + 1$ and $f_2(x) = -x - 1$ for $-2 \leq x \leq 2$ on the same graph. (Hint: Use **plot** with syntax for a multiple plot.)

11.   Assign *A* and *B* to plots for $y = x + 1$ and $y = -x - 1$, respectively, along $-2 \leq x \leq 2$.

12.   Superimpose and display both plots with **display**.

8.3.3 Parametric Plots

Consider the pair of functions $x(t) = \cos t$ and $y(t) = \sin t$. Both $x(t)$ and $y(t)$ are called ***parametric functions***. Unlike with graphs of multiple functions, each parametric function determines the coordinate value of a different axis. In the example in this section, different values of a *parameter t* produce pairs of *x* and *y* coordinates on an *xy*-plot.

Enter **plot([fh, fv, t=range], opts)** to plot the horizontal and vertical parametric functions **fh** and **fv**, respectively, for parameter **t**:

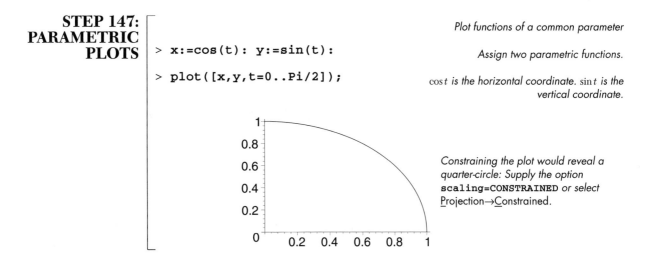

STEP 147:
PARAMETRIC
PLOTS

Plot functions of a common parameter

```
> x:=cos(t): y:=sin(t):
```

Assign two parametric functions.

```
> plot([x,y,t=0..Pi/2]);
```

$\cos t$ *is the horizontal coordinate.* $\sin t$ *is the vertical coordinate.*

Constraining the plot would reveal a quarter-circle: Supply the option `scaling=CONSTRAINED` *or select* <u>P</u>rojection→<u>C</u>onstrained.

Never confuse **plot([*funcs*],*h*)**, the command for plotting multiple functions, with **plot([*funcs*,*t*])**, the command for plotting parametric functions! Consult **?plot[parametric]** for more options.

PRACTICE!

13. Plot $x = \cos t$ and $y = \sin t$ for $0 \le t \le 2\pi$. What shape does this graph have?

14. Plot both $f(t) = \cos t$ and $g(t) = \sin t$ for $0 \le t \le 2\pi$ on the same graph. What is the difference between this graph and that of the previous problem?

8.4 THREE-DIMENSIONAL PLOTS

This section introduces aspects of three-dimensional, or **3D**, plotting.

8.4.1 Syntax

Many two-dimensional plot commands have 3D versions. Just append "**3d**" to a function name to call its 3D version. For functions expressed in the form $z = f(x, y)$, enter **plot3d(*expr*,*x=range*,*y=range*,*opts*)** to plot values of z. In general, **plot3d** plots a surface above and below the xy-plane:

STEP 148:
PLOTTING
THREE-
DIMENSIONAL
EXPRESSIONS

Demonstrate 3D plots.

```
> restart:
```

Clear all assignments.

```
> opts:=axes=FRAME,shading=zgrayscale,title="3D PLOT":
```

Assign options.

```
> plot3d(cos(x)^2+sin(y)^2,x=0..2*Pi,y=0..2*Pi,opts);
```

Plot expression.

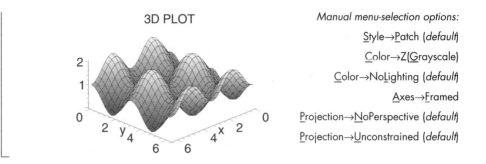

3D PLOT

Manual menu-selection options:
Style→Patch (*default*)
Color→Z(Grayscale)
Color→NoLighting (*default*)
Axes→Framed
Projection→NoPerspective (*default*)
Projection→Unconstrained (*default*)

8.4.2 Customizing

Review Step 140 and **?plot3d[options]** for many of the options available for 3D plots. Also, consult **?setoptions3d**, **?plot3d[colorfunc]**, and **?plot3d [coords]** for more information.

8.4.3 Orientation

Orientation, an important option of 3D plots, measures how plots rotate about each axis. Maple denotes the following angles, shown in Figure 8.3:

- ϑ (cursive *theta*) = rotation in the xy-plane
- φ (cursive *phi*) = rotation from the z-axis

After a plot is selected, these symbols appear on the Tool Bar.

Change a 3D plot's orientation by selecting the plot. While holding down the left mouse button, move the mouse. The plot will slowly spin. Monitor the angles next to ϑ and φ on the toolbar. Retain these angles by entering the option **orientation=[a,b]**, where $\vartheta = a$ and $\varphi = b$:

Figure 8.3.
3D Orientation

STEP 149: CHANGING ORIENTATION

Rotate a 3D plot.

```
> with(plots):
```
In Step 148, you entered restart, so you must reload the plots package.

```
> opts:=axes=BOXED,tickmarks=[2,2,2],labels=["x","y","z"],
  grid=[5,5]:
```
Choose options.

```
> P:=plot3d(exp(x*y),x=0..1,y=0..1,opts):
```
Assign a 3D plot.

```
> display3d(P); display3d(P,orientation=[145,75]);
```
Display plots.

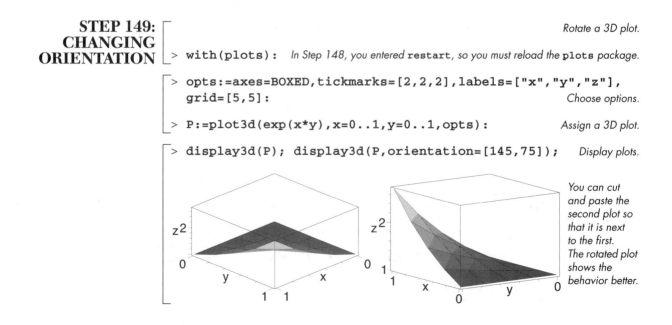

You can cut and paste the second plot so that it is next to the first. The rotated plot shows the behavior better.

PRACTICE!

15. Plot $f(x, y) = e^{(x^2 - y^2)}$ for $-1 \le x \le 1$ and $-1 \le y \le 1$.

16. Describe the surface $f(x, y) = x + y$.

17. Plot $f(x, y) = \ln(x - y^2)$ for $1 \le x \le 1.5$ and $1 \le y \le 1.1$. Set appropriate options to see "drip marks."

8.5 MISCELLANEOUS

This section reviews other common Maple plotting functions.

8.5.1 Text

Besides table titles, you can annotate plots by plotting text strings. Enter **textplot ([x,y,string])** to add text to a plot. The values **x** and **y** are the horizontal and vertical coordinates of **string**:

STEP 150:
TEXT PLOTS

Plot strings and names inside a plot.

Enter **with(plots)** *if you have not already done so.*

textplot belongs to the **plots** *library package.*

> **T:=textplot([Pi/2,3/2,"maximum"]):**   *Plot the string "maximum" at* $x = \pi/2$ *and* $y = 3/2$.

STEP 151:
COMBINE
TEXT AND
GRAPHICAL
PLOTS

Superimpose text and graphical plots.

> **opts:=tickmarks=[3,2]:**   *Assign plotting options.*

> **G:=plot(sin(x),x=0..Pi,opts):**   *Assign a graphical plot.*

> **display({G,T});**   *Superimpose the sine graph with the text plot.*

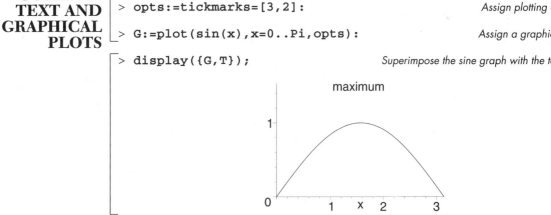

Vertically and horizontally align **string** about **x** and **y** with the option **align={vert, horz}**. Enter **ABOVE** or **BELOW** for **vert**. Enter **RIGHT**, **CENTER**, or **LEFT** for **horz**. Change fonts with the command **font=[FONT,STYLE,SIZE]** option. Consult **?plots[textplot]** and **?plots[textplot3d]** for more information.

8.5.2 Points

A point is represented in two dimensions with the notation $[x, y]$. For instance, you would enter the coordinate $(x, y) = (1, 2)$ as **[1,2]** in Maple. Collect n data points inside a list of lists in the format $[[x_1, y_1], [x_2, y_2], \ldots, [x_n, y_n]]$:

STEP 152: PLOTTING POINTS

Plot a list of points.

```
> L := [[1,2],[2,1]]:
```
Assign a list of points. Each point is also a list: $[x_i, y_i]$.

```
> plot(L,thickness=3);
```
Plot the points. Maple automatically creates lines between the points.

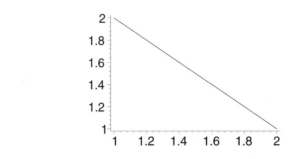

Also, consult **?plots[pointplot]**, **?plottools[point]**, **?geometry[point]**, and **?geom3d[point]** for more information.

8.5.3 Coordinate Systems

Cartesian graphs plot functions along mutually perpendicular x-, y-, and z-axes. However, other coordinate systems provide better visual tools for plotting certain functions. For instance, ***cylindrical coordinates*** are good for modeling circular objects:

STEP 153: COORDINATE SYSTEMS

Specify a coordinate system other than Cartesian.

```
> opts := coords=cylindrical,style=WIREFRAME:
```
Choose cylindrical coordinates.

```
> plot3d(1,theta=0..2*Pi,z=0..1,opts);
```
Specify $r = 1$ for $0 \le \theta \le 2\pi$ and $0 \le z \le 1$.

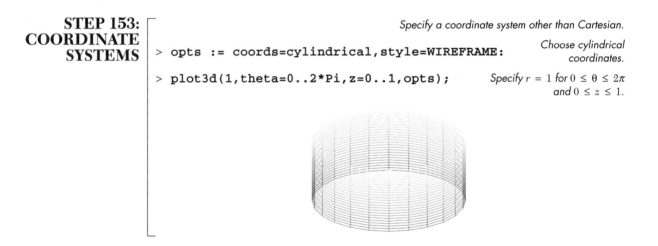

Consult **?coords** and **?plot[coords]** for further description and information on many related functions.

8.5.4 Implicit Plots

Maple provides functions for plotting entire equations. For instance, let $F(x,y)$ represent the entire equation $y^3 + xy = 1$. $F(x, y)$ is called an ***implicit function***, which is a function of mutually dependent variables. So, you can set $F(x, y) = (x^3 + xy = 1)$. Implicit functions simultaneously vary x and y values to satisfy the equation, now represented by F. Enter **implicitplot(*F,h,v,opts*)** to implicitly graph *F*:

STEP 154:
IMPLICIT PLOTS

Plot equations stored as implicit functions.

implicitplot *belongs to the*
plots *library package.*

Enter **with(plots)** *if you have not already done so.*

> **implicitplot(y^3+x*y=1,x=-10..10,y=-3..3);** *Plot* $F(x,y) = y^3 + xy = 1$.

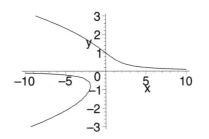

Consult **?plots[impliciplot3d]** for information on 3D implicit plots.

8.5.5 Geometric Objects

Maple provides several library packages for drawing geometric objects:

- **plots**: Graph polygons with **polygonplot** and **polygonplot3d**.
- **plottools**: Construct many common geometric shapes and modify other plots.
- **geometry**: Define and assign 2D shapes. Consult **?geometry[draw]** for information on graphics.
- **geom3d**: Define and assign 3D shapes. Consult **?geom3d[draw3d]** for information on graphics.

8.5.6 Animated Plots

Maple can display functions that vary with time t as ***animation***, which is a sequence of images that simulate motion. Animated plots flash a sequence of changing "snap-shots" that simulate actual motion for different values of time t. Time-dependent functions, such as $f(x, t) = x\sin(xt)$, produce functions that change in space x as well as time t. Note that time-dependent functions, like $f(x, t)$, have three overall coordinates:

- Two spatial coordinates that are typically represented as x and y. Spatial coordinates are plotted on horizontal and vertical axes.
- One temporal coordinate that is typically represented as time t. As time changes, Maple redraws (x, y) coordinates for new values of t.

For instance, enter **animate(f,x=x1..x2,t=t1..t2)** to animate $f(x, t)$, where and $x_1 \le x \le x_2$ and $t_1 \le t \le t_2$:

STEP 155:
ANIMATION

Animate plots.

animate *is stored inside the*
plots *library package.*

Enter **with(plots)** *if you have not already done so.*

> **animate(x*sin(x*t),x=0..10,t=0..2*Pi);** *Animate the function*
$f(x, t) = x\sin(xt)$ *for* $0 \le x \le 10$ *and* $0 \le t \le \pi$.

A plot appears as shown in Figure 8.4.

Select the plot. Then, select A̲nimation→P̲lay.
Also, try the PLAY icon.

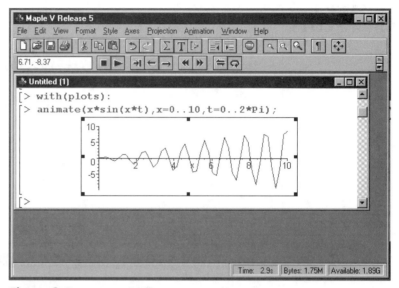

Figure 8.4. Animated Plot

The toolbar icons resemble music-player icons. You may select an animated plot and then press the play icon ▶, stop icon ■, and other icons, as shown in Figure 8.4. To take instantaneous "snapshots" of a plot at various times without animating the entire plot, supply **display** with the **insequence=false** option:

STEP 156:
ANIMATION

Display animated plots as sequences of images.

Enter **with(plots)** *if you have not already done so.*

> **opts:=axes=NONE,labels=[" "," "],frames=6:**   *Take six "snapshots".*

> **P:=animate(x*sin(x*t),x=0..10,t=0..3,opts):**   *Store the animated plot.*

> **display(P,insequence=false);**

animate and **display** *belong to the* **plots** *library package.*

insequence=false tells Maple not to animate in real time.

For more details, consult **?plots[animate]** and **plots[animate3d]**.

PRACTICE!

18. Plot the functions $f(x) = x$ and $f(x) = x^2$ on the same graph. Label each function inside the plot.

19. Plot a triangle. Use the coordinates $(0, 0)$, $(1, 1)$, and $(2, 0)$ as its vertices.

20. Plot $r(\theta, z) = z - \theta^2$. Hint: Consult **?plot3d[coords]**.

21. Plot the circle $x^2 + y^2 = 1$ using an implicit plot.

22. Plot a circle using Maple's **plottools** package. Hint: Consult **?circle**.

23. Animate $f(x, t) = \tan(xt)$ for $0 \leq x \leq 100$ and $0 \leq t \leq 1$. Display only 10 frames. Restrict the vertical height to $-20 \leq y \leq 20$. Hint: Consult **?animate**.

8.6 APPLICATION: PIPELINE FLOW

This section demonstrates Maple's plotting capabilities using an example regarding pipeline flow.

8.6.1 Background

Pipelines carry water, gas, oil, and effluents. Not only do the characteristics of the flowing substance affect flow, but other factors, such as flow rates, pipe roughness, elevation changes, and bends, can greatly change flow behavior as well. While theoretical approaches to the analysis of flow behavior exist, many empirical techniques also greatly assist such analysis. For instance, the Weymouth equation predicts reasonable values for the flow rate Q of natural gas in a pipe, where C_Q = a constant, T_b = temperature base, P_b = pressure base, D = internal diameter of the pipe, G = relative gas density, T_f = average flowing temperature, L = length, P_1 = upstream pressure, and P_2 = downstream pressure:

$$Q = C_Q \frac{T_b}{P_b} D^{\frac{8}{3}} \left(\frac{P_1^2 - P_2^2}{GT_fL} \right)^{\frac{1}{2}}. \tag{8-1}$$

8.6.2 Problem

Given C_Q = 0.0037477, T_b = 293 K, P_b = 1.060 Kg/cm^2, D = 305 mm, G = 0.600, T_f = 300 K, and L = 130 km, describe the relationship between Q, P_1, and P_2.

8.6.3 Methodology

First, restart Maple:

STEP 157: INITIALIZE MAPLE

Initialize system variables.

```
> restart:
```

Restart your Maple session.

For this application, first assign the model to keep the equation free of variable assignments for later study:

STEP 158: MODEL

Assign the system model.

```
> Q:=Cq*(Tb/Pb)*D1^(8/3)*((P1^2-P2^2)/(G*Tf*L))^(0.5);
```

$$Q := \frac{CqTbD1^{\left(\frac{8}{3}\right)} \left(\frac{P1^2 - P2^2}{GTfL} \right)^{.5}}{Pb}$$

Assume that flow rate is a function of pressure.

Now, assign pertinent data:

STEP 159: SEPARATE AND STATE

Assign the system data.

```
> Cq:=0.0037477:Tb:=293:Pb:=1.06:D1:=305:G:=0.6:Tf:=300:L:=130:
```

Check the expression for Q:

STEP 160:
CHECK

Check the system model.

```
> Q1:=evalf(Q,2);
```
Calculate with two floats and evaluate Q.

$$Q1 := .43\ 10^{7}(.000044P1^{2} - .000044P2^{2})^{.5}$$

Now, you can plot the function. Because Q is a function of two independent variables, use **plot3d** to create a three-dimensional plot. Whereas the pressures are represented by the "bottom" axes, the height of the plot represents Q. You might need to adjust the ranges for $P1$ and $P2$ to display relevant features that illustrate the model's physical aspects:

STEP 161:
SOLVE AND
REPORT

Plot the model of the system.

```
> plot3d(Q1, P1=100..120, P2=0..100, title="Pipe Flow",
         axes=BOXED, gridstlye=RECTANGULAR,
         orientation=[135,65], tickmarks=[2,2,4]);
```

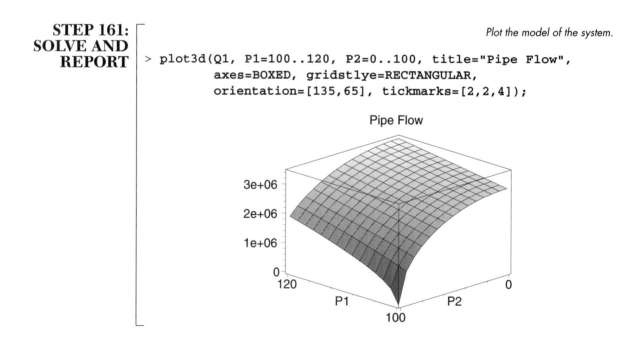

8.6.4 Solution

The plot shows that large pressure differences generate large flow rates. From Section 4.5, you can conclude that electrical-current flow and pipe flow have analogous relationships. Also, as the voltage potential drives electrical-current flow, differences in pressures, called "pressure drops," drive pipe flow, as shown in the plot. Therefore, as the pressure difference decreases, the flow rate diminishes, all other factors being equivalent.

Learning is difficult! Avoid the "lone-wolf" mentality by seeking help from professors and teaching assistants when your need is dire.

Also, consider checking with classmates. Classmates suffer through the same problems that you have. Perhaps a friend knows a trick that you missed. Trading help also helps you learn. Better yet, finding another student to work with is a cinch. Just look around your lab! Developing teamwork skills is crucial for later success in the marketplace. Try applying teamwork to these tasks:

❑   Homework:
Avoid blatant copying. Find other motivated students to work with, but beware of leeches, or people who seek only to benefit from your labors! Work alone, and then meet with your team to discuss results and stumbling blocks. In fact, teaching one another will strengthen your own knowledge.

❑   Tests:
Never join a study-group until you have studied alone. Bring questions to the group. Address stumbling blocks. Quiz each other. Above all else, stay focused. Give yourselves hourly breaks. Be careful, for group study easily degenerates into socializing.

❑   Projects:
With all projects, brainstorm, choose a leader, set firm schedules, and stay focused on goals ... details come later. Project work involves good "group dynamics," or how people work together. Beware that you will have rough periods after going through the initial formalities. Although conflict yields better work, always respect each other's feelings. Remember always to share the burden and encourage each other.

SUMMARY

This chapter has reviewed a variety of Maple's graphical tools for visualizing mathematical functions. Functions are either specified as expressions or in functional notation. If you prefer to use equation form, use implicit plots. You can also supply infinite ranges for plots. Plot multiple and parametric functions with **plot** and **plot3d**, but beware of "**[]**" syntax! Customize your plots with command-line arguments, menu selections, and toolbar icons. Assigning plots to plot structures for use in the **display** command helps plotting multiple functions. Many other graphing tools require that library packages, like **plots**, are loaded.

KEY TERMS

2D	horizontal axis	plot structures
3D	implicit function	plots
Animation	multiple plots	vertical axis
Cartesian graphs	orientation	
cylindrical coordinates	parametric functions	

Problems

1. What is a Maple plot?
2. Demonstrate how to apply a vertical range to a two dimensional plot.
3. What is a coordinate system?
4. Give an example of all options that are listed in **?plot[options]**. For example, **plot(x+1,x=0..1,title="I am an example!")** demonstrates the title option.

5. Plot the functions $y = \cos^2 t$ and $y = \sin^2 t$ on the same graph for $0 \le t \le \pi$.

6. Plot the parametric functions $x = \cos^2 t$ and $y = \sin^2 t$ for $0 \le t \le \pi$.

7. How do multiple plots and parametric plots differ? Explain in reference to Problems 5 and 6.

8. Plot a circle of radius 1 and origin $(0, 0)$:

    8a. Use **implicitplot** for the equation $x^2 + y^2 = 1$. (Remember to first load **plots**.)

    8b. Use a parametric plot.

    8c. Use **circle**. (Hint: Remember to first load **plottools**.)

9. The Gaussian-distribution, or normal-distribution, function is popular in statistical models:

    $$f(x) = \frac{1}{\sigma\sqrt{2\pi}} \exp\left(\frac{-(x-m)^2}{2\sigma^2}\right),$$

    where $\sigma > 0$ and $-\infty < x < \infty$. Plot $f(x)$ for standard deviation $\sigma = 7.5$ and mean $m = 65$. (Hint: Pick "reasonable" ranges to produce a clear plot.)

10. Repeat the problem in Section 8.6, but use only $P_2 = 50$ Kg/cm^2. Instead, plot the function for $100 \le D \le 400$ mm and the given variation of P_1.

11. Plot the functions $f(t) = \sin t$ and $f(t) = \sin(t + \theta)$ on the same plot for $\theta = 45°$. Let $0 \le t \le 10$, and label both plots. What effect does θ have on the second plot?

12. Plot the results of Problem 6.8 for values of h, b_1, and b_2 that yield a trapezoidal area of 10. (Hints: Use an implicit plot with **implicitplot3d** because the function has three independently ranging variables. Remember to load the **plots** library package! Choose ranges such as $0 \le b_1 \le 20$, $0 \le b_2 \le 20$, and $0 \le h \le 20$, though you might wish to try other spans that better demonstrate the function's features.)

13. Due to the centripetal force on vehicles, curved roadways are banked at a superelevation angle ϕ. You can calculate the necessary superelevation for a bank using the formula

    $$\tan\phi = \frac{v^2}{gr},$$

    where v is vehicle-velocity and r is the roadway-radius of curvature. Given $g = 32.2$ ft/s^2, $45 \le v \le 75$ miles per hour, and $500 \le r \le 1000$ ft, plot ϕ. Be sure to rotate the plot to illustrate important features.

14. Given elevation above sea level E (m) and air temperature t_a (°C), you can compute air density ρ_a (kg/m^3) as

    $$\rho_a = \frac{353(1 - 0.2257 \times 10^{-4}E)^{5.255}}{t_a + 273}.$$

    Plot ρ_a with respect to both E and t_a. (Hint: Use **plot3d**.) Explain how changes to both elevation and air temperature qualitatively affect air density.

15. Draw a "smiley-face" ⌣ using Maple. (Hints: Store each portion as a separate plot structure. Enter **display({P1,P2,P3,P4},options)** to display the entire plot. Do not forget to first load the **plots** library package! Use circles for the face and eyes. An arc or a pair of parametric functions can define the smile. Consult **?circle** and **?arc**. Be sure to enter **with(plottools)** before using **circle** or **arc**! For plot options, set **axes=NONE**.)

16. Consider the plot of experimentally measured data shown in Figures 6-2 and 6-3. How would you determine the most appropriate line to draw through the scattered points? A common method to determine such lines is the least-squares formula for n pairs of dependent and independent variables, x and y:

    $$y = a_1 x + a_0,$$

    where

    $$a_1 = \frac{(n)\left(\sum\limits_{i=1}^{n} x_i y_i\right) - \left(\sum\limits_{i=1}^{n} x_i\right)\left(\sum\limits_{i=1}^{n} y_i\right)}{(n)\left(\sum\limits_{i=1}^{n} x_i^2\right) - \left(\sum\limits_{i=1}^{n} x_i\right)^2}$$

and

$$a_0 = \frac{\left(\sum\limits_{i=1}^{n} y_i \right)}{n} - (a_1) \left(\frac{\sum\limits_{i=1}^{n} x_i}{n} \right).$$

Using this formula, solve the following problems:

16a.   Assign the data in Table 8-1 for u and w using sequences. For instance, you could assign `DP:=1,2,3,4,5` (though unnecessary):

TABLE 8-1   Mass-Spring Experimental Data

DATA POINT	1	2	3	4	5
w (Newtons)	0.00	5.00	10.0	20.0	50.0
u (cm)	0.00	0.51	0.98	1.21	5.16

16b.   Investigate Maple's **add** function. Why can this function help perform the sums inside the least-squares formula? (Hint: try `add(DP[i],i=1..5)`.)

16c.   Evaluate a_1 and a_0.

16d.   Assign the least-squares formula, using w, u, a_1, and a_0 as variables. Is your result linear or nonlinear?

16e.   Assign a plot of the individual data points to a plot structure.

16f.   Assign a plot of your least-squares formula to another plot structure.

16g.   Display both plot structures superimposed together. (Hint: Use **display** for multiple plots.)

16h.   How does the point plot relate to the line plot of the least-squares formula?

16i.   Find Maple's statistics library package for performing a least-square fit. (Hint: Look inside **?stats** for a linear regression function.)

16j.   Evaluate the least-squares formula using Maple's statistics functions. Compare Maple's formula to the one that you generated in Problem 16d.

9

Substituting, Evaluating, and Solving

9.1 INTRODUCTION

Recall the definition of **equations**, or expressions in the form **expr1=expr2**, from Section 5.5. Thus far, you have simulated many equations with assignments by using **name:=expr**. For instance, simulate the equation for a line $y = mx + 6$:

OBJECTIVES

After reading this chapter, you should be able to:

- Substitute values into expressions
- Evaluate expressions
- Solve equations for symbolic values
- Solve equations for numerical values
- Verify solutions

In a multibillion-dollar construction industry, accidents account for about 6% of all construction related costs in the United States of America. Overall, about one out of 10 workers will be injured in some fashion every year. Construction-safety engineers combine ergonomics, biology, and mechanics to design work environments and devices that protect people from accidents throughout the world. Courtesy of Thornton Thomasetti Engineers

STEP 162:
EXPRESSION
ASSIGNMENTS

> `restart:`

> `y:=m*x+b:`

> `x:=1: m:=2: b:=0: y;`

$$2$$

Use assignments to simulate equations.

Clear all previous assignments.

Assign an expression.

Assign parameter values.

Now, the expression is evaluated.

You also have simulated equations with functional notation by using **f:=name->expr**. Given instead the line-equation in terms of a function, try the following input:

STEP 163:
FUNCTIONAL
NOTATION

> `restart: f:=(x,m,b)->m*x+b:`

> `f(1,2,0);`

$$2$$

Use functional notation to simulate equations.

Assign an expression using functional notation.

Select parameter values.

Now, the expression is evaluated.

Unfortunately, these methods become cumbersome for larger problems. This chapter reviews techniques that ease input of expressions, such as *substitution, evaluation,* and *solving*.

9.2 SUBSTITUTION

Recall that expressions are composed of subexpressions. Substituting for these subexpressions with other expressions helps manipulate equations, as introduced in this section.

9.2.1 Syntactic Substitution

Syntactic substitution replaces operands of expressions with other expressions. Enter **subs(old=new,expr)** to substitute each occurrence of **old** with **new** inside **expr**. Both **old** and **new** are often individual names:

STEP 164:
SYNTACTIC
SUBSTITUTION

> `restart:`

> `A:=(x*y^2)*sin(x*t);`

$$A := xy^2\sin(xt)$$

> `subs(x=a,A);`

$$ay^2\sin(at)$$

> `subs(x=1,A);`

$$y^2\sin(t)$$

Substitute expressions inside another expression.

Clear variable assignments.

Assign an expression.

Ensure that you first entered `restart`.

Replace x with the new expression a.

Maple swapped x for a.

Replace x with the new expression 1.

Maple performed the substitution and, then, simplified the result.

Recall that Maple considers equations as expressions that include the equals sign (=). Therefore, each input *old=new* forms an equation expression, as denoted by commands reviewed later in this chapter. Also, consult **?subs**, **?alias**, **?subsop**, and **?trigsubs** for more information.

9.2.2 Assignments

The **subs** function uses *local variables*, which are variables that do not carry global assignments. (See Section 5.4.) When a function that uses a local variable finishes evaluating, Maple resets the local variable to an unassigned state. Thus, substituted names inside **subs** have no global assignments. For instance, you may check the current values of x and A from Step 164:

STEP 165:
SUBSTITUTION
NEVER ASSIGNS!

> `x, A;`

$$x, xy^2\sin(xt)$$

Substitution does not change expression trees.

Test the values of x and A.

No assignments were performed.

However, you can preserve your results by assigning them to a new name:

STEP 166:
ASSIGN RESULTS
OF subs

> `B:=subs(x=1,A);`

$$B := y^2\sin(t)$$

Assign a name to the results of substitution.

Assign B to the results of `subs(x=1,A)`.

Now, B is assigned to the new expression.

9.2.3 Evaluation and Simplification

In general, **subs** does not evaluate expressions:

STEP 167:
SUBSTITUTION
DOES NOT
EVALUATE!

> `subs(x=Pi/3,sin(x));`

$$\sin\left(\frac{1}{3}\pi\right)$$

> `sin(Pi/3);`

$$\frac{1}{2}\sqrt{3}$$

subs leaves substituted expressions unevaluated.

Substitute $x = \frac{\pi}{3}$ into $\sin x$.

Maple did not evaluate the expression.

Evaluate $\sin\frac{\pi}{3}$.

Maple did evaluate the expression.

However, **subs** still automatically simplifies expressions:

STEP 168:
SUBSTITUTION
PERFORMS
AUTOMATIC
SIMPLIFICATION

> `subs(x=1,x+x);`

$$2$$

subs simplifies some expressions.

Arithmetic expressions are automatically simplified.

Maple simplified $1 + 1$.

9.2.4 Multiple Substitutions

Enter **subs({eqns},{exprs})** to perform multiple substitutions. Both **eqns** and **exprs** can consist of a sequence or single input, where:

- **{eqns}**, or **{eqn1,eqn2,...}**, is a set of simultaneous substitutions
- **{exprs}**, or **{expr1,expr2,...}**, is a set of expressions provided for the substitutions

Note that each **eqn** inside **{eqns}** takes the form **old=new**, where the **new** expression replaces the **old** expression. For instance, substitute $a = 1$ and $b = 2$ simultaneously into the expressions $a + b$ and ab:

STEP 169:
MULTIPLE
SUBSTITUTIONS

> `subs({a=1,b=2},{a+b,a*b});`

$$\{2,3\}$$

Substitute multiple variables and expressions.

Substitute $a = 1$ and $b = 2$ into the expressions $a + b$ and ab.

Sets have no order, so you could have entered **[a+b,a*b]** *instead to produce* $[3,2]$ *instead of* $\{2,3\}$.

You can also enter **subs(eqn1,eqn2,...,{exprs})** to perform each substitution in sequence, rather than simultaneously.

9.2.5 Algebraic Substitution

Substitution sometimes fails because Maple attempts substitution for *surface* operands and individual names. To see an instance of this failure, try substituting for a more complicated subexpression:

STEP 170:
SUBSTITUTION
SOMETIMES
FAILS

> `subs(x*y=1,A);`

$$xy^2\sin(xt)$$

subs usually handles only operands in surface types.

Substitute $xy = 1$ into $xy^2\sin(xt)$. See Step 164.

subs *failed!*

Why did **subs** fail? Investigate the failure by displaying the main operands of the expression $xy^2 \sin(xt)$ with **op(expr)**:

STEP 171:
CHECKING
OPERANDS

> `op(A);`

$$x, y^2, \sin(xt)$$

Investigate why **subs** *failed.*

Display operands of an expression's surface type.

xy does not explicitly appear inside A as an operand.

The expression xy does not explicitly appear in the expression, and thus, **subs** fails. For a successful substitution, try *algebraic substitution* with the **algsubs** function. Algebraic substitution searches for expressions not explicitly recognized as surface-type operands:

STEP 172:
ALGEBRAIC
SUBSTITUTION

> `algsubs(x*y=1,A);`

$$\sin(xt)y$$

When **subs** *fails, try* **algsubs**.

Substitute 1 for each occurrence of xy inside $xy^2\sin(xt)$.

algsubs *found that $xy^2\sin(xt) = (xy)y\sin(xt)$.*

Consult **?simplify[siderel]** for more information. For instance, try **simplify (A,{x*y=1})** for Step 172.

PRACTICE!

1. Assign *EQN* to the expression $y = mx + b$.
2. Substitute the values $x = 1$, $m = 2$, and $b = 0$ into *EQN*.
3. What output does the input **subs(x=0,sin(x))** produce? Why is the answer not 0?
4. Substitute $ab = c$ into abc. Will entering **subs(a*b=c,a*b*c)** produce useful results? Why or why not? What command should you enter instead?

9.3 EVALUATION

Evaluation breaks expressions into subexpressions, replaces variables with assigned values, and then, computes the result. Although Maple uses *full evaluation* for most expressions (see Chapter 4), some types are only partially evaluated (see the subsections entitled "Vectors" and "Matrices" in Chapter 10). Furthermore, some functions, such as **subs**, do not evaluate resulting expressions, though automatic simplification typically works. Use the functions introduced in this section to force Maple into evaluating unevaluated expressions.

9.3.1 Basic Evaluation

Consider the basic substitution statement shown in Step 167, for which entering **subs(x=Pi/3,sin(x))** yields $\sin\left(\frac{1}{3}\pi\right)$. To manually force full evaluation of *expr*, enter **eval(expr)**:

STEP 173:
FORCE
EVALUATION

> `restart:`

> `S:=subs(x=Pi/3,sin(x)):`

> `eval(S);`

$$\frac{1}{2}\sqrt{3}$$

Enter **eval** *to force evaluation.*

Substitute $x = \frac{\pi}{3}$ into $\sin x$. Maple produced

$\sin\left(\frac{1}{3}\pi\right)$ *in Step 167.*

Fully evaluate S.

Maple evaluated the expression.

Also, consult **?student[value]** for more information. Consult Table 9-1 and Mathematics...Evaluation... for details on other evaluation functions, such as **evalf** and **evalr**, from other chapters.

TABLE 9-1   Common Evaluation Functions

FUNCTION	DESCRIPTION	EXAMPLE
eval	evaluate expression	eval(*expr*)
evalb	evaluate boolean	evalb(1<2)
evalc	evaluate complex	evalc((a+b*I)*(c+d*I))
evalf	evaluate floating-point	evalf(Pi/2,3)
evalm	evaluate matrix	evalm(vector([1,2])+vector([3,4]))
evaln	evaluate to a name	*name*:=evaln(*name*)
evalr	evaluate range	evalr(INTERVAL(1..2)+INTERVAL(3..4))

9.3.2 Numerical Evaluation

Other chapters introduced the "evaluate-float" command **evalf**. Enter **evalf(*expr,n*)** to numerically evaluate and report *expr* in *n* digits:

STEP 174:
NUMERICAL
EVALUATION

> evalf(S,3);

.865

Enter **evalf** *for numerical evaluation.*

Numerically evaluate $\sin\left(\frac{1}{3}\pi\right)$ *and report in three digits.*

Maple produced a floating-point result.

Recall, also, that entering decimal values into expressions typically forces numerical evaluation.

9.3.3 Substitution and Evaluation

Enter **eval(*expr,old=new*)** to substitute a new expression for an old one and evaluate the resulting expression. Maple substitutes expression ***new*** for each occurrence of expression ***old***. Then, Maple evaluates the revised expression:

STEP 175:
EVALUATION

> eval(sin(x),x=Pi/3);

$$\frac{1}{2}\sqrt{3}$$

Enter **eval** *for evaluation of substituted expressions.*

Substitute $x = \frac{\pi}{3}$ *into* $\sin x$.

Confirm by entering **sin(Pi/3)**.

But, as **subs** cannot assign a local variable, neither can **eval**:

STEP 176:
EVALUATION
NEVER ASSIGNS!

> x;

x

eval does not assign local variables.

Check the value of x.

Entering **eval(sin(x),x=Pi/3)** *did not assign* x.

As with **subs**, refer to *old=new* as *eqn*. Hence, you should enter **{eqns}** instead of *eqn* when evaluating multiple equations. Note, also, that evaluation functions have difficulty with algebraic substitutions.

PRACTICE!

5. Evaluate $x^2 + \cos x$ for $x = 2$.
6. Evaluate $\dfrac{x^2 - y^2}{x + y}$ for $x = 2$ and $y = 3$. Assign B to the result.
7. Evaluate $xy = 1$ for $xy^2 \sin(xt)$. Does **eval** work?

9.4 SOLVING

In previous sections, you manipulated expressions with commands, like **subs** and **eval**. This section presents techniques that solve equations for individual expressions.

9.4.1 Exact Solutions

Solving manipulates equations in order to isolate desired variables. For instance, manually solving an equation $y = mx + b$ for the variable x yields $x = \dfrac{y - b}{m}$. In general, enter **solve(eqn,var)** to solve equation *eqn* *exactly* for variable *var*:

STEP 177:
SOLVE
EQUATION

> `restart;`

> `solve(p=k*u,k);`

$$\frac{p}{u}$$

Solve one equation for one unknown variable.

Clear all assignments.

Solve $p = ku$ for k.

Maple reports the solution $k = \dfrac{p}{u}$.

Beware that **solve** does not assign solutions! As with **subs** and **eval**, **solve** uses local variables during the solution process. For Step 177, check the value of your solved variable:

STEP 178:
solve DOES
NOT ASSIGN!

> `k;`

$$k$$

solve does not assign variables that you solve equations for.

Make sure that you performed Step 177. Check the value of k.

Maple did not assign k.

To assign a single solution, you have to specify an assignment. For instance, assign the name S to the solution of **solve(p=k*u,k)** that you performed in Step 177:

STEP 179:
ASSIGN A
SINGLE
SOLUTION

> `S:=solve(p=k*u,k);`

$$S := \frac{p}{u}$$

*Assign a name to results of the **solve** function.*

Solve $p = ku$ for k. Assign the name S to the results.

S now stores the results.

Because **solve** uses local variables, you could have even entered **k:=solve (p=k*u,k)** in Step 179! Also, note that a single equation is known as a *scalar equation*, as opposed to multiple equations that Chapter 10 reviews. For more information, consult **?solve** and **?solve[scalar]**. Investigate related functions in **?eliminate**, **?isolve**, **?isolate**, and **?solvefor**.

9.4.2 Multiple Solutions to Single Equation

Some equations, such as polynomials, yield multiple results. For instance, the equation $x^2 - 4 = 0$ has two solutions: $x = 2$ and $x = -2$. Try finding these solutions using **solve**:

STEP 180: MULTIPLE SOLUTIONS

> *Solve a single, or scalar, equation with multiple solutions.*

```
> solve(x^2-4=0,x);
```
Solve $x^2 - 4 = 0$ for x.

$$2, -2$$
Maple reports multiple solutions as a sequence.

If you expect or discover multiple solutions, use braces in the syntax **solve ({eqn},{var})** to present clearer solutions:

STEP 181: USE BRACES FOR MULTIPLE SOLUTIONS

> *Surround items inside* **solve** *with braces ({}) if you expect multiple solutions.*

```
> solve({x^2-4=0},{x});
```
Solve $x^2 - 4 = 0$ for x. Supply braces to collect solutions.

$$\{x = 2\}, \{x = -2\}$$
Specifying {} produces solutions as sets.

Consult Chapter 10 for information on solving *multiple equations*.

9.4.3 Polynomials

Find polynomial roots with **solve** or **roots** by entering **solve(poly=0,name)** or **roots(poly)**, respectively. Also, you may review the root-finding functions described in Chapter 6.

9.4.4 Lost Solutions

If **solve** fails to find a solution, Maple produces no output. However, if you suspect that **solve** missed some solutions, check if Maple assigned a global variable called **_SolutionsMayBeLost** to the Boolean value *true*. Consult with **?solve** for more details.

9.4.5 Extracting Solutions

Many equations produce multiple solutions. Use square brackets (**[]**) to extract solutions as you would select expressions from a sequence, list, or set. First, assign the sequence of solutions to a name like **Sols**:

STEP 182: ASSIGN SOLUTIONS

> *Assign the results of an equation's solution to a name.*

```
> Sols:=solve({x^2-4=0},{x});
```
Solve $x^2 - 4 = 0$ for x.
Assign Sols to the solutions.

$$Sols := \{x = 2\}, \{x = -2\}$$
Sols is a sequence of sets.

Because `Sols` holds an expression sequence, you can select individual solutions by using indices:

STEP 183:
EXTRACTING
SOLUTIONS

> *Select solutions from the solution sequence generated by* `solve`.

```
> Sols[1];
```
Extract the first solution from `Sols`.

$$\{x = 2\}$$
This expression is the first solution.

Each solution—Sol_1 and Sol_2—forms an equation in the form **var=val**. Also, recall that **eval(expr,var=val)** replaces **var** with **var** inside **expr**. Since the single name **var** is also an expression, you can enter **eval(var,var=val)** to extract the value of **var**. Here, `Sols[1]` stores the equation $x = 2$. To extract the value 2 from the expression x, enter the following:

STEP 184:
EXTRACTING
VALUES FROM
SOLUTIONS

Extract the value from a solution.

```
> eval(x,Sols[1]);
```
Substitute for $x = 2$ into the expression x. Then, evaluate the result.

$$2$$
$Sols_1$ is $\{x = 2\}$. Maple extracted the value 2.

Also, try **lhs(Sols[1])** and **rhs(Sols[1])** to extract the name x and value 2, respectively.

9.4.6 Related Commands

Consult Mathematics…Finding Roots, Factorization, and Solving… and **?solve** for information on numerous related functions. Example worksheets that demonstrate many of **solve**'s techniques are contained in **?examples[solve]**.

PRACTICE!

8. Solve the equation $\sin x = \frac{1}{2}\sqrt{3}$ for x.
9. Solve the quadratic equation $ax^2 + bx + c = 0$ for x.
10. Extract the first and second solutions of the quadratic equation. Assign $x1$ and $x2$ to each solution, respectively.
11. Solve $\sin x = 0$ for x. Produce all possible values of x. Hint: Consult **?solve** for information on the environment variable **_EnvAllSolutions**.

9.4.7 Numerical Solutions

Not all equations have exact answers. You may find approximate results with **numerical solutions**. Enter "floating-point solve" **fsolve(eqn,var)** to obtain numerical results:

STEP 185:
NUMERICALLY
SOLVE
EQUATIONS

Solve for floating-point results.

```
> fsolve({x^2=2},{x});
```
Numerically solve $x^2 = 2$ for x.

$$\{x = -1.414213562\}, \{x = 1.414213562\}$$
Maple reports the answers as floats.

You may also supply additional options to control **fsolve**'s behavior. For instance, enter **fsolve(*eqn*, *var*, *range*)** to search for solutions within a specific interval *range*:

<table>
<tr>
<td>

STEP 186:
FIND
SOLUTION
WITHIN A
SPECIFIED
INTERVAL

</td>
<td>

Supply the range option to **fsolve**.

> `fsolve({tan(x)=x},{x},Pi..2*Pi);`   *Numerically solve* $\tan(x) = x$ *for* x.

$\{x = 4.493409458\}$ *Maple reports the answers contained within* $\pi \le x \le 2\pi$.

</td>
</tr>
</table>

Another method involves entering numbers as floats inside **solve**, as discussed in **?solve[float]**. Also, consult **?Digits**, **?evalf**, and **?fnormal** for more information.

PRACTICE!

> **12.** Solve $x^x = 2$ for a numerical value of x. Use both **fsolve** and **solve**.
> **13.** Solve $\sin(x) = 0$ for a value of $10 \le x \le 20$.
> **14.** Solve $\sin(x) = 0$. Avoid $x = 0$ and $x = \pm\pi$. Hint: Consult **?fsolve**.

9.5 VERIFICATION

Computer programs are not perfect, so always check your work! This section discusses Maple functions for solution **verification**, or how you can check your output.

9.5.1 Checking Results

Substituting solutions back into equations should produce **identities** of the form LHS = RHS. For instance, substitute $\dfrac{y-b}{m}$ for x inside $y = mx + b$. After rearranging the equations, you will produce the identity $y = y$. Using Maple, you can enter **eval(*orginal_eqn*, *sol*)** to verify that *sol* solves *orginal_eqn*. Recall that *sol* is of the form *var=val*. Now, verify the solution from Step 181:

<table>
<tr>
<td>

STEP 187:
VERIFY
SOLUTIONS

</td>
<td>

Check solutions by backsubstituting into the original equation.

> `EQN := x^2-4=0:`   *Assign EQN to the equation* $x^2 - 4 = 0$.

> `Sols:= solve({EQN},{x});`   *Solve* $x^2 - 4 = 0$ *for* x. *Assign Sols to the solutions.*

$Sols := \{x = 2\}, \{x = -2\}$ *Maple found two solutions.*

> `eval(EQN,Sols[1]), eval(EQN,Sols[2]);`   *Substitute the solutions into EQN.*

$0 = 0, 0 = 0$ *Maple produces identities for both solutions.*

</td>
</tr>
</table>

9.5.2 Multiple Substitutions

Try **map(subs,[*Sols*],*EQN*)** for multiple substitutions. Maple expands this command as the sequence **subs(*Sols*[1],*EQN*),subs(*Sols*[2],*EQN*),...,** **subs(*Sols*[n],*EQN*)** for *n* solutions. Use **[*Sols*]** instead of *Sols* because **map** requires a list:

STEP 188:
VERIFY ALL
SOLUTIONS

*Use **map** to verify all solutions in one statement.*

```
> map(subs,[Sols],EQN);
```
*Substitute each solution into EQN. Use lists with **map**!*

$$[0 = 0, 0 = 0]$$
The solutions produce identities.

Remember that **subs** does not evaluate expressions! Extract and evaluate individual results when **subs** does not produce identities. Consult **?map** for more information.

PRACTICE!

15. Solve $x^2 + 4x + 3 = 0$ for x. Verify each solution individually.

16. Verify both solutions in the previous problem by using **map**.

9.6 MISCELLANEOUS

This section introduces features of **solve** and related commands.

9.6.1 RootOf

Solving for roots sometimes produces odd-looking results. For example, find the roots of $x^4 + x + 1$:

STEP 189:
RootOf

RootOf *roots of high-order polynomials.*

```
> x:='x':
```
Clear any value stored in x.

```
> S:=solve(x^4+x+1=0,x);
```
Find the roots of $x^4 + x + 1$.

$$S := \text{RootOf}(\_Z^4 + \_Z + 1)$$
Maple produces a "placeholder" for the results.

RootOf(*expr*) is a "placeholder" for the actual roots of ***expr***. The _Z values represent the roots of the original expression. Enter **allvalues(*expr*)** to find all _Z values:

STEP 190:
FIND ALL
ROOTS

*Find all roots from a **RootOf** expression.*

```
> S2:=allvalues(S);
```
allvalues *symbolically evaluates all **RootOf** values.*

You will see very lengthy results! They are omitted here in order to conserve space.

Use a colon next time.

Maple often breaks up long output into ***labels***, which are names that start with a percent sign (%). My version of Maple produced $\%1 := 108 + 12I \sqrt{687}$. If your version produced this label, you can now enter **%1** as a valid name in an expression. You might have to select Options→OutputDisplay→TypesetNotation to activate labeling. Investigate **?labeling** or **?interface** for information on labeling options.

Finally, you can evaluate numerical results:

STEP 191:
EVALUATE
FLOATING-
POINT RESULTS

> `evalf(S2,2);`

Find numerical values of your solutions.

Find all floating-point values of the roots. Use only 2 digits during the computation.

$$.75 - 91I, .75 + 91I, -.74 - .39I, -.77 + .39I$$

Maple found only complex roots.

You could have also entered `Digits:=2: evalf(S2);` to achieve similar results. Consult `?evalf`, `?convert[RootOf]`, `?convert[radical]`, and `?type[RootOf]` for more information.

9.6.2 Inequalities

Inequality expressions contain `<`, `<=`, `>`, and `>=`, as discussed in Section 5.5. The `solve` function can solve relations of a single inequality:

STEP 192:
SOLVE AN
INEQUALITY

> `solve(2*abs(x)>1,{x});`

Find a solution to an inequality relationship.

Solve $2|x| > 1$.

$$\left\{\frac{1}{2} < x\right\}, \left\{x < \frac{-1}{2}\right\}$$

Maple automatically converts inequalities into "<" form.

Consult `?solve[ineq]` for more details. Also, consult `?simplex` and `?plots[inequal]` for information about solving relations with multiple inequalities.

9.6.3 Extrema

Extrema are extreme values of an expression, either the most negative or the most positive. Find candidates for extrema of an expression by entering `minimize(expr)` and `maximize(expr)`:

STEP 193:
FIND MINIMUM
AND MAXIMUM
VALUES

> `A:=sin(x):`

> `minimize(A),maximize(A);`

Find the extrema of an expression.

Assign a function.

Find the possible extrema of $\sin x$.

$$-1, 1$$

You should further investigate these values to confirm whether they are truly extrema or not.

Also, consult `?extrema` and `?max` or `?min` for more information.

PRACTICE!

17. Evaluate RootOf($\_Z^2 + 1$). Find all possible values.

18. Find the roots of $x^5 + x + 1$ in floating-point notation.

19. Verify the roots of the previous problem.

20. Solve $x^2 > 1$.

21. What are the extrema of $\cos x$? What are the extrema of $\tan x$?

9.7 APPLICATION: PILES

This section solves a problem involving soil mechanics that requires the solution of a fourth-order polynomial equation.

9.7.1 Background

Landscaping and construction often require structures to shore up and block portions of the ground from collapsing. Very often, temporary *piles* help protect workers on construction sites. Figure 9-1 illustrates a *sheet pile* driven into sandy soil. The weight of the ground creates a force P that pushes the pile to left and causes different pressure distributions to the left and right of the pile.

Balancing these pressure distributions according to the soil properties yields the proper depth that one should drive the pile into soil. Given unit weight γ (force/volume), find the necessary pile depth D from the following equation:

$$D^4 - \frac{8P}{\gamma(K_p - K_a)} D^2 - \frac{12PL}{\gamma(K_p - K_a)} D - \left(\frac{2P}{\gamma(K_p - K_a)}\right)^2 = 0. \tag{9-1}$$

The coefficients

$$K_a = \tan^2\left(45° - \frac{\phi}{2}\right) \tag{9-2}$$

and

$$K_p = \tan^2\left(45° + \frac{\phi}{2}\right) \tag{9-3}$$

help determine the pressure that the soil places on the pile. The angle ϕ represents the soil's friction.

9.7.2 Problem

Given $\gamma = 18$ kN/m³, $\phi = 30°$, $L = 3$ m, and $P = 30$ kN/m, determine the necessary depth at which to drive the sheet pile shown in Figure 9.1.

Figure 9.2. Sheet Pile

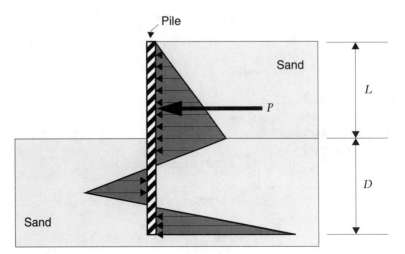

9.7.3 Methodology

First, state and assign pertinent variables:

STEP 194: INITIALIZE MAPLE

Initialize system variables.

> `restart:` *Restart your Maple session.*

STEP 195: RESTATE AND SEPARATE

Initialize problem variables.

> `unprotect(gamma):gamma:=18*kN/m^3:` *Maple predefines γ, so remove the protection before assigning γ. In general, you should unprotect only variables of small problems.*

> `phi:=convert(30*degrees,radians):` *Assign the flow height.*

> `theta:=convert(45*degrees,radians):` *Assign the notch angle, but use radians!*

> `L:=3*m:  P:=30*kN/m:` *Assign length and force.*

To simplify data entry, assign the model for Eq. 9-1 first:

STEP 196: MODEL

Assign the model for finding the depth of the sheet pile.

> `Eqn:=(Dp^4)-C1*(Dp^2)-C2*(Dp)-C3^2=0;` *Remember that Maple protects D.*

Like γ, you could unprotect D as well. I just want to demonstrate different methods.

$$Dp^4 - C1 Dp^2 - C2 Dp - C3^2 = 0$$ *Use Dp to replace D in the model.*

Now, assign the coefficients $C1$, $C2$, and $C3$:

STEP 197: MODEL

Assign the model's coefficients. See Eqs. 9-2 and 9-3.

> `Ka:=tan(theta-phi/2)^2;` $K_a = \tan^2\left(45° - \frac{\phi}{2}\right)$

> `Kp:=tan(theta+phi/2)^2;` $K_p = \tan^2\left(45° + \frac{\phi}{2}\right)$

$$\frac{1}{3}$$ *Check your results before continuing.*

$$3$$ *Check your results before continuing.*

STEP 198: MODEL

Assign the model's coefficients. See Eq. 9-1.

> `C1:=8*P/(gamma*(Kp-Ka)):` $C1 = \frac{8P}{\gamma(K_p - K_a)}$

> `C2:=12*P*L/(gamma*(Kp-Ka)):` $C2 = \frac{12PL}{\gamma(K_p - K_a)}$

> `C3:=2*P/(gamma*(Kp-Ka)):` $C3 = \frac{2P}{\gamma(K_p - K_a)}$

After suppressing so much output, you should check your work so far:

STEP 199:
CHECKING

> *Check your work in progress.*

> `Eqn;`   *What has Maple assigned to the variable Eqn?*

$$Eqn := Dp^4 - 5m^2 Dp^2 - \frac{45}{2}\, m^3 Dp - \frac{25}{16}\, m^4 = 0$$ *Note how the units all balance to m^4.*

Now, solve the fourth-order polynomial equation for the pile depth Dp:

STEP 200:
SOLVE

> *Find a solution to the problem.*

> `S:=solve(Eqn,Dp);`   *Solve the model for Dp.*

$$S := \frac{1}{2}\, RootOf(\_Z^4 - 25 - 180\_Z - 20\_Z^2)m$$

Remember that Maple solves many higher order polynomials in terms of the placeholder `RootOf`.

You need a more exact answer!

STEP 201:
REPORT

> *Convert your solution into a more comprehensible form.*

> `S2:=allvalues(S);`   *Force Maple to produce all solutions from Step 200.*

A very long solution appears...   *This impractical solution is too long to print in entirety here. Normally, you would use a colon to suppress the output.*

The previous answer, though "exact," is unwieldy. Use **evalf** to produce a more compact and useful numerical form:

STEP 202:
REPORT

> *Convert your "exact" solution into an more comprehensible floating-point form.*

> `S3:=evalf(S2,3);`   *Force Maple to evaluate a floating-point solution from Step 201.*

$$S3 := 3.44m, -.0750m, (-1.68 + 1.92I)m,$$ *This answer is much better!*
$$(-1.68 - 1.92I)m$$

9.7.4 Solution

Of course, negative and imaginary pile depths make no physical sense. Therefore, choose the required pile depth found by Maple as 3.44 m.

PROFESSIONAL SUCCESS: TECHNICAL PRESENTATIONS

Does public speaking make you nervous? Presentations are common in many professions. Consider some of the following suggestions to calm your nerves:

☐ Preparation:

Treat presentations as you would written reports. *Brainstorm*, *outline*, *write*, and *rewrite*. Break larger tasks into smaller subtasks if the work seems daunting.

☐ Organization:

- **Tell them what you'll tell them**. Commence with a title, abstract, and overview. Next, provide an introduction and some background material.
- **Tell them**. Focus the scope of the problem. Include relevant theory, methodology, experiments, and examples. Compare expected and actual results.
- **Tell them what you told them**. Summarize your presentation. Discuss conclusions and recommendations. Always leave enough time for questions.

☐ Material:

Never write down everything that you will say. Instead, summarize important concepts and points with brief bulleted statements, and spruce up your talk with many graphics. Also, people should actually be able to see the writing on such displays! Avoid having to say, "Well, you probably can't see this, but it says, ..."

☐ Style:

Look up, and look around. Pretend that everyone is wearing nothing but underwear. Never memorize every word. Speak slowly and calmly. Avoid habits such as head scratching, nail biting, and, certainly, nose picking. Above all else, smile!

SUMMARY

This chapter has reviewed further techniques for manipulating expressions. Both substitution and evaluation help avoid tedious name assignments that simulate equations. Substitution swaps operands in an expression for other expressions. You can substitute one or many expressions in one or many other expressions. When **subs** fails, try **algsubs**. Use **eval** when you wish to evaluate expressions. You can also substitute with **eval**. Use **solve** to solve equations. Though Maple prefers to display exact solutions, you may force it to produce numerical results with **fsolve**. You can also generate numerical results by using floats inside **solve**. As with all techniques, verify your solutions.

KEY TERMS

algebraic substitution	identities	solving
equations	labels	syntactic substitution
evaluation	numerical solutionsn	verification
extrema	scalar equatio	

Problems

1. Explain the differences between Maple's substitution, evaluation, and solving procedures.
2. When should you use syntactic substitution as opposed to an algebraic substitution?
3. Describe cases in which you would use **eval** in place of **subs**.

4. Perform the following substitutions using the **subs** command. (Hint: You might wish to check your results by assigning expressions as demonstrated in Section 9.1):

   4a. Find $f(2)$ given $f(x) = 1 + x$.

   4b. Find $f(2)$ given $f(x) = \dfrac{x + c}{2}$.

   4c. Find $f(1,2)$ given $f(x,y) = x - y^2$.

   4d. Find $f(0)$ given $f(x) = \dfrac{\sin(x)}{x}$.

   4e. Find $f(2)$ and $g(2)$ given $f(x) = 1 + x^2$ and $g(x) = \sqrt{f(x)}$.

   4f. Find $f(2)$ and $g(2)$ given $f(x) = 1 + x^2$ and $g(x) = f(x + 1)$.

5. Repeat Problem 9.4 using the **eval** command instead of **subs**.

6. Replace the subexpression $\dfrac{a}{c}$ with x inside the expression $\dfrac{ab}{c}$ using a substitution. (Hint: You should try **subs**, but that function will fail. Use **algsubs** instead.)

7. Solve the problem in Section 4.5 using the **subs** function for Case 1 and Case 2.

8. Find the numerical value of π to 5 decimal places without changing the value of **Digits**. (Hint: Use **evalf**.)

9. Try solving Problem 5.9 by using **evalf**. Why does Maple generate the following output that results?

```
> restart:
> evalf(2*1.05,2); # Step 1
              2.1
> a:=1.05: evalf(2*a,2); # Step 2
              2.2
```

10. Solve the following equations for exact solutions when possible. Otherwise, find floating-point answers. (Hints: In general, use **solve**. You might wish to find numerical solutions from **fsolve** when **solve** fails. Note also that some equations might generate complex solutions.)

    10a. Solve $y = mx + b$ for x.

    10b. Solve $y = 5x - 1$ for x.

    10c. Solve $11x^2 - 0.17x = -5.4$ for x.

    10d. Solve $\sin\left(x + \dfrac{\pi}{3}\right) = 1$ for x.

    10e. Solve $\ln\left(\dfrac{x}{x + y}\right) + x = 1$ for y.

    10f. Solve $\sqrt{x} + 2\sqrt{x} - \sin(x + 1) = 0$ for x. Produce a complex result.

11. Verify the solutions for Problem 9.10. (Hints: Try to substitute the solutions back into the original equations. Note that you might need to simplify or expand various subexpressions.)

12. Solve $x^5 - 3x^3 + x - 1 = 0$ for x. (Hints: Applying **solve** yields two solutions. Use **allvalues** on the more complicated of the two. Then, use **evalf**.)

13. Find a general formula for solving a general third-order polynomial, such as

$$a_0 + a_1 x + a_2 x^2 + a_3 x^3 = 0,$$

for x. (Hints: Use **solve**, and surround the variable x with curly braces. You can use either arbitrary constants or the constants a_i that are shown above. For instance, to output a_2, you would enter **a[2]**. Also, you might wish to activate Maple's labeling feature.)

14. Repeat the problem in Section 9.7 given $\phi = 25°$ and $P = 35$ kN. Verify your results using Maple.

15. Thermodynamics provides many equations for relating the physical properties of substances. Given volume v, temperature T, pressure P, gas constant R, and arbitrary constant C, the equation

$$v = \frac{RT}{P} - \frac{C}{T^3}$$

defines the equation of *state* for a gas. Find the temperature T in terms of the other variables. (Hint: You might wish to activate Maple's labeling feature.)

16. What interest rate i will convert a current payment $P = \$12,000$ into an annual cost $A = \$2400$ for a 10-year period? (Hint: Refer to Section 3.4.)

17. Repeat Problem 7.10, but use **solve** to find values of τ from $\tau^3 - A\tau^2 + B\tau - C = 0$.

18. Given $\gamma = 18$ kN/m^3, $\phi = 30°$, $\theta = 45°$, $L = 3$ m, and $P = 24$ kN/m, determine the necessary depth at which to drive the sheet pile shown in Figure 9.1.

19. Snow fences help prevent snow drifts from accumulating on roads. Given fence length L_f, fence height H, storage capacity Q_c, and storage capacity for an infinitely long fence $Q_{c,inf}$, engineers have developed the following empirical equation:

$$\frac{Q_c}{Q_{c,inf}} = 0.288 + 0.039\left(\frac{L_f}{H}\right) - 0.0009\left(\frac{L_f}{H}\right)^2 + \frac{\left(\frac{L_f}{H}\right)^3}{133333} \text{ for } 5 \le \frac{L_f}{H} \le 50$$

Assuming a factor $Q_c/Q_{c,inf} = 0.8$ and a fence height $H = 6$ ft, solve for the required length L_f. (Hint: Follow a similar procedure that Section 9.7 demonstrates.)

20. The "loudness" of sound L (decibels, or dB) can be estimated using a logarithmic intensity ratio:

$$L = 10\log_{10}\left(\frac{I}{I_0}\right).$$

I is the intensity (W/m^2, or Watts per square meter). The threshold of human hearing is defined as the intensity $I_0 = 1 \times 10^{-12}$ W/m^2.

20a. In general, a sound that has intensity $I = 1$ reaches the threshold of pain in humans. ITo what level of loudness L does this intensity correspond? (Hints: Evaluate the equation for L given $I = 1$ and $I_0 = 1 \times 10^{-12}$. Note that you are using a base-10 logarithm. Also, beware of Maple's aliased value of I! Use a different name. You should compute 120 dB.)

20b. In 1994, the heavy metal band *MANOWAR* claimed to achieve a world record loudness of 130 dB at a concert. What value of intensity I did the band reach? (Hint: Use **solve** or **fsolve**.)

10

Systems of Equations

10.1 SIMULTANEOUS EQUATIONS

Increasing the complexity of a model introduces more variables. This section introduces multivariable models and solution methods. Before solving a model, however, you will first need to develop it. An example of this process is shown in Section 10.1.1.

OBJECTIVES

After reading this chapter, you should be able to:

- Describe and model systems of equations
- Solve systems of equations by hand
- Solve systems of equations with Maple plots
- Use linear algebra with vectors and matrices
- Solve systems of equations with Maple's linear-algebra functions

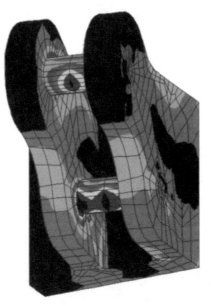

The boundary-element method (BEM), a versatile analysis technique, solves problems, such as the stress analysis of a bracket with hinges shown in the accompanying figure. BEM models discretize a body's surface into elements that contribute to the overall system behavior. The analysis of behavior using only surfaces provides BEM's greatest advantage over volumetric-discretization techniques. Not only are BEM models easier to produce, but important system behaviors typically occur on surfaces. Courtesy of Boundary Element Software Technology Corporation, Getsville, NY 14068-0310

10.1.1 Building a Model

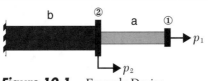

Figure 10.1. Example Device

A device composed of two elastic bars capped with rigid plates is shown in Figure 10.1. Loads are statically applied on both plate ① and plate ②. For now, you will call the connections at ① and ② *nodes*.

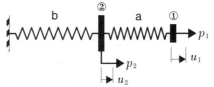

Figure 10.2. Model of Device

You can model elastic bars as springs, as shown in Figure 10.2. Assume that Hooke's Law ($p = ku$) governs the bars' force-displacement behavior, as discussed in Chapter 6. Thus, bar a has force p_a and displacement u_a. Similarly, bar b has force p_b and displacement u_b.

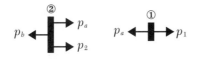

$$p_b = p_2 + p_a \qquad p_a = p_1$$
$$\quad = p_1 + p_2$$

Figure 10.3. Free-Body Diagrams

After the loads are slowly applied, the bars deform and reach a new resting, or *equilibrium*, position. The applied loads (p_1 and p_2) and internal forces of the bars (p_a and p_b) must balance according to equilibrium. Assume no twisting or rotation of the plates occurs. See Figure 10.3.

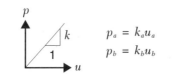

$$p_a = k_a u_a$$
$$p_b = k_b u_b$$

Figure 10.4. Hooke's Law

From Hooke's Law, illustrated in Figure 10.4, relate each spring's internal force to its *relative displacement*, the measure of how much each spring stretches. Bars a and b have relative displacements u_a and u_b, respectively.

10.1.1 Building a Model (cont.)

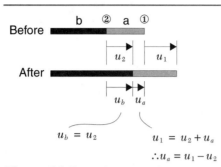

The displacement at ② (u_2) stretches spring b and compresses spring a. The displacement at ① (u_1) stretches spring a. Therefore, determine a's "relative stretch" by subtracting node ②'s displacement from that of node ①, as shown in Figure 10.5.

$$u_b = u_2 \qquad u_1 = u_2 + u_a$$
$$\therefore u_a = u_1 - u_2$$

Figure 10.5.   Relative Displacements

$$p_1 = p_a$$
$$= k_a u_a = k_a(u_1 - u_2)$$
$$p_2 = p_b - p_1$$
$$= k_b u_2 - k_a(u_1 - u_2)$$
$$= -k_a u_1 + (k_a + k_b)u_2$$

Ease your analysis by expressing the equations in terms of nodal values, as shown in Figure 10.6. Combine equilibrium, Hooke's Law, and displacement relations into two equations in terms of p, k, and u.

Figure 10.6.   Combine Equations

10.1.2 Systems of Equations

The equations in Figure 10.6 may be rearranged into the following **system of equations**:

$$k_a u_1 - k_a u_2 = p_1 \tag{10-1}$$
$$-k_a u_1 + (k_a + k_b)u_2 = p_2. \tag{10-2}$$

A system of equations collects simultaneous equations with common unknown variables, also called *unknowns* or *indeterminates*. The system in Eqs. 10-1 and 10-2 has two unknowns, u_1 and u_2. Assume that all other variables have predetermined values.

Linear systems contain all first-order equations in the form $a_0 = a_1 x_1 + \ldots + a_n x_n$. Both Eqs. 10-1 and 10-2 contain terms with powers no greater than unity, and thus, the equations constitute a linear system. On the other hand, **nonlinear systems** of equations contain terms with powers higher than unity.

10.1.3 Gaussian Elimination

Solve for the unknowns u_1 and u_2, as shown in Figure 10.7. First, assume the values $k_a = 2$, $k_b = 3$, $p_1 = 10$, and $p_2 = 20$ in Step ①. Apply **Gaussian elimination**, as demonstrated by Steps ②, ③, and ④. By adjusting coefficients, you can eliminate common terms. After dividing out leading coefficients, solve for unknowns by backsubstitution.

10.1.4 Dependency

The following conditions characterize a **linearly independent** system of equations:

- The number of equations match the number of unknowns.
- No equation is a multiple of another equation in the system.

A linearly independent system produces only one, or unique, solution for each unknown, as demonstrated in Figure 10.7. You might encounter systems with duplicates of equations, such as the system $x + y = 1$ and $2x + 2y = 2$. Such a system produces an infinite number of x and y solutions and is called **linearly dependent**.

① Substitute values into Eqs. 10-1 and 10-2.	② Reduce the second equation by adding the first.	③ Divide equations by the first, or leading, coefficient.	④ Backsubstitute results into the first equation.
$2u_1 - 2u_2 = 10$ $-2u_1 + 5u_2 = 20$	$2u_1 - 2u_2 = 10$ $3u_2 = 30$	$u_1 - u_2 = 5$ $u_2 = 10$	$u_1 = 15$ $u_2 = 10$

Figure 10.7. Gaussian Elimination

10.2 GENERAL EQUATION SOLVING

This section demonstrates the application of **solve** to linear and nonlinear systems of equations.

10.2.1 Multiple Equations

To solve systems of equations, enter **solve({eqns},{vars})**, where

- **{eqns}** is the set of simultaneous equations in terms of **vars**.
- **{vars}** is the set of unknown variables that you wish to find.

Try solving the spring model from the previous section:

STEP 203:
SOLVE LINEAR
SYSTEM

> `restart:`

> `eqn1:= 2*u1-2*u2 = 10:`

> `eqn2:= -2*u1+5*u2 = 20:`

> `sols:=solve({eqn1,eqn2},{u1,u2});`

$$sols := \{u2 = 10, u1 = 15\}$$

Solve a system of linear equations.

Begin a new Maple session.

Assign eqn1 to $2u_1 - 2u_2 = 10$.

Assign eqn2 to $-2u_1 + 5u_2 = 20$.

Solve the system of equations.

Maple produces both answers.

Consult **?solve[system]** and **?solve[linear]** for more information.

10.2.2 Verifying Solutions

Check your work! Recall Section 9.5, which provided information on backsubstitution methods using the **subs** function:

STEP 204:
CHECKING
SOLUTIONS

> `subs(sols,{eqn1,eqn2});`

$$\{10 = 10, 20 = 20\}$$

Verify your results.

Backsubstitute solutions into original equations.

Identities indicate correct results.

10.2.3 Assigning Solutions

The **solve** function never assigns the unknowns for which you solve. In general, assign unknowns with **assign(expr)**, where **expr** is a list or set that contains the sequence of solutions, **var1=val1, var2=val2,...**. For instance, enter **assign(sols)** to assign $u1$ and $u2$:

STEP 205: ASSIGNING SOLUTIONS		
		Assign unknown-variable names to solved values.
	`> assign(sols);`	*sols is $\{u1 = 15, u2 = 10\}$. Assign $u1$ to 15 . Assign $u2$ to 10.*
	`> u1,u2;`	*Check the values of $u1$ and $u2$.*
	15, 10	*The names were correctly assigned.*

Consult **?assign** for more information.

10.2.4 Nonlinear Equations

Use **solve** for nonlinear systems. You can mix linear and nonlinear equations in a system, though mixed systems are still considered nonlinear systems:

STEP 206: SOLVE NON-LINEAR SYSTEM		
		Solve linear and nonlinear equations together.
	`> A:= x^2+y^2=1:`	*Assign A to a circle $x^2 + y^2 = 1$.*
	`> B:= x+y=1:`	*Assign B to a line $x + y = 1$.*
	`> solve({A,B},{x,y});`	*Solve equations for common variables.*
	$\{x = 1, y = 0\}, \{x = 0, y = 1\}$	*The line crosses the circle in two places!*

10.2.5 Numerical Solutions

You can enter **fsolve({eqns},{vars},options)** to obtain floating-point results of linear and nonlinear systems of equations.

PRACTICE!

1. Solve the system $2x + 3y + z = 0$, $2y + z = -1$, and $x + z = 2$.
2. Verify and assign the solutions in the previous problem. Show values of x, y, and z.
3. Solve the system $x + y = \pi$ and $\sin(x) = y$ for x and y.
4. Can you "solve" the system $x + y = 1$ and $2x + 2y = 2$?

10.3 GRAPHICAL SOLUTION

Both Eqs. 10-1 and 10-2 are mutually dependent equations of u_1 and u_2. Recall that **implicitplot** graphs functions with mutually dependent variables. Thus, you can enter **implicitplot({eqns},h,v)** to display a graphical solution of **eqns**:

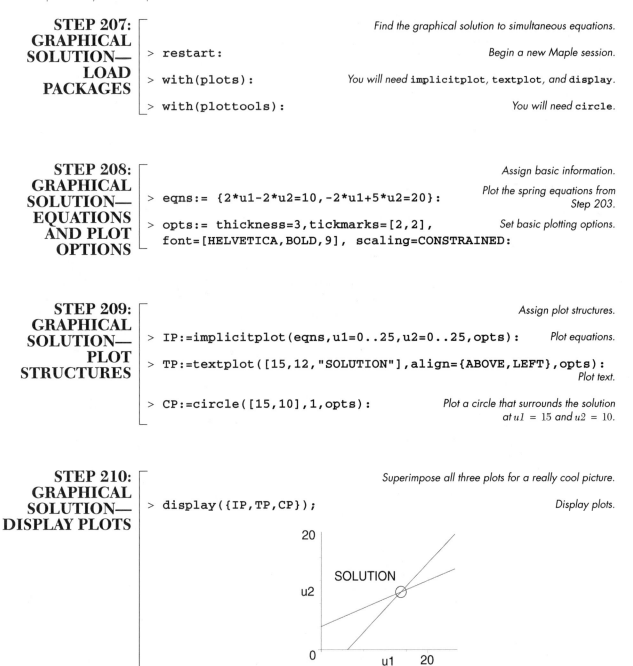

STEP 207:
GRAPHICAL
SOLUTION—
LOAD
PACKAGES

Find the graphical solution to simultaneous equations.

```
> restart:
```
Begin a new Maple session.

```
> with(plots):
```
You will need `implicitplot`, `textplot`, *and* `display`.

```
> with(plottools):
```
You will need `circle`.

STEP 208:
GRAPHICAL
SOLUTION—
EQUATIONS
AND PLOT
OPTIONS

Assign basic information.

```
> eqns:= {2*u1-2*u2=10,-2*u1+5*u2=20}:
```
Plot the spring equations from Step 203.

```
> opts:= thickness=3,tickmarks=[2,2],
  font=[HELVETICA,BOLD,9], scaling=CONSTRAINED:
```
Set basic plotting options.

STEP 209:
GRAPHICAL
SOLUTION—
PLOT
STRUCTURES

Assign plot structures.

```
> IP:=implicitplot(eqns,u1=0..25,u2=0..25,opts):
```
Plot equations.

```
> TP:=textplot([15,12,"SOLUTION"],align={ABOVE,LEFT},opts):
```
Plot text.

```
> CP:=circle([15,10],1,opts):
```
Plot a circle that surrounds the solution at u1 = 15 and u2 = 10.

STEP 210:
GRAPHICAL
SOLUTION—
DISPLAY PLOTS

Superimpose all three plots for a really cool picture.

```
> display({IP,TP,CP});
```
Display plots.

The axes represent each unknown variable in the equations. The lines cross at the common solution to both equations. Having only one common point to both equations indicates a unique solution.

PRACTICE!

5. Graphically solve $3x + 2y = -4$ and $-x + 3y = 5$.

6. Can you graphically solve $x^2 + y^2 = 1$ and $y = 2$? Do the equations intersect?

10.4 VECTORS AND MATRICES

When solving many equations, data entry becomes tedious. Thankfully, computers and mathematics have provided powerful tools for solving systems of equations. This section briefly reviews vectors and matrices, both data structures needed to efficiently solve equations.

10.4.1 Maple's Linear-Algebra Package

Many functions demonstrated in this section require the **linalg** library package:

STEP 211:
LOAD linalg

> *Load the linear-algebra library package.*

```
> with(linalg):
```
linalg contains many vector and matrix functions.

```
Warning, new definition for norm
```
Ignore this error message.

```
Warning, new definition for trace
```
Ignore this error message, too.

Consult **?linalg** and Appendix D for more information.

10.4.2 Vectors

A *vector* represents a quantity with both direction and magnitude. For instance, represent the solution $(u_1, u_2) = (15, 10)$, as shown in Figure 10.8:

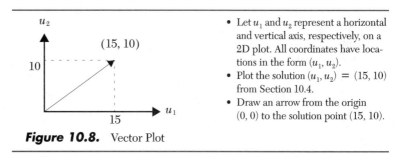

- Let u_1 and u_2 represent a horizontal and vertical axis, respectively, on a 2D plot. All coordinates have locations in the form (u_1, u_2).
- Plot the solution $(u_1, u_2) = (15, 10)$ from Section 10.4.
- Draw an arrow from the origin $(0, 0)$ to the solution point $(15, 10)$.

Figure 10.8. Vector Plot

Consider the arrow shown in Figure 10.8. Compute vector magnitude as length using the Pythagorean Theorem:

$$\sqrt{u_1^2 + u_2^2} = \sqrt{15^2 + 10^2}.$$

Also, provide vector direction with the coordinates $(u_1, u_2) = (15, 10)$. Therefore, the arrow drawn to the solution point represents a vector!

10.4.3 Vector Notation

Let u represent the arrow drawn from $(0, 0)$ to any coordinate (u_1, u_2). Denote vector u as

$$u = \begin{bmatrix} u_1 \\ u_2 \end{bmatrix}, \tag{10-3}$$

where u_1 and u_2 are called ***vector components***. The component indices 1 and 2 label the vector rows and axes, respectively, in a solution plot. Vertical vectors, like u, are called *column vectors*. Horizontal vectors, like $v = [v_1\ v_2]$, are called *row vectors*.

When writing vectors by hand, distinguish vectors from other quantities with arrow notation, such as $\vec{u}$ or $\vec{u}$. Also, vectors with unitary magnitudes (length of one, or unity) are often written as unit vectors, such as $\hat{u}$.

10.4.4 Vector Syntax

Enter **vector(*list*)** to create a vector:

STEP 212:
CREATE
VECTOR

Assign vectors in Maple. Ensure that `linalg` *is loaded using* `with(linalg)`.

```
> u := vector([15, 10]);
```

$$u := [15, 10]$$

Assign u to the vector $\begin{bmatrix} u_1 \\ u_2 \end{bmatrix}$.

Maple prints vectors horizontally.

Consult with **?vector**, **?linalg[vector]**, **?type[vector]**, and **?array** for more information. Unfortunately, Maple rarely distinguishes between column and row vectors. Investigate **pvac** inside **?share[contents]** for information on how to print column vectors vertically.

10.4.5 Vector Components

Use indexed names in the form ***name[index]*** to access individual vector components. Indices start from 1. For instance, you can extract the first component of u with **u[1]**:

STEP 213:
EXTRACT
VECTOR
COMPONENTS

Access vector components. Indices start from 1.

```
> u[1],u[2];
```

15, 10

Extract u_1 and u_2 from vector u.

Vector components $u_1 = 15$ and $u_2 = 10$.

PRACTICE!

7. Assign p to the vector

$$\begin{bmatrix} p_1 \\ p_2 \end{bmatrix}.$$

8. Check p's type.
9. Assign p_1 to 10 and p_2 to 20. Now, extract p_1 and p_2 from p.

10.4.6 Matrices

Vectors store information in one dimension, either horizontally or vertically. A ***matrix*** stores information in two dimensions inside a rectangular array much like a spreadsheet or table does.

10.4.7 Matrix Notation

Values stored inside matrices are commonly called *matrix elements*. Row and column element positions are indicated by two indices. For instance, matrix K,

$$K = \begin{bmatrix} K_{11} & K_{12} \\ K_{21} & K_{22} \end{bmatrix}, \qquad (10\text{-}4)$$

has four elements organized into two rows and two columns. Element K_{11} corresponds to row 1, column 1. Element K_{12} corresponds to row 1, column 2, and so forth. *Square matrices*, like K, have equal numbers of rows and columns.

10.4.8 Maple Syntax

A matrix is entered as a list of lists in the form `matrix([list1,list2,..., listn])`. Each `list` represents a matrix row. Separate rows and row elements with commas!

STEP 214: CREATE MATRIX

Assign matrices in Maple. Ensure that `linalg` *is loaded.*

```
> K:=matrix([[2,-2],[-2,5]]);
```
Assign K to $\begin{bmatrix} 2 & -2 \\ -2 & 5 \end{bmatrix}$.

$$K := \begin{bmatrix} 2 & -2 \\ -2 & 5 \end{bmatrix}$$

Maple created a 4-by-4 matrix.

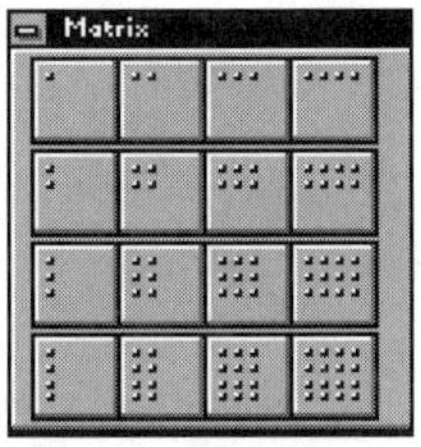

Figure 10.9.
Matrix Palette

Consult `?matrix` for an alternative syntax. Also, select View→Palettes→MatrixPalette (see Figure 10.9) to ease entry. Consult `?linalg[matrix]`, `?type[matrix]`, and `?array` for more information. Investigate `?matrixplot` for information on how to create a graphical matrix representation.

10.4.9 Matrix Elements

Enter `name[row,col]` to extract a matrix element from `row` and `col` of the matrix assigned to `name`:

STEP 215: MATRIX ELEMENTS

Extract matrix elements.

```
> K[1,1],K[1,2],K[2,1],K[2,2];
```
Extract K_{11}, K_{12}, K_{21}, and K_{22} from matrix K in Step 214.

$$2, -2, -2, 5$$

Remember that matrix indices have the order `row,col`.

PRACTICE!

10. Enter the matrix

$$A = \begin{bmatrix} 1 & 2 & 3 \\ 4 & 5 & 6 \end{bmatrix}.$$

11. How many rows and columns compose A?

12. Extract elements A_{12} and A_{23}.

10.4.10 Displaying Vectors and Matrices

Maple employs *last-name evaluation* for large objects, like vectors and matrices. Last-name evaluation evaluates expressions, but stops just before displaying the results in order to conserve space. Enter either the evaluate-matrix command **evalm(*expr*)** or **print(*expr*)** to override last-name evaluation and force a display:

STEP 216: DISPLAY MATRIX AND VECTOR CONTENTS

Print expressions that hide because of last-name evaluation.

> V:=vector([1,2]): V;   *Assign V to a vector. Check V's value.*

$$V$$

Maple will not display V's contents!

> evalm(V);   *Force Maple to display V's contents.*

$$[1, 2]$$ **evalm** *forces Maple to disable last-name evaluation.*

See also Appendix E for other expression types that use last-name evaluation.

10.4.11 Functions and Operations

Table 10-1 summarizes many common functions and operations for vectors and matrices. Most functions belong to the **linalg** library. Remember first to load the **linalg** library package. Enter **with(linalg)** or consult Appendix D for other methods. Beware that many operations require **evalm(*expr*)** to evaluate *expr*. For instance, add two vectors:

STEP 217: VECTOR ADDITION

Add two vectors together. Use the rule $a_i + b_i = c_i$.

> a:=vector([1,2]): b:=vector([-1,1]):   *Assign two vectors.*

> a+b;   *Attempt vector addition.*

$$a + b$$ *Maple refuses to evaluate the result.*

> evalm(a+b);   *Forcibly evaluate the sum $a + b$.*

$$[0, 3]$$ $\begin{bmatrix} 1 \\ 2 \end{bmatrix} + \begin{bmatrix} -1 \\ 1 \end{bmatrix} = \begin{bmatrix} 0 \\ 3 \end{bmatrix}.$

Another common operation is matrix–vector multiplication. Enter **multiply(*M*, *v*)** to multiply matrix *M* by vector *v*:

STEP 218: MATRIX AND VECTOR MULTIPLICATION

Multiply a matrix by a vector.

> K := matrix([[2,-2],[-2,5]]):   *Assign a matrix $K = \begin{bmatrix} 2 & -2 \\ -2 & 5 \end{bmatrix}$.*

> u := vector([15,10]):   *Assign a vector $u = \begin{bmatrix} 15 \\ 10 \end{bmatrix}$.*

> multiply(K,u);   *Find Ku.*

$$[10, 20]$$ $Ku = \begin{bmatrix} (2)(15) + (-2)(10) \\ (-2)(15) + (5)(10) \end{bmatrix} = \begin{bmatrix} 10 \\ 20 \end{bmatrix}.$

Order is crucial! When you need to find *Mv*, never evaluate *vM*!

TABLE 10-1 Vector and Matrix Operations

OPERATION	DEFINITION	SYNTAX
	ARITHMETIC	
Equality	$V_i = V_i$ $M_{ij} = M_{ij}$	`equal(V1,V2)` Maple reports *true* or *false*.
Addition	$A_i + B_i = C_i$ $A_{ij} + B_{ij} = C_{ij}$	`evalm(A+B)` `matadd(A+B)`
Subtraction	$A_i - B_i = C_i$ $A_{ij} - B_{ij} = C_{ij}$	`evalm(A-B)` `matadd(A-B)`
Scalar Multiplication	cA_{ij}	`evalm(c*A)` `scalarmul(A,C)`
	VECTORS	
Dot Product	$A \cdot B = \sum_i A_i B_i$	`dotprod(A,B)`
Cross Product	$A \times B = \begin{bmatrix} A_2 B_3 - A_3 B_2 \\ A_3 B_1 - A_1 B_3 \\ A_1 B_2 - A_2 B_1 \end{bmatrix}$	`crossprod(A,B)` Vectors must have exactly three elements each.
Magnitude	$\|A\| = \sqrt{\sum_i A_i^2}$	`norm(A,frobenius)`
Angle	$\theta = \cos^{-1}\left(\dfrac{A \cdot B}{\|A\|\|B\|}\right)$	`angle(A,B)`
	MATRICES	
Multiplication	$AB = \sum_k A_{ik} B_{kj}$ $AB \neq BA$	`evalm(A&*B)` `multiply(A,B)`
Transposition	$A_{ij} = A_{ji}$	`transpose(A)`

Inversion	A^{-1}	`evalm(1/A)`
		 `evalm(A^(-1))`
		 `inverse(A)`

Determinant	$\|A\|$	`det(A)`
Identity Matrix	$I_{ij} = \begin{cases} 1 \text{ if } i = j \\ 0 \text{ if } i \neq j \end{cases}$	`&*()` Enter `alias(Id=&*())` for clarity.

PRACTICE!

13. Evaluate

$$\begin{bmatrix} 1 & 2 \\ 2 & 1 \end{bmatrix} + 2\begin{bmatrix} -1 & 0 \\ 0 & -1 \end{bmatrix} - \begin{bmatrix} 3 & 1 \\ 1 & 3 \end{bmatrix}.$$

14. Evaluate Abc, where

$$A = \begin{bmatrix} 1 & 2 \\ 2 & 1 \end{bmatrix},$$

$$b = \begin{bmatrix} x \\ y \end{bmatrix}, \text{ and}$$

$$c = \begin{bmatrix} -1 \\ 1 \end{bmatrix}.$$

10.5 LINEAR ALGEBRA

This section introduces linear algebra, a collection of methods and techniques that solve linear equations and systems. Ensure that you have loaded **with(linalg)** for this section.

10.5.1 Systems of Equations

Systems of linear equations may be converted into matrix form, as shown in Figure 10.10. Separate u and p terms into vectors. Store the remaining square array of constants inside a matrix K.

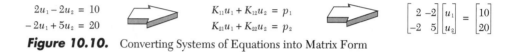

$$2u_1 - 2u_2 = 10$$
$$-2u_1 + 5u_2 = 20$$

$$K_{11}u_1 + K_{12}u_2 = p_1$$
$$K_{21}u_1 + K_{22}u_2 = p_2$$

$$\begin{bmatrix} 2 & -2 \\ -2 & 5 \end{bmatrix} \begin{bmatrix} u_1 \\ u_2 \end{bmatrix} = \begin{bmatrix} 10 \\ 20 \end{bmatrix}$$

Figure 10.10.   Converting Systems of Equations into Matrix Form

Denote the resulting "matrix form" of the equations as

$$Ku = p, \tag{10-5}$$

where matrix multiplication and equality are implied. Each term is described as follows:

System $Ku = p$	The **system of equations** $Ku = p$ is a set of simultaneous linear equations.
Coefficient Matrix $K = \begin{bmatrix} 2 & -2 \\ -2 & 5 \end{bmatrix}$	The **coefficient matrix** K collects the constants in front of unknowns: • Square matrices, such as K, require the same number of unknowns and equations. • Elements of these matrices typically reflect models' physical parameters.
Source Vector $p = \begin{bmatrix} 10 \\ 20 \end{bmatrix}$	The **source vector** p applies modeled inputs, or "sources," to the system: • In the spring example, these source terms are loads. • Source values are typically known or assumed.
Solution Vector $u = \begin{bmatrix} u_1 \\ u_2 \end{bmatrix}$	The **solution vector** u collects the unknown variables that you wish to find: • The matrix formulation separates known and unknown variables. • Manipulating the coefficient matrix and source vector with linear-algebra techniques, like Gaussian elimination (see Figure 10.7), finds the unknowns.

Consult **?genmatrix** for information on methods that convert equations directly into matrix form.

10.5.2 Manual Solution

As demonstrated in Section 10.1.3, you can perform Gaussian elimination to solve the system of equations that Eq. 10-5 represents. But, why should you use the matrix formulation? Vectors and matrices store equation data in a compact form that computer programs can readily manipulate. Though more complex techniques exist, you can solve the matrix formulation with ***row reduction***, which is a method that mimics Gaussian elimination, as demonstrated in Table 10-2.

TABLE 10-2 Row Reduction

STEP	MATRIX FORMULATION	OPERATIONS	RESULTS
①	$\begin{bmatrix} 2 & -2 \\ -2 & 5 \end{bmatrix}\begin{bmatrix} u_1 \\ u_2 \end{bmatrix} = \begin{bmatrix} 10 \\ 20 \end{bmatrix}$	$2u_1 - 2u_2 = 10$ $-2u_1 + 5u_2 = 20$	$2u_1 - 2u_2 = 10$ $-2u_1 + 5u_2 = 20$
②	$\left[\begin{array}{cc|c} 2 & -2 & 10 \\ -2 & 5 & 20 \end{array}\right]$		
③	$\left[\begin{array}{cc|c} 2 & -2 & 10 \\ 0 & 3 & 30 \end{array}\right]$	$\begin{array}{r} 2u_1 - 2u_2 = 10 \\ + \quad -2u_1 + 5u_2 = 20 \\ \hline 0u_1 - 3u_2 = 30 \end{array}$	$2u_1 - 2u_2 = 10$ $3u_2 = 30$
④	$\left[\begin{array}{cc|c} 1 & -1 & 5 \\ 0 & 1 & 10 \end{array}\right]$	$\frac{1}{2}(2u_1 - 2u_2 = 10) \rightarrow u_1 - u_2 = 5$ $\frac{1}{3}(0u_1 + 3u_2 = 30) \rightarrow u_2 = 10$	$u_1 - u_2 = 5$ $u_2 = 10$
⑤	$\left[\begin{array}{cc|c} 1 & 0 & 15 \\ 0 & 1 & 10 \end{array}\right]$	$\begin{array}{r} u_1 - u_2 = 5 \\ + \quad u_2 = 10 \\ \hline u_1 + 0u_2 = 15 \end{array}$	$u_1 = 15$ $u_2 = 10$

The following steps explain row reduction:

- Step ①: Cast the equations into a matrix formulation, as discussed in Section 10.5.1.
- Step ②: Rewrite the system into a matrix that includes the source vector written to the right. You may draw a vertical bar to serve as a reminder to separate the coefficient matrix.
- Step ③: Row reduction dictates that you may add a row to any other row. So, add the top row to the bottom row. This process is equivalent to adding an equation to another equation within the given system.
- Step ④: Row reduction also dictates that you can multiply any row by any constant. So, divide the top row by 2, and divide the bottom row by 3. You can perform this action in conjunction with adding rows to each other.
- Step ⑤: You keep performing row reduction until the coefficient matrix becomes the *identity matrix*, a matrix with values of 1 on the diagonal and 0 elsewhere. The final values in the right-hand column of the matrix represent the solution vector.

Note that a linearly dependent system of equations will yield at least one row that contains only values of zero.

10.5.3 Maple Solution
Enter **linsolve(A, b)** to solve a *linear* system of equations $Ax = b$ for the solution vector ***x***. Matrix ***A*** is the coefficient matrix, and vector ***b*** is the source vector. Remember to assign the solution-vector name to the result! For instance, solve the problem stated in Figure 10.10:

STEP 219:
SOLVE LINEAR
SYSTEM IN
MATRIX FORM

linsolve belongs to `linalg`.

```
> K := matrix([[2,-2],[-2,5]]):
```

Assign K to $\begin{bmatrix} 2 & -2 \\ -2 & 5 \end{bmatrix}$.

```
> p := vector([10,20]):
```

Assign p to $\begin{bmatrix} 10 \\ 20 \end{bmatrix}$.

```
> u := linsolve(K,p);
```

Solve Ku = p for u = $\begin{bmatrix} u_1 \\ u_2 \end{bmatrix}$.

$$u := [15, 10]$$

Maple found u = $\begin{bmatrix} 15 \\ 10 \end{bmatrix}$. *Check with Figure 10.7.*

If `linsolve` produces no result, then the system is unsolvable.

10.5.4 Linearly Dependent Systems

Generally, you should ensure that the number of equations equals the number of unknowns. Beware of duplicated equations that create a linearly dependent system. Given too few equations, or a linearly dependent system, `linsolve` produces parametric solutions in terms of "_t" variables. For example, solve $x_1 + x_2 = 2$ and $2x_1 + 2x_2 = 4$:

STEP 220:
SOLVE
LINEARLY
DEPENDENT
SYSTEM

Solve $\{x_1 + x_2 = 2, 2x_1 + 2x_2 = 4\}$.

```
> A := matrix([[1,1],[2,2]]):
```

Assign A to $\begin{bmatrix} 1 & 1 \\ 2 & 2 \end{bmatrix}$.

```
> b := vector([2,4]):
```

Assign b to $\begin{bmatrix} 2 \\ 4 \end{bmatrix}$.

```
> x := linsolve(A,b);
```

Solve Ax = b for x = $\begin{bmatrix} x_1 \\ x_2 \end{bmatrix}$.

$$[2 - \_t_1, \_t_1]$$

Maple "parameterized" the solution.

The unknown x_1 *is, in turn, a function of* $x_2 = \_t_1$.

Assign "_t" variables to other expressions to eliminate linear dependency and generate nonparametric solutions.

10.5.5 Verification

Check your work! After finding the solution vector u, multiply Ku. Compare Ku with p using `equal(M1,M2)`, where *M1* and *M2* are two vectors or two matrices:

STEP 221:
CHECK LINEAR
SYSTEM OF
EQUATIONS

`multiply` *and* `equal` *belong to* `linalg`.

```
> Ku := multiply(K,u):
```

Multiply matrix K by vector u.

```
> equal(Ku,p);
```

Check if Ku = p.

$$true$$

Your solution vector u is correct.

Beware that **equal** has trouble with simplification. You might need to extract and compare individual vector components, first. Also, consider the alternative approach demonstrated in Table 10-3.

PRACTICE!

15. Solve the system of equations $\{x + y = 2, x - y = 0\}$ with **solve**.

16. Now, try a graphical approach.

17. Convert the system to matrix form and use **linsolve** to solve it.

18. Finally, check your solutions by backsubstituting the solution vector.

TABLE 10-3 Solvability of Linear Equations

STEP	SINGLE EQUATION	MAPLE INPUT	MULTIPLE EQUATIONS	MAPLE INPUT
Assign Equation	$ax = b$	`eqn := a*x=b`	$Ax = b$	`A:=matrix(...)` `b:=vector(...)`
Invert Coefficients	$a^{-1}ax = a^{-1}b$ $x = a^{-1}b$	`(1/a)*eqn`	$A^{-1}Ax = A^{-1}b$ $x = A^{-1}b$	`Ai:=inverse(A)` `multiply(Ai,b)`

10.6 APPLICATION: MECHANICAL DESIGN

This sections expands notions developed throughout the text and applies many Maple functions to a design problem.

10.6.1 Background

Review the development in Section 10.1. This section involves analysis of the two bars shown in Figure 10.1.

10.6.2 Problem

Given the model in Figure 10.1, determine the bar-stiffness values such that the model uses a minimum of material. Let $p_1 = 25,000$ lb and $p_2 = 15,000$ lb. Use Young's Modulus $E = 30 \times 10^6$ lb/in^2 and bar lengths $L_a = 25$ in and $L_b = 30$ in. Also, restrict individual deflections of both bars to 0.1 in.

10.6.3 Methodology

First, initialize Maple and load the linear-algebra library package:

STEP 222:
INITIALIZE
MAPLE

Initialize Maple.

```
> restart:
```
Restart your Maple session.

```
> with(linalg):
```
Load Maple's linear-algebra library package.

```
Warning, new definition for norm
```
Do not fear these error messages.

```
Warning, new definition for trace
```
They are quite natural.

STEP 223:
MODEL

> `K:=matrix([[ka,-ka],[-ka,ka+kb]]):`

Assign the coefficient matrix.
Use [row,row,...]
notation: $K = \begin{bmatrix} k_a & -k_a \\ -k_a & k_a + k_b \end{bmatrix}$.

> `p:=vector([p1,p2]):`

$p = \begin{bmatrix} p_1 \\ p_2 \end{bmatrix}$.

> `u:=linsolve(K,p);`

Solve for vector u such that Ku = p.

$$u := \left[\frac{kap2 + kap1 + p1kb}{kakb}, \frac{p2 + p1}{kb} \right]$$

Maple produces a symbolic form.

Now, state your known parameters:

STEP 224:
STATE AND
SEPARATE

Initialize known model variables.

> `p1:=25000*lb: p2:=15000*lb:`

Assign loads.

> `E:=30e6*lb/inch^2: La:=25*inch: Lb:=30*inch:`

Assign geometry.

> `u[1],u[2];`

Evaluate current forms of displacements.

$$\frac{40000kalb + 25000lbkb}{kakb}, 40000 \frac{lb}{kb}$$

Maple is keeping track of units.

Note the value of u_2. By simple rearrangement, you know that $k_b = \frac{40000}{u_2}$ lb. Now, set $u_2 = 0.1$, which is the maximum acceptable value. Therefore, you can now solve for k_b:

STEP 225:
SOLVE—
INITIAL
VALUE

Solve for k_b.

> `kb_init:=kb*u[2]/(0.1*inch);`

Substitute maximum value for u_2.

$$kb\_init := 400000. \frac{lb}{inch}$$

Assign the initial value.

Given a "worst-case" k_b, solve for k_a:

STEP 226:
SOLVE—
INITIAL
VALUE

Solve for the initial k_a.
Solve k_a in terms of k_b.

> `ka:=solve(u[1]=0.1*inch,ka);`

This formula will help you

$$ka := 250000. \frac{lbkb}{-400000.lb + inchkb}$$

find k_a, given different values of k_b.

To search for acceptable values of stiffness coefficients, you need to create a sequence of test cases. Each case adds another increment to the previous case. First, assign the sequence of cases by using an increment size of 5%, or 1/20:

STEP 227: SOLVE— ITERATE

Increment values for testing.

```
> S_kb:=kb_init*(1+p/20) $ p=1..40:
```
Create a sequence of k_b values that adds 5% of the initial value to each case.

```
> S_ka:=subs(kb=S_kb[p],ka) $ p=1..40:
```
Create a sequence of k_a values by substituting each k_b value into the expression for k_a.

Now, you can calculate the volume for all test cases. For tension members, $k = AE/L$, and, thus, area $A = kL/E$. Therefore, you can find volume from the equation $V = AL = kL^2/E$. Add both bars' volumes to get the total volume:

STEP 228: SOLVE—ALL VOLUMES

Solve for the total bar volume for each test case.

```
> S_Vol:=((S_ka[p]*La/E)*La+(S_kb[p]*Lb/E)*Lb)/
inch^3 $ p=1..40;
```

This output is really long and is omitted here to conserve space.
Note that by dividing by cubic inches, you can check for unit consistency.

STEP 229: SOLVE— MINIMUM VOLUME

Find the smallest volume from all test cases.

```
> min(S_Vol);
```
Find the minimum value of a sequence—the volumes, in this case.

33.02115384

This value is the 13th entry in the sequence.

Before believing your output, you should plot your results. You should plot each case as a point. First, create a list of all data points using the **seq** function:

STEP 230: CHECKING— COLLECT POINTS

Check your work in progress.

```
> x:=S_ka[p]*(inch/lb): y:=S_kb[p]*(inch/lb): z:=S_Vol[p]:
> S:=seq([x,y,z],p=1..40):
```
Collect all test cases in a list of three-item lists.

Then, prepare for plotting:

STEP 231:
CHECKIN—
PLOT DATA

Check your work in progress.

```
> with(plots):
```
Load the plots library package.

```
> opts:=thickness=3,connect=true,axes=BOXED,
        tickmarks=[8,8,2],orientation=[-135,45],
        labels=["Ka","Kb","Vol"],title="Design Problem":
```
Set plot options. Set connect=true to connect the points.

Finally, plot your test cases. Note that volume is your dependent variable:

STEP 232:
CHECKING—
GRAPHICALLY
REPRESENT
YOUR DATA

Check your work in progress.

```
> pointplot3d([S],opts);
```
Plot your results in three dimensions.

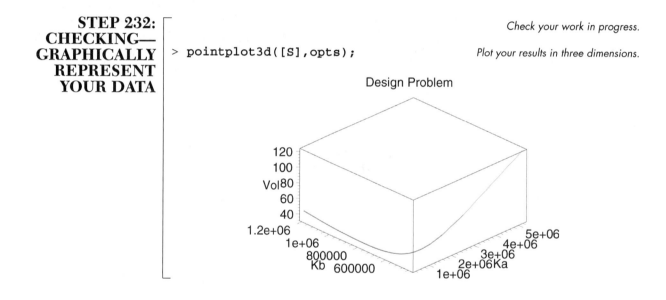

10.6.4 Solution

From your plot in Step 232, you may determine that your approximated minimum volume of about 33 in³ is reasonable. For more accurate results, try programming a "do loop," as demonstrated in Appendix E.

SUMMARY

This chapter has presented different techniques for solving systems of equations. Systems of equations contain multiple equations with common unknown variables. Solution approaches search for values that satisfy all equations in the given system. Linear systems involve polynomial equations with powers no greater than unity. **solve** directly solves linear and nonlinear systems. **implicitplot** is a graphical function for "small" systems. **linsolve** is more efficient for linear systems stored in matrix form. The matrix form separates terms and coefficients into a coefficient matrix, source vector, and solution vector.

Do you wish to perform well on homework, projects, and tests? Then, attend class! Here are some related tips:

❐ Go to class:

Where are you going to find out the assignment? Go to class. What material does the homework cover? Go to class. What material will be tested? Go to class. Students often ask me on due dates, "When is the homework due?" Usually, I look at my watch and retort, "In about five minutes." Go to class!

❐ Learn beforehand:

Some classroom boredom arises from bafflement and wandering thoughts. Prepare ahead of time! Skim the textbook a few times. After all, repetition aids learning. (Go to class!)

❐ Listen:

Listen to your professor. Guess what usually shows up on tests? Students who stay alert and listen perform well.

❐ Take notes:

Combine note taking with listening. Let your professor's voice guide your writing. Later, combine assigned reading with lecture notes.

❐ Ask questions:

When material confuses you, raise your hand! At least half of your class will thank you. Someone's paying good money for your education, so get your money's worth!

❐ Now, go to class!

KEY TERMS

coefficient matrix	linearly independent	solution vector
Gaussian elimination	matrix	source vector
last-name evaluation	matrix element	system of equations
linear systems	nonlinear systems	vector
linearly dependent	row reduction	vector components

Problems

1. Distinguish a scalar quantity from a vector quantity.
2. Describe the difference between Maple's lists and vectors.
3. Explain the difference between vectors and matrices.
4. Considering matrix size, when can you multiply two matrices?
5. Assign the vectors

$$x = \begin{bmatrix} 3 \\ -2 \\ 0 \end{bmatrix}$$

and

$$y = \begin{bmatrix} -5 \\ 2 \\ 4 \end{bmatrix}.$$

Evaluate the following expressions and check your work, ensuring that Maple prints the solutions:

5a.	$x + y$	5e.	$(2x + 3y) \cdot (-x)$
5b.	$x - y$	5f.	$\lvert x \rvert$
5c.	$x \cdot y$	5g.	$\lvert x \times y \rvert$
5d.	$x \times y$	5h.	Find the angle between x and y in degrees.

6. Assign the vector

$$c = \begin{bmatrix} 1 \\ 2 \end{bmatrix}$$

and matrices

$$A = \begin{bmatrix} 1 & 2 \\ 2 & 1 \end{bmatrix}$$

and

$$B = \begin{bmatrix} -2 & -1 \\ 3 & 0 \end{bmatrix}.$$

Evaluate the following expressions and check your work, ensuring that Maple prints the solutions:

6a.	$A + B$.	6e.	$\lvert A \rvert$.
6b.	$A - B$.	6f.	B^T.
6c.	AB and BA. Do the results differ? Why or why not?	6g.	Ac. Can you also evaluate cA? Why or why not?
6d.	BB^{-1}. Do you obtain an identity matrix? Why or why not?	6h.	ABA. (Hint: Beware of the order of operations.)

7. Is the system of equations $\{x + 2y = 5, -2x - 4y = -10\}$ linearly dependent or independent? Why or why not? Check for linear independence or dependence using Maple.

8. Can you solve the system of equations $\{x - y = 2, \sin x + y = 10\}$ using linear solution techniques? Why or why not? Solve for x and y, and verify your results.

9. Use any method you see fit to solve the following systems of equations, and be sure to verify your results:

9a. $\begin{cases} x + 2y = 13 \\ -2x - 4y = -26 \end{cases}$

9d. $\begin{cases} w + 2x - y + 3z = 4 \\ -x + 4y + 5z = 10 \\ w + x + 7z = -9 \\ -4w - x - 3y + 12z = -8 \end{cases}$

9b. $\begin{cases} 10x - 17y = 13.2 \\ -6.5x + 0.11y = -7.1 \end{cases}$

9e. $\begin{cases} x + 2y = 4 \\ -2x + y = -3 \end{cases}$

9c. $\begin{cases} x + 2y - 3z = 14 \\ -3y + 11z = -2 \\ x = 0 \end{cases}$

9f. $\begin{cases} x + y + z = 6 \\ x - y - z = -4 \\ -x - y + z = 0 \end{cases}$

10.   Recall the equation

$$Z = R - \frac{j}{\omega C}$$

from Problem 5.16. The components of the complex number Z form a vector called a *phasor* when plotted along a real and imaginary axis. Treat the real axis as horizontal and the imaginary axis as vertical. Solve the following problems using the information in Problem 5.16:

10a.   Identify and assign the horizontal and vertical components of Z.

10b.   Find the magnitude of the vector Z.

10c.   Find the angle at which Z rotates from the real (horizontal) axis in radians.

11.   You can use vectors to solve *equilibrium* problems, which involve static bodies that do not move. The two cables shown in Figure 10.11 balance a suspended weight of $W = 100$ N:

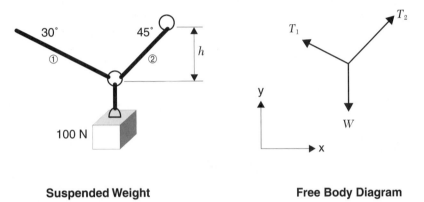

Suspended Weight   **Free Body Diagram**
Figure 10.11.   Equilibrium Problem

Answer the following questions:

11a.   Resolve both cable forces into horizontal and vertical components. (Hint: Use trigonometry and the indicated axes in Figure 10.11. For instance, $(T_1)_x = -T_1\cos 30°$.) Report your results in Maple text.

11b.   Assign the variables T_{1x} and T_{1y} to the horizontal and vertical components of cable force $\vec{T}_1$, respectively. If you prefer, you may skip the subscripts.

11c.   Assign the variables T_{2x} and T_{2y} to the horizontal and vertical components of cable force $\vec{T}_2$, respectively. If you prefer, you may skip the subscripts.

11d.   What is the value of W_x, the horizontal component of force W? What is the value of W_y, the horizontal component of force W? Assign the variables W_x and W_y to their appropriate values.

11e.   The sum of the forces in the x direction must balance. Express this relationship in Maple using horizontal components of each force. (Hint: Assign variable *Eqn1* to the equation $T_{1x} + T_{2x} + W_x = 0$.)

11f.   The sum of the forces in the y direction must balance. Express this relationship in Maple using horizontal components of each force. (Hint: Assign variable *Eqn2* to the equation $T_{1y} + T_{2y} + W_y = 0$.)

11g.   Solve for both cable forces, and check your work by comparing the results from various approaches. Do you achieve the same answers?

11h.   Project: Let the height $h = 1$ m in Figure 10.11. Assume that you cannot allow each cable's displacement to exceed 1% of h (1 cm). Assuming circular cross-sections for the cables, find the maximum diameter of each cable using Maple.

Hints:

- Assume that the cables behave in accordance with Hooke's Law for axial members,

$$T = \frac{AE}{L}\, u,$$

  where force T stretches the cable with displacement u. The other parameters are circular cross-sectional area A, length L, and Young's modulus E (force/area). See also Problem 3.12 for more information.

- Assume that both cables have the same value of $E = 300 \times 10^6$ Pa (N/m^2). Beware that each cable might have different parameters. Use different names for areas, like $A1$ and $A2$, and so forth. You will have to solve for the lengths and iterate for displacements and areas!

- Assume that the weight moves with a "small" displacement Δ. Therefore, the deformed geometry does not appreciably alter the original geometry. Better yet, you can apply original equilibrium forces to the deformed system.

- Both cables must have compatible displacements. That is, the cables must stay connected. You should resolve displacement Δ into x and y components: let $u = \Delta_x$ and $v = \Delta_y$. Sum the contributions for each cable as $\Delta_1 = u_1 + v_1$ and $\Delta_2 = u_2 + v_2$, according to the geometry.

11

Introduction to Calculus

11.1 INTRODUCTION

Recall from Chapter 1 that models represent mathematical abstractions of physical systems. Analyzing the equations in models helps engineers and scientists predict, analyze, and design the real physical systems. This section introduces how calculus helps model changes in physical systems.

11.1.1 Change

Models encompass many features of physical systems, such as *change* in space, time, and other physical characteristics. Consider a rocket shooting towards space. Engineers must account for increasing velocity, decreasing gravity, decreasing mass of fuel, vibrating components, and many other factors. ***Calculus*** provides a mathematical methodology for modeling these changes in equations.

11.1.2 Maple Calculus Functions

Consult Mathematics...Calculus... inside the Help Browser. Also, `?examples[index]` and `?share[contents]` provide information on commands and examples that pertain to Maple's calculus functions. The `student` library package provides commands for learning calculus. Enter `?student` or `?calculus` for a description.

OBJECTIVES

After reading this chapter, you should be able to:

- Understand how calculus models change in physical states
- Identify smoothness and continuity on functions
- Understand the notion of a limit
- Demonstrate how derivatives model changes by finding slopes
- Demonstrate how integrals model sums by finding areas and volumes
- Demonstrate how differentiation and integration are inverse operations

Earthquake-damage mitigation presents a major challenge for structural engineers. Devices such the shake-table shown in the accompanying figure simulate the ground motion and acceleration during an earthquake. Building small-scale structural models helps engineers test new technologies. Courtesy of Multidisciplinary Center for Earthquake Engineering Research (MCEER)

Great feats rarely occur overnight, especially that of learning Maple in entirety tonight for tomorrow's test. Break projects into "baby steps," or tiny steps whose sum encompasses your goals. Consider these aspects of this process:

- Conception:
  Imagine your goals. As you would when writing a paper or project report, brainstorm your ideas. Eventually, your objectives might shift, but you need a starting point. Starting is half the battle!

- Clarification:
  Stay realistic. Follow guidelines and understand your main objectives. Double your time expectations when struggling to meet deadlines.

- Baby Steps:
  Attempt everything all at once, and you will never finish. Instead, outline your tasks. Decompose each step into smaller steps. After all, smaller tasks are easier to complete.

- Procrastination:
  Start with the easiest tasks. Whether your first job involves cleaning your desk or labeling your files, simply *starting* will provide necessary momentum for more important tasks.

- Work:
  Set a schedule and stick to it. When stuck, never be afraid or ashamed to seek help. No one is an omnipotent, omniscient superbeing!

- Life:
  Balance your life. Reward yourself when finishing tasks. Talk a walk. Call a loved one. People need companionship and personal time. Stay human, and your goals will flourish.

STEP 233:
student
LIBRARY
PACKAGE

```
> restart:

> with(student):
```

`student` *contains many introductory calculus functions.*

Restart your Maple session.

Load `student` *library package.*

11.2 FUNCTIONS

Functions embrace change by modeling different physical states given different variable values. Consider Hooke's Law, $p = ku$, which models the interaction between the displacement u and the force p in a linear spring. Changing u or p produces new physical states. You can plot each state as a point in (u, p) coordinates. This section studies how functions vary between states.

11.2.1 Limits

Limits investigate function behavior near a point. As $x \to c$ (x "approaches" a value c), the limit of $f(x)$ approaches L, or

$$\lim_{x \to c} f(x) = L. \tag{11-1}$$

Although L might approximate or, perhaps, equal $f(c)$, the limit depends on whether you approach from the right or left along the x-axis. Enter `limit(f,x=c)` to find the limit of f as x approaches c:

STEP 234:
LIMITS

Find limits of functions.

> `limit(sin(x),x=Pi/2);`

Find $\lim\limits_{x \to \frac{\pi}{2}} \sin x$.

1

$\sin x$ has no other values near $x = \frac{\pi}{2}$. Therefore, use $\sin \frac{\pi}{2}$.

Consult **?Limit**, **?limit**, and Mathematics...Calculus...Limits... for more information.

11.2.2 Continuity

Continuous functions have limits that match function values:

$$\lim_{x \to c} f(x) = f(c). \tag{11-2}$$

In Figure 11.1, $f(x)$ is continuous between points A, B, and C. However, at points C and C' the function $f(x)$ has no unique value, and thus, loses continuity. Moreover, the limit of $f(x)$ at points C and C' depends on whether you approach those points from the left or the right. Except for points C and C', however, all other points along $f(x)$ are continuous. Consult **?discont**, **?fdiscont**, **?iscont**, and **?singular** for more information.

11.2.3 Smoothness

Smooth functions contain no abrupt changes in slope. As shown in Figure 11.1, the slopes of $f(x)$ to the left and right of point B change, but point B suffers a slopeless fate. Point B forms a cusp, which is a sharp point with no slope. In general, smooth functions lack cusps. Functions, like $f(x) = mx + b$ and $f(x) = \sin x$, have continuous and defined slopes, and thus, are good examples of smooth functions. Functions, like $f(x) = |x|$, have undefined slopes at some locations, and are thus non-smooth.

11.2.4 Piecewise Functions

You might wish to investigate **?piecewise** to create *piecewise* functions of your own that resemble Figure 11.1. A piecewise function is composed of a set of functions that depend on different ranges of the independent variable. By combining functions with

Figure 11.1. Non-Continuous Function

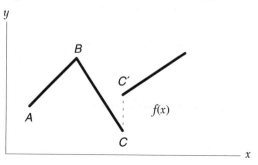

different slopes, you can create points that lack smoothness. Furthermore, by specifying disconnected ranges for the independent variable, you will create a non-continuous function as well.

PRACTICE!

1. Plot $\tan x$ for $0 \le x \le 2\pi$. Hint: See **?plot** regarding the **discont** option.
2. Find

$$\lim_{x \to \frac{\pi}{2}} \tan x$$

   Hint: See **?limit** and **?limit[dir]**.
3. What values of x make $\tan x$ discontinuous? Hint: See **?discont**.

11.3 SLOPE

Derivatives measure rate, or how quickly functions change. This section first introduces the familiar concept of slope: slope measures change.

11.3.1 Change and Slope

Slope measures change. Recall the various definitions of slope for a linear equation $y = f(x)$:

$$\text{slope} = \frac{\text{rise}}{\text{run}} = \frac{\Delta y}{\Delta x} = \frac{y_2 - y_1}{x_2 - x_1}. \tag{11-3}$$

Many formulas employ slope to help model physical systems that change. For instance, consider the plot and formulas of Hooke's Law shown in Figure 11.2. The spring stiffness k measures how the load p changes linearly with the displacement u. When using the **student** library package, enter **slope(*eqn, dep_var, indep_var*)** to find an expression for the slope of an equation *eqn*:

STEP 235:
SLOPE

> *Determine the slope of an equation.* **slope** *belongs to the* **student** *library package.*

> **slope(p=k*u,p,u);**   *Find the slope of $p = ku$, where p is dependent and u is independent.*

$$k$$

The slope is the parameter k.

Figure 11.2. Slope for Hooke's Law

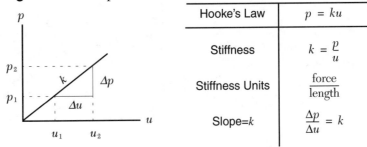

Hooke's Law	$p = ku$
Stiffness	$k = \dfrac{p}{u}$
Stiffness Units	$\dfrac{\text{force}}{\text{length}}$
Slope=k	$\dfrac{\Delta p}{\Delta u} = k$

Consult **?slope** for information on other syntax. Typically, you can enter **slope(f(x))** or **slope(y=f(x))**, as well. Also, **slope** works for both linear and nonlinear equations.

11.3.2 Tangents

Linear equations in the form $y = mx + b$ have a constant slope m. Varying x and y does not change m. What is the slope of a nonlinear equation? For nonlinear equations, measure slope at individual points by drawing a ***tangent*** to the curve. A tangent's slope matches the original equation's slope at the point where the tangent touches the original equation.

The spring example can demonstrate a nonlinear curve and tangent lines. The equation for potential energy of a spring,

$$E_s = \frac{1}{2} ku^2, \tag{11-4}$$

is nonlinear because of the u^2 expression. Assuming a value of $k = 2$, suppose you wish to draw a tangent to the curve at $u = 4$. Before plotting the curve and tangent, you must first assign expressions and values for Eq. 11-4:

STEP 236:
ASSIGN DATA

> `k:=2: u:='u':`

> `Es:=(k*u^2)/2;`

$$Es := u^2$$

Create an expression for E_s.

Assign k to the value 2. Unassign u.

Let $E_s = \frac{1}{2} ku^2$.

Remember that you assigned k to 2.

The function **showtangent(f,var=val)** displays the tangent of the expression **f** at the point **var=val**. To draw the tangent to E_s at $u = 4$, enter the following:

STEP 237:
SHOW TANGENT

> `showtangent(Es,u=4);`

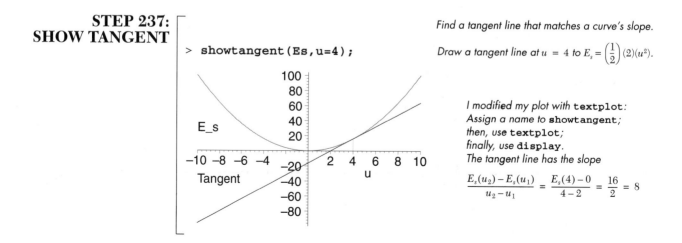

Find a tangent line that matches a curve's slope.

Draw a tangent line at $u = 4$ to $E_s = \left(\frac{1}{2}\right)(2)(u^2)$.

I modified my plot with **textplot**:
Assign a name to **showtangent**;
then, use **textplot**;
finally, use **display**.
The tangent line has the slope

$$\frac{E_s(u_2) - E_s(u_1)}{u_2 - u_1} = \frac{E_s(4) - 0}{4 - 2} = \frac{16}{2} = 8$$

At $u = 4$, you can determine the slope of E_s is 8, as shown in Step 237.

You can also find the slope of a curve by using Maple's **slope** function. You need to express your function for E_s in terms of an equation. Using Eq. 11-4, you would enter **Es=(1/2)*k*u^2** as your equation, where E_s is the dependent variable, and u is the dependent variable. Now, try the following commands to find the value of slope at $u = 4$ for the example discussed in this section:

STEP 238:
FIND SLOPE

*Find the slope of an equation using **slope**.*

`> restart:`   *Restart Maple.*

`> with(student):`   *Load the **student** library package to access **slope**.*

`> p:=slope(Es=(1/2)*k*u^2,Es,u);`   *Find the slope at any point along $E_s = \frac{1}{2}ku^2$.*

Indicate that E_s and u are the dependent and independent variables, respectively.

$$p := ku$$ *Maple assigned p to the expression for slope ku.*

`> subs({k=2,u=4},p);`   *Determine the value of ku for $k = 2$ at the point $u = 4$.*

$$8$$ *The slope $ku = (2)(4) = 8$.*

Methods inside Steps 237 and 238 produce the same value of slope. In general, the slope function is easier to implement, though calculus provides a more general approach that the next section demonstrates.

PRACTICE!

4. Draw a tangent at $x = \frac{\pi}{2}$ for $f(x) = \sin x$.
5. What is the slope of $f(x) = ax^2 + bx + c$?

11.4 DERIVATIVES

This section introduces differentiation, or how derivatives produce a function's slope.

11.4.1 Relating Slopes and Derivatives

Calculus provides an analytical method for finding tangents and, in turn, slopes. Consider the curve $f(u)$ shown in Figure 11.3. Find the slope of line ab with Eq. 11-3:

$$m_{ab} = \frac{f(u_b)-f(u_a)}{u_b-u_a} = \frac{f(u_a+\Delta u)-f(u_a)}{(u_a+\Delta u)-(u_a)} = \frac{f(u_a+\Delta u)-f(u_a)}{\Delta u}. \tag{11-5}$$

Apply mathematical limits such that Δu shrinks, or $\Delta u \to 0$. Then, the line ab approaches the tangent to point a:

$$m_{\text{Tangent}} = \lim_{\Delta u \to 0}\frac{f(u_a+\Delta u)-f(u_a)}{\Delta u}. \tag{11-6}$$

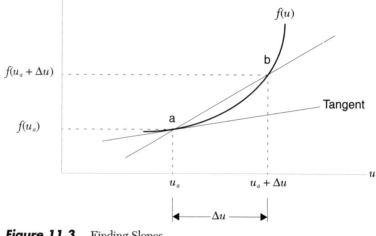

Figure 11.3. Finding Slopes

Equation 11-6 represents the formula for a **derivative**. Derivatives measure slope as the instantaneous rate of change of a function at a point. Note that derivatives exist only where a function is smooth and continuous.

11.4.2 Notation

Using $\Delta y/\Delta x$ only approximates slope, but you can improve your accuracy. Let $y = f(x)$. The **first derivative** of y with respect to x finds the exact, *instantaneous* slope anywhere on $f(x)$:

$$\textbf{First Derivative}: y' = f'(x) = \frac{dy}{dx} = \frac{d}{dx}f(x). \qquad (11\text{-}7)$$

Whereas Δ indicates a "large" change, d indicates an infinitesimal change in a variable. Thus, derivatives provide exact slopes.

11.4.3 Physical Interpretation

Derivatives determine rates, or how functions change, and thus, provide useful tools for analysis and design. Consider the formula for the potential energy of a spring:

$$E_s = \frac{1}{2}ku^2.$$

The original equation models a physical system $E_s = f(u)$, where some parameters, like E_s and u, vary, whereas others, like k, do not. Taking the derivative E_s' measures how E_s changes whenever the displacement u changes. From Step 238, you can determine that $E_s' = 2u$ for $k = 2$. The derivative $2u$ now provides a new formula for measuring how E_s changes as u varies.

11.4.4 Maple Syntax

Enter `diff(func,var)` to find the derivative of **func** with respect to **var**. For instance, given a function $y = f(x) = ax^2$, you would enter `diff(y,x)` or `diff(f(x),x)` to compute y'. Try the spring example using Eq. 11-4:

STEP 239:
FIRST
DERIVATIVE—
CLEANUP

> > `k:='k': u:='u':`

Prepare for work.

Clear k and u assignments.

STEP 240: FIRST
DERIVATIVE—
ASSIGN

> > `Es:=(1/2)*k*u^2:`

Assign the expression for spring energy.

Assign E_s to $\frac{1}{2}ku^2$.

STEP 241:
FIRST
DERIVATIVE—
EVALUATE

> > `diff(Es,u);`

$$ku$$

Find the slope of the energy function of the spring.

Find the first derivative E_s' from $\frac{1}{2}ku^2$

Does this expression look familiar? See Steps 237 and 238.

In functional notation, use parentheses such that $E_s(u) = \frac{1}{2}ku^2$:

STEP 242:
FIRST
DERIVATIVE—
FUNCTIONAL
NOTATION

> > `Es:=u->(1/2)*k*u^2:`

Assign the expression for spring energy.

Assign $E_s(u)$ to $\frac{1}{2}ku^2$.

STEP 243:
FIRST
DERIVATIVE—
EVALUATE

> > `diff(Es(u),u);`

$$ku$$

Find the slope of the energy function of the spring.

Find the first derivative $E_s'(u)$.

Does this expression look familiar?

Also, try **`implicitdiff(eqn,y,x)`** to directly differentiate the equation $f(x, y) = c$, where both y and x vary independently given constant c.

11.4.5 Higher Order Derivatives

Differentiating derivatives creates ***higher order derivatives***. For instance, a second derivative measures how much a first derivative changes with respect to the independent variable. Thus, the second derivative of y with respect to x yields

$$y'' = \frac{d}{dx}\left(\frac{dy}{dx}\right) = \frac{d^2y}{dx^2}. \tag{11-8}$$

Enter **diff(*func*,*var*,*var*)** or just **diff(*func*,*var*\$2)** to calculate second derivatives. The input **var\$2** abbreviates the sequence **var,var**:

STEP 244:
SECOND
DERIVATIVE

> *Take a derivative of a derivative of a function.*

> `diff(Es(u),u,u);`

> *Evaluate $E_s''(u)$.*

$$k$$

> *Also, try* `diff(diff(Es(u),u),u)`.

Enter **diff(*func*,*var*\$n)** for *n*th-order derivatives. Table 11-1 organizes common notations for many types of derivatives. Beware of the syntax change when using functional notation.

TABLE 11-1 Differentiation

OPERATION	STANDARD MATH	MAPLE NOTATION
First derivative of y with respect to x	$\frac{dy}{dx}$ and y'	`diff(y,x)`
First derivative of $f(x)$ with respect to x	$\frac{d}{dx}f(x)$ and $f'(x)$	`diff(f(x),x)`
First derivative of y with respect to time t	$\frac{dy}{dt}$ and $\dot{y}$	`diff(y,t)`
Second derivative of y with respect to x	$\frac{d^2y}{dt^2}$ and y''	`diff(y,x,x)` `diff(y,x$2)`
Second derivative of y with respect to time t	$\frac{d^2y}{dt^2}$ and $\ddot{y}$	`diff(y,t,t)` `diff(y,t$2)`
nth derivative of y with respect to x	$\frac{d^ny}{dx^n}$ and $y^{(n)}$	`diff(y,x,x,...)` `diff(y,x$n)`
Partial derivative of $f(x,y)$ with respect to x	$\frac{\partial}{\partial x}f(x,y)$	`diff(f(x,y),x)`
Partial derivative of $f(x,y)$ with respect to y	$\frac{\partial}{\partial x}f(x,y)$	`diff(f(x,y),y)`
Partial derivative of $f(x,y)$ with respect to x and y	$\frac{\partial^2}{\partial x\partial y}f(x,y)$	`diff(f(x,y),x,y)` `diff(f(x,y),y,x)`

11.4.6 Partial Derivatives

Maple does not output derivatives using the "*d*" syntax. Instead, Maple prefers **partial derivatives**, which take the form $\frac{\partial}{\partial x}f(x)$. Partial derivatives assume that functions might have multiple independent variables. For only one independent variable, you can assume that

$$\frac{\partial}{\partial x}f(x) = \frac{d}{dx}f(x).$$

For instance, enter **Diff(f(x),x)**:

STEP 245:
PARTIAL
DERIVATIVES

> `Diff(f(x),x);`

$$\frac{\partial}{\partial x}\, f(x)$$

Display a partial derivative, Maple's default derivative notation.

Display, but do not evaluate, $\frac{\partial}{\partial x}\, f(x)$.

`Diff` *is an inert function that Maple does not directly evaluate.*

Consult `?student[value]` for information on how to evaluate `Diff` and other inert expressions.

11.4.7 Miscellaneous

Consult these references for more information:

- Differential Operators: `?D`, `?operators[D]`, and `?difforms`
- Vector Calculus: `?curl`, `?diverge`, `?grad`, and `?laplacian`
- Differential Equations: Mathematics...Differential Equations... and `?dsolve`

PRACTICE!

> **6.** Find the first derivative of $f(x) = ax^2 + bx + c$ with respect to x.
> **7.** What is the slope of $f(x) = ax^2 + bx + c$ at $x = 2$?
> **8.** Find the second derivative of $f(x) = ax^2 + bx + c$ with respect to x.
> **9.** What is the first derivative of $f(x, y) = xy^2 + x^2y$ with respect to x?

11.5 AREA

The concepts of area that are discussed in this section will clarify the integration methods in the next section.

11.5.1 Summation

Let s represent a sequence of values:

$$s = s_1, s_2, \ldots, s_n. \tag{11-9}$$

The summation of all values in s is represented using sigma notation Σ:

$$\sum_{i=1}^{n} s_i = s_1 + s_2 + \ldots + s_n, \tag{11-10}$$

where s_i denotes each individual element of the sequence s. The index i ranges from 1 to n, where n is the last element in the sequence. To calculate the summation of a sequence *seq* over a particular range *range*, enter `sum(seq,index=range)`:

STEP 246:
SUMMATION

> *Sum values in a sequence.*

> ```
> S:=2,4,6,8: i:='i':
> ```
Assign S to a sequence. Clear any assignment on i.

> ```
> sum(S[i],i=1..4);
> ```
Sum each value in the sequence s_1, s_2, s_3, s_4.

$$20$$
$2 + 4 + 6 + 8 = 20$.

If Maple reports "`Error, invalid subscript selector`", go back and unassign the index **i** with **i:='i'** before evaluating the summation. Or, instead, enter **sum(S['i'],'i'=1..4)**. Refer to Section 4.4.4 for an explanation of the forward quotes.

11.5.2 Area

Suppose that you wish to approximate the **_area_**, or the amount of space, underneath the function $p = ku$ to the u-axis. Assume $k = 2$ and the range $0 \le u \le 4$. Enter **middlebox(f,range,b)** to approximate the area with **b** "boxes" that slice the area:

STEP 247:
DRAW
APPROXIMATE
AREA WITH
RECTANGLES

> *Divide the area below a curve with rectangles.*

*Ensure that you have already entered **with(student)**. The **middlebox** function belongs to **student**.*

> ```
> middlebox(2*u,u=0..4,6);
> ```
Slice $p = 2u$ into six "boxes."

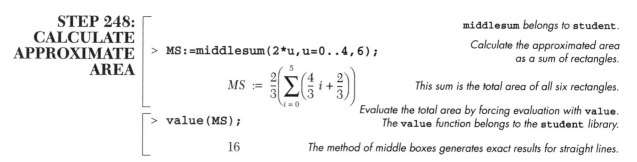

Enter **middlesum(f,range,b)** to evaluate the approximation:

STEP 248:
CALCULATE
APPROXIMATE
AREA

> *middlesum belongs to **student**.*

> ```
> MS:=middlesum(2*u,u=0..4,6);
> ```
Calculate the approximated area as a sum of rectangles.

$$MS := \frac{2}{3}\left(\sum_{i=0}^{5}\left(\frac{4}{3}i + \frac{2}{3}\right)\right)$$

This sum is the total area of all six rectangles.

*Evaluate the total area by forcing evaluation with **value**.*

> ```
> value(MS);
> ```
*The **value** function belongs to the **student** library.*

$$16$$
The method of middle boxes generates exact results for straight lines.

Consult **?student** for information on "left" and "right" box approximations. See, also, **?student[simpson]** and **?student[trapezoid]** for details regarding further numerical techniques.

11.6 INTEGRALS

Area-approximation methods provide background for integration, as discussed in this section.

11.6.1 Relating Area and Integrals

Consider the general function $f(u)$ shown in Figure 11.4. Approximate the area below $f(u)$ with a sequence of rectangular "slices" $A_i = f(\bar{u}_i)\Delta u_i$. Represent the total approximated area $\bar{A}$ under $f(u)$ as the sum

$$\bar{A} = f(\bar{u}_1)\Delta u_1 + f(\bar{u}_2)\Delta u_2 + f(\bar{u}_3)\Delta u_3 + f(\bar{u}_4)\Delta u_4, \tag{11-11}$$

or

$$\bar{A} = \sum_{i=1}^{4} A_i = \sum_{i=1}^{4} f(\bar{u}_i)\Delta u_i. \tag{11-12}$$

Improve your results by shrinking each Δu_i to an infinitesimal size. The limit as $\Delta u_i \to 0$ yields

$$A = \lim_{\Delta u \to 0} \sum_{i=1}^{n} f(\bar{u}_i)\Delta u_i, \tag{11-13}$$

where A provides the exact, total area. Equation 11-13 defines an **integral**, which is the limit of a sum of infinitesimal "slices". In general, integrals measure the area below a curve to the axis of the independent variable.

11.6.2 Notation

Assume you have defined a function $y = f(x)$. Let x and y represent the independent and dependent variables, respectively. Borrowing from the notation used for differentiation, you may denote infinitesimal changes in a variable x as dx. Now, consider the following implications:

- The width of each infinitely slim "slice" is the term dx.
- The height of each infinitely slim "slice" is the function value $f(x)$.
- The area of each infinitely slim "slice" is the product $f(x)dx$.

Between end points, there exist an infinite number of "slim slices" of width dx and height $f(x)$. The total area between end points $x = a$ and $x = b$ must be the sum of all segments of area $f(x)dx$. Calculus denotes this sum with an integral in the form:

$$\textbf{\textit{Integral}}: \int_{a}^{b} f(x)dx, \tag{11-14}$$

Figure 11.4. Approximated Area

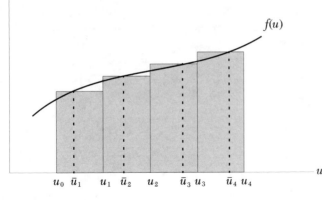

	Δu_i	$f(\bar{u}_i)$	$A_i = f(\bar{u}_i)\Delta u_i$
	$\Delta u_1 = u_1 - u_0$	$f(\bar{u}_1)$	$f(\bar{u}_1)\Delta u_1$
	$\Delta u_2 = u_2 - u_1$	$f(\bar{u}_2)$	$f(\bar{u}_2)\Delta u_2$
	$\Delta u_3 = u_3 - u_2$	$f(\bar{u}_3)$	$f(\bar{u}_3)\Delta u_3$
	$\Delta u_4 = u_4 - u_3$	$f(\bar{u}_4)$	$f(\bar{u}_4)\Delta u_4$

where $\int$ is the integral sign. The integral sign resembles a funny looking "S" that stands for *sum*.

11.6.3 Physical Interpretation

Integrals help measure cumulative effects of changes, or how much a model varies. Consider the definition of work = force × displacement. In integral form, this definition is $W = \int p du$. From the spring example in Section 11.3, the load p pulls the spring to a displacement u. Assuming no energy loss—for example, due to friction—the spring stores all of the work by the load p as potential energy:

$$E_s = \frac{1}{2} ku^2.$$

Releasing the spring would cause the spring to release the stored energy by snapping back.

By slowly pulling the spring, one would cause the load and displacement to increase gradually, according to Hooke's Law $p = ku$. Each increment of load and displacement stores more energy: $\Delta E_s = \Delta p \Delta u$. These energy increments contribute to the total energy stored inside the spring. Moreover, $\Delta p \Delta u$ slices the area under $p = ku$ into "boxes", as shown in Step 247. An exact sum of the areas of the boxes is the total area, or the integral

$$E_s = \int p du = \frac{1}{2} ku^2.$$

11.6.4 Definite Integration

A ***definite integral*** sums the area below a curve between two points along the independent variable ***var***. Find the integral of a function ***f*** between two points ***a*** and ***b*** with `int(f,var=a..b)`:

STEP 249: **DEFINITE** **INTEGRATION**	`> int(2*u,u=0..4);`	*Find the integral of a function between two end points.* *Evaluate $\int_{0}^{4} 2u du$.*
	16	*Maple finds the area below u^2 along $0 \le u \le 4$.*

Consult **?int** and **?student[int]** for more information.

11.6.5 Indefinite Integration

An ***indefinite integral*** has no specified bounds. This integral produces functions that compute the area below a curve for any set of bounds. Enter **int(*expr*, *var*)** to generate an indefinite integral:

STEP 250: **INDEFINITE** **INTEGRATION**	`> Indef:=int(k*u,u);`	*Integrate a function with no specified bounds.* *Evaluate $\int k u du$.*
	$Indef := \frac{1}{2} ku^2$	*This integral produces the area of the triangle below ku.*

Maple does not add a generic constant to results, although the addition of this constant is common practice in hand calculations.

11.6.6 Multiple Integrals

When integrating multivariable functions, like $f(x, y)$, use multiple integrals. For instance, enter `Doubleint(f(x,y),x,y)` to evaluate $\iint f(x,y)dxdy$. Consult `?student [Doubleint]`, `?student[Tripleint]`, and `?value` for more information.

11.6.7 Miscellaneous

Consult Mathematics…Calculus…Integration… inside the Help Browser for more details pertaining to integration. Also, consult `?evalfint` and `?student` for more information.

PRACTICE!

> **10.** Integrate $\sin x$ along $0 \leq x \leq \frac{\pi}{2}$.
> **11.** Determine the indefinite integral of $\sin x$.
> **12.** Compute the area above and below the x-axis for $\sin x$ along $0 \leq x \leq 2\pi$.

11.7 FUNDAMENTAL THEOREM OF CALCULUS

This section shows how derivatives and integrals represent inverse operations.

11.7.1 Force and Work

Consider the equations for the spring example in the previous sections inside this chapter. Force is described as $p = ku$. The energy of the spring is $E_s = \frac{1}{2}ku^2$, and in previous steps, you found that

- the derivative of E_s is $\frac{dE_s}{du} = ku$. Thus, differentiating energy (and work) yields force.
- the integral of p is $\int ku\,du = \frac{1}{2}ku^2$. Thus, integrating force yields work.

The general formulas $W = \int p\,du$ and $p = \frac{dW}{du}$ relate work and force. Integration and differentiation are indeed inverse operations!

11.7.2 Antiderivatives

Differentiating an indefinite integral of a function $f(x)$ produces the original function $f(x)$. Thus, indefinite integrals are sometimes called antiderivatives. The antiderivative of $f(x)$ is denoted as $F(x)$. Given a continuous function $f(x)$ along $a \leq x \leq b$, the **Fundamental Theorem of Calculus** (FTC) states:

$$\int_a^b f(x)dx = F(b) - F(a). \tag{11-15}$$

$F(x)$ represents the function determined by the indefinite integral $\int f(x)dx$.

PRACTICE!

> **13.** Demonstrate the FTC with k and $p = ku$ for the spring example that this chapter employs.
> **14.** Demonstrate the FTC with $f(x) = \sin x$ for $0 \leq x \leq 2\pi$.

11.8 APPLICATION: DIFFERENTIAL EQUATIONS

Maple provides an excellent tool for solving calculus-based models. This section introduces how calculus provides a tool for modeling dynamic systems with differential equations.

11.8.1 Background

Many branches of engineering, science, and other fields model changing systems with *differential equations*, which are equations that include differentials as parameters. One common differential equation models systems that grow or decay in proportion to their present amount:

$$\text{rate of } Q(t) \propto Q(t). \tag{11-16}$$

Given a quantity $Q(t)$ at time t, the derivative $Q(t)$ with respect to t models the rate of change of $Q(t)$. Thus, a changing quantity may be represented by $\frac{dQ(t)}{dt}$. Next, because $Q(t)$ changes in proportion to the current amount, you can state the system's governing model as

$$\frac{dQ(t)}{dt} = kQ(t). \tag{11-17}$$

Equation 11-17 assumes a linear relationship represented by the growth rate k. Note that Eq. 11-17 is an *ordinary differential equation* (ODE), an equation expressed in terms of one independent variable, which is t in Eq. 11-17.

11.8.2 Problem

Let $Q(0) = Q_0$. Solve Eq. 11-17.

11.8.3 Methodology

First, state and assign pertinent variables:

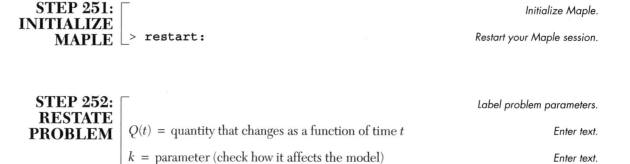

STEP 251: INITIALIZE MAPLE		Initialize Maple.
	`> restart:`	Restart your Maple session.

STEP 252: RESTATE PROBLEM		Label problem parameters.
	$Q(t)$ = quantity that changes as a function of time t	Enter text.
	k = parameter (check how it affects the model)	Enter text.

You can solve *separable* ODEs by rearranging the dependent and independent variables. Divide the entire equation by $Q(t)$. Next, multiply both sides by the differential dt:

$$\frac{dQ(t)}{Q(t)} = kdt. \tag{11-18}$$

You can express this equivalent ODE in Maple. First, assign the left-hand side of Eq. 11-18:

STEP 253:
SEPARATE
THE LHS

> `LHS := diff(Q(t),t)/Q(t);`

$$LHS := \frac{\frac{\partial}{\partial t} Q(t)}{Q(t)}$$

Rearrange the left-hand side of your equation.

Assign LHS to $\frac{dQ(t)}{Q(t)}$.

Recall that Maple prefers partial-differential notation.

Why does Maple use the partial-differential symbol ∂ instead of "d"? Maple cannot distinguish variables that depend upon only one independent variable from those that depend on multiple independent variables. However, Maple will still properly solve the equation.

Next, assign the right-hand side of Eq. 11-18. You should not include the differential dt! Step 255 will demonstrate why:

STEP 254:
SEPARATE
THE RHS

> `RHS := k;`

$$k$$

Rearrange the right-hand side of your equation.

Assign RHS to k.

Do not include dt.

Recall that integrals reverse differentiation. Therefore, to solve the equation, simultaneously integrate both sides of Eq. 11-18:

$$\int_0^T \frac{dQ(t)}{Q(t)} = \int_0^T k\,dt. \tag{11-19}$$

Do you see how the RHS automatically includes dt as part of the integral? Both integrals use the limits of integration $t_{initial} = 0$ and $t_{final} = T$, as indicated by the problem statement. Now, integrate with Maple's `int(expr, var=range)` function:

STEP 255:
MODEL

> `Temp:=int(LHS,t=0..T)=int(RHS,t=0..T);`

$$Temp := \ln(Q(T)) - \ln Q(0) = kT$$

Solve the differential equation.

Integrate both sides.

You will need to simplify this result.

Why does Maple report a natural logarithm? Maple knows that the integral $\int \frac{dx}{x} = \ln x$. Now, use **solve** to derive an expression for Q(T):

STEP 256:
SOLVE AND
REPORT

> `Temp2:=solve(Temp,Q(T));`

$$Temp2 := \frac{Q(0)}{\mathbf{e}^{-kT}}$$

Simplify your result.

Try `solve` *to rearrange your result.*

Well, you still have a little more work.

Note that $e^{kt} = \exp(kt)$ as discussed in Section 6.4.

11.8.4 Solution

Finally, substitute Qo for $Q(0)$, which is the model's initial condition. The solution to Eq. 11-17 is the exponential equation from Section 2.5:

STEP 257:
DONE!

> `Model:=simplify(subs(Q(0)=Qo,Temp2));`

$$Model := Qo\mathbf{e}^{kT}$$

Clean up your result a bit more.

Substitute the initial condition Q_0

and simplify the results.

Congratulations! You solved a differential equation.

SUMMARY

This chapter has introduced calculus, which embodies various mathematical tools for modeling change. Measuring slope and area helps predict changes in functions. In turn, these predictions help to model changes in physical systems. Derivatives compute slope, which describes how functions change with respect to independent variables. Apply derivatives when you need to predict changes in a model as variables change. Integrals compute area, or the space below functions to the axis of the independent variable. Apply integrals to sum the effects of changes to a model. Differentiation and integration are inverse operations related by the Fundamental Theorem of Calculus.

KEY TERMS

area	first derivative	limits
calculus	Fundamental Theorem of Calculus (FTC)	partial derivatives
continuous functions	higher order derivatives	slope
definite integral	indefinite integral	smooth functions
derivative	integral	tangent

Problems

1. Under what conditions can you take the derivative of a function?
2. Describe how the processes of differentiation and integration relate.
3. Use Maple to find the first derivative for each of the following expressions with respect to the variable x. (Hint: Review `?diff`.)

    3a. x

    3b. cx

    3c. $cx^2 + x$

3d. $\sqrt{x}$

3e. $x + \dfrac{1}{x}$

3f. xy

4. Use Maple to evaluate the following derivatives that each problem indicates. (Hint: Review **?diff**.)

    4a. Let $y = x^2 + 2x$. Find $\dfrac{dy}{dx}$.

    4b. Let $y = x^2 + 2x$. Find $\dfrac{d^2y}{dx^2}$.

    4c. Let $y = e^x$. Find $\dfrac{d^2y}{dx^2}$. Hint: Recall that e is the exponential function.

    4d. Let $y = \sin(2x)$. Find $\dfrac{d^3y}{dx^3}$.

    4e. Let $z = xy$. Find $\dfrac{\partial z}{\partial x}$.

    4f. Let $z = xy$. Find $\dfrac{\partial z^2}{\partial x \partial y}$.

5. Use Maple to evaluate the following indefinite integrals:

    5a. $\int x\,dx$

    5b. $\int x^2\,dx$

    5c. $\int \dfrac{1}{x}\,dx$

    5d. $\int x \sin x\,dx$

6. Use Maple to evaluate the following definite integrals:

    6a. $\int_0^2 x\,dx$

    6b. $\int_0^\pi \cos x\,dx$

    6c. $\int_1^2 \int_0^2 xy\,dx\,dy$ (Hint: This is called a *double-integral.*)

    6d. $\int_{-\infty}^\infty e^{\left(\frac{-x^2}{2}\right)}$ (Hint: Use the exponential function.)

7. Given a displacement $u(t)$ and time t, the derivative $\dot{u}(t)$ computes velocity, and the derivative $\ddot{u}(t)$ computes acceleration. Let $u(t) = t^2 + 4t - 6$ m. Perform the following steps using Maple:

    7a. Assign the variable u to the function $t^2 + 4t - 6$.

    7b. What kind of units would you normally expect the displacement u to have?

    7c. Find the velocity $\dot{u}$ by evaluating the derivative of u with respect to time t. Assign the name v to your results. (Hints: Use **diff(*something*,t)**.)

    7d. What kind of units would you normally expect the velocity v to have?

    7e. Find the acceleration $\ddot{u}$ by evaluating the derivative of $\dot{u}$ with respect to time t. Assign the name a to your results. (Hints: Use **diff(*something*,t)** or **diff(u,*something*)**.)

    7f. What kind of units would you normally expect the acceleration a to have?

8. Confirm your results in Problem 11.7. Note that you must use the *initial conditions* $u(0) = -6$ and $\dot{u}(0) = 4$ to properly check your expressions:

    8a. Starting with acceleration, integrate $\ddot{u}$ with respect to time t. (Hint: Try **int(a,t)**. You will find an expression for v. Now, modify v with the proper initial condition.)

    8b. Next, integrate $\dot{u}$ with respect to time t. (Hint: You will find an expression for u. Now, modify u with the proper initial condition.)

    8c. Do your results match the equations in Problem 11.7?

9. Consider the *electric field E*, the force per unit charge, that the charged rod in Figure 11.5 exerts on any point P along the rod's axis. From physics, assuming a charge per unit length of λ,

$$\Delta E = \frac{k\Delta q}{x^2} = \frac{k\lambda\Delta x}{x^2},$$

given unit charge Δq. To derive an equation for E, let ΔE and Δx shrink to infinitesimal sizes, dE and dx, respectively. Thus,

$$dE = \frac{k\lambda dx}{x^2}.$$

Using Maple, find an equation for E using the geometry indicated in Figure 11.5. You should obtain the result that

$$E = \frac{k\lambda L}{(d+L)d}.$$

(Hints: Enter **int(1,E)** to prove that integrating dE yields just E. You now need to solve a definite integral for $k\lambda dx/x^2$ along the range $d \le x \le d + L$.)

Figure 11.5. Electric Field of Charged Rod

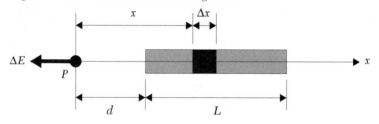

10. The Clapeyron equation relates a changing pressure P and temperature T of a substance. An ordinary differential equation expresses a simplified form of the relationship

$$\frac{dP}{P} = \frac{h_g - h_0}{R}\frac{dT}{T^2}$$

for the constants h_g, h_0, and R. Given initial values P_1 and T_1 and final values P_2 and T_2, solve this equation. (Hints: Follow the steps in Section 11.8. You might also wish to try **dsolve**.)

11. As shown in Figure 11.6, the *bending moment* M_0, with units of *force · length*, twists the cantilever beam in the xy-plane. Bending moments are defined as forces that act upon bodies and cause twisting about an axis. The differential equation

$$\frac{d^2y}{dx} = \frac{M}{EI}$$

relates the beam's deflection y with respect to the distance x, the bending moment M, and the flexural stiffness EI. Assuming constant EI, the solution to the differential equation yields

$$y = \frac{M_0 x^2}{2EI},$$

where both M and y are functions of x. Answer the following questions using Maple:

11a. Solve for the bending moment as a function of x. (Hint: Use the equation for y and the differential equation. You will need a second derivative.)

11b. Plot both the moment M and the displacement y as a function of x on the same graph. (Hint: Pick unit values for the constants.)

11c. Does the moment change as a function of position x?

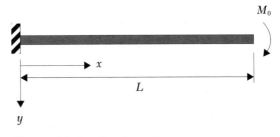

Figure 11.6. Cantilever Beam

11d. What is the shape of the deflection curve? (Hint: Consider the nature of the independent variable x.)

11e. Does the top of the beam experience compression or tension? Why or why not?

12. Repeat the problem in Section 11.8 for these values: $k = 2$ and $k = -2$. Explain the difference between choosing positive and negative values of k. You might also wish to supply plots that illustrate your answer.

13. Demonstrate how spring force $p = ku$ and spring energy $E_s = \frac{1}{2}ku^2$ are related. (Hint: Use the FTC.)

14. Consider the motion of a mass connected to a spring, as shown in Figure 11.7. (See also Figure 6.1). The mass will bounce up and down after the hand releases the mass. Whereas gravity initially pulls the mass downward, the spring reacts by pulling upward. Newton's second law states that the rate of change of momentum, $m\,\frac{du}{dt}$, experienced by a mass equals the force F_u acting on the mass m. Thus,

$$\sum F_u = ma_u,$$

where acceleration

$$a_u = \frac{d^2u}{dt^2} = \ddot{u}.$$

given displacement u and constant mass. Solve the following problems to describe the motion of the mass:

14a. Express a_u in Maple as a function of displacement $u(t)$. (Big hint: Restart Maple, and then, enter `a:=diff(u,t,t)`.)

14b. From Newton's Second Law and the free-body diagram as shown in Figure 11.7, $W - S = m\ddot{u}$. Using your expression for $\ddot{u}$, assign the name NSL to this equation. Why should you use the name *Weight* instead of W? Maple should output

$$NSL := Weight - S = m\left(\frac{\partial^2}{\partial t^2}\,u(t)\right).$$

14c. Using Hooke's Law and spring stiffness k, the weight provides an initial static displacement u_0. Thus, you can relate the weight and static displacement:

$$W = ku_0.$$

Substitute this equation for weight into your expression for NSL. Assign $NSL2$ to the results. Maple should output

$$NSL2 := ku0 - S = m\left(\frac{\partial^2}{\partial t^2}\,u(t)\right).$$

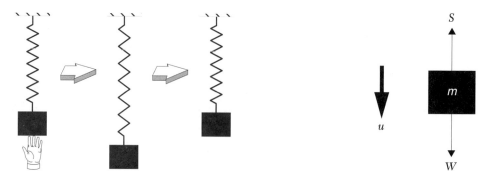

Dynamic Model   Free Body Diagram

Figure 11.7. Mass-Spring Model

14d. The total displacement that the mass experiences at any time t is the sum $u(t) + u_0$. You may now express the spring force S in terms of k and displacements $u(t)$ and total displacement of the mass as

$$S = k(u(t) + u_0).$$

Substitute this equation for weight into your expression for *NSL2*. Assign *NSL3* to the results. Maple should output

$$NSL3 := ku0 - k(\mathrm{u}(t) + u0)S = m\left(\frac{\partial^2}{\partial t^2}\,\mathrm{u}(t)\right).$$

14e. Based on the expression *NSL3*, show that $m\ddot{u} + ku = 0$ using Maple. Maple should output

$$ODE := -k\mathrm{u}(t) = m\left(\frac{\partial^2}{\partial t^2}\,\mathrm{u}(t)\right).$$

Based on these results, discuss whether initial static displacement affects the system's model.

14f. Express *ODE* as $ODE2 := -\mathrm{u}(t)\omega^2 = \frac{\partial^2}{\partial t^2}\,\mathrm{u}(t)$. (Hints: Substitute $\omega^2 = \frac{k}{m}$ with an algebraic substitution into $\frac{ODE}{m}$ Also, that's an omega, not a "w"!)

14g. Solve your differential equation using **dsolve**. Assign U to the results. You should obtain

$$U := \mathrm{u}(t) = \_C1\,\cos(\omega t) + \_C2\,\sin(\omega t).$$

(Maple might swap the coefficients *_C1* and *_C2*.)

14h. Assign V to the velocity $v(t)$, which is defined as $\dot{u}(t)$. (Hint: Use **diff** on the expression U.) You should obtain

$$V := \frac{\partial}{\partial t}\,\mathrm{u}(t) = \_C1\,\sin(\omega t)\omega + \_C2\,\cos(\omega t)\omega.$$

14i. Let displacement $u(0) = U_0$ and velocity $\dot{u}(0) = v(0) = V_0$. Express U and V in terms of U_0 (**Uo**) and V_0 (**Vo**). (Hints: You need to solve for the coefficients *_C1* and *_C2*. Separate out the RHS of U and V and evaluate the expressions for $t = 0$. You might wish to try **eval** and **solve**.) You should obtain

$$\mathrm{u}(t) = Uo\,\cos(\omega t) + \frac{Vo\,\sin(\omega t)}{\omega}.$$

and

$$\frac{\partial}{\partial t} u(t) = -Uo \, \sin(\omega t)\omega + Vo \, \cos(\omega t).$$

14j. Let $U_0 = 1$, $V_0 = 0$, and $m = k = 1$. Plot both $u(t)$ and $v(t)$ on the same graph for $0 \le t \le 2\pi$. Be sure to label your plots.

14k. What is the amplitude of the mass? That is, what is the magnitude of the maximum and minimum displacements?

14l. What is the velocity whenever the mass reaches its maximum or minimum displacement?

A

Symbols

A.1 KEYBOARD CHARACTERS*

!	Exclamation Point, *Bang*	(	Left Parenthesis, *Open Paren*
@	At Sign	)	Right Parenthesis, *Close Paren*
#	Pound Sign, *Sharp*, *Hash*	[	Left Square Bracket
$	Dollar Sign	]	Right Square Bracket
%	Percent Sign	{	Left Brace Bracket, *Left Curly Brace*
^	Circumflex, Caret	}	Right Brace Bracket, *Right Curly Brace*
&	Ampersand, *And*	<	Left Angle Bracket, *Less Than*
*	Asterisk, *Star*	>	Right Angle Bracket, *Greater Than*
+	Plus Sign, *Add*	/	Forward Slash, Virgule, *Slash*
=	Equals Sign	\	Backslash, *Switch*
~	Tilde	:	Colon
?	Question Mark	;	Semicolon
|	Vertical Line, *Bar*, *Pipe*	`	Back Quotation Mark, Grave Accent
_	Underscore, Underline	'	Single Quotation Mark, Aspostrophe
-	Hyphen, Minus Sign, *Dash*	"	Double Quotation Mark
.	Period, *Dot*	,	Comma

*Italicized names indicate common labels and other jargon.

A.2 GREEK CHARACTERS*

A	Alpha	α	alpha
B	Beta	β	beta
Γ	Gamma, **GAMMA**	γ	gamma
Δ	Delta	δ	delta
E	Epsilon	ε	epsilon
Z	**ZETA**	ζ	Zeta, zeta
H	Eta	η	eta
Θ	Theta	θ	theta
I	Iota	ι	iota
K	Kappa	κ	kappa
Λ	Lambda	λ	lambda
M	Mu	μ	mu
N	Nu	ν	nu
Ξ	Xi	ξ	xi
O	Omicron	o	omicron
Π	PI	π	Pi, pi
P	Rho	ρ	rho
Σ	Sigma	σ	sigma
T	Tau	τ	tau
Y	Upsilon	υ	upsilon
Φ	Phi	ϕ	phi
X	CHI	χ	chi
Ψ	Psi	ψ	psi
Ω	Omega	ω	omega

*Beware of names, such as **Pi** and **gamma**, that have pre-defined values in Maple. Enter **type(*name*,protected)** to check whether ***name*** has a predefined meaning.

B

Help!

Familiarize yourself with Maple's on-line help. The Help windows document most features.

B.1 HELP MENU

Use Maple's Help menu to become familiar with Maple. When first using Maple, select Help→BalloonHelp. Little balloons with helpful information will appear when you touch any icon and menu option.

B.2 TUTORIALS

New Maple users should select Help→NewUser'sTour and Help→Introduction for an overview of Maple features.

B.3 HELP BROWSER

Maple provides an excellent tool for finding help on commands with the Help Browser as shown in Figure B-1. You can open the Help Browser with the following actions:

- Select Help→UsingHelp and other menu selections like Help→Introduction.
- Enter ? or ?? at the Maple prompt (>).
- Find help on commands using ?*command* or a text or topic search under Help (See the following sections.)

The Help Browser organizes many of Maple's resources in categories called *topics*. Typically, *topics* describe commands with help on syntax, usage, and examples. Click once on topics listed as Topic . . . in the left column to open *subtopics* that will appear to the right of the topics. You can also click on the toolbar icons that appear below the workspace menus to move forward and backwards along topics.

B.4 SECTIONS AND SUBSECTIONS

Help topics typically organize information with *sections*, indicated by the icons ✚ and ▬. Sections collect text, execution groups, and other sections. *Subsections* are sections that are contained inside other sections.

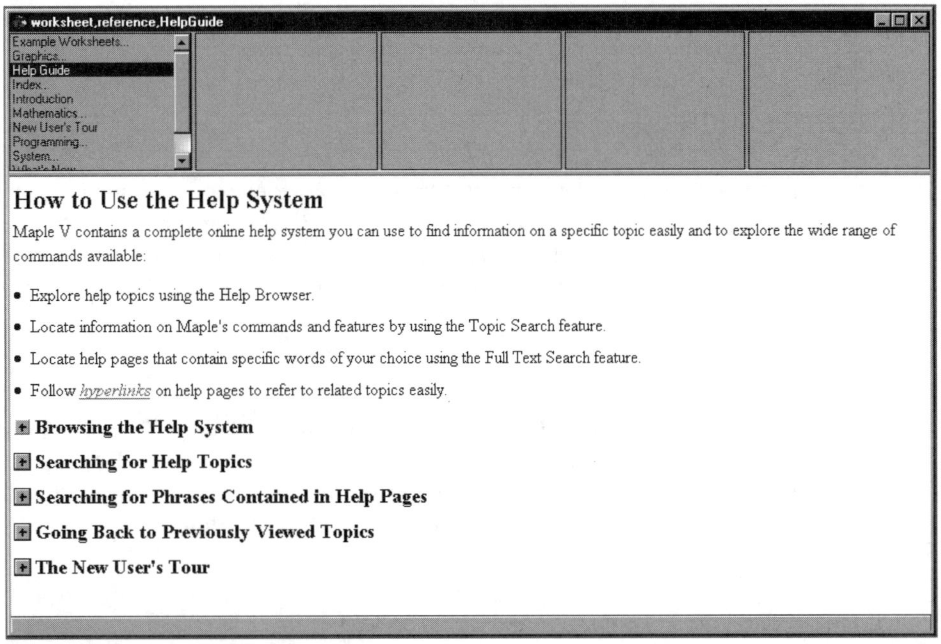

Figure B.1.   Help Browser

- Click once on the ➕ icon to expand a section.
- Click once on the ➖ icon to collapse a section.

Also, investigate WorksheetInterface . . . DocumentingYourWork . . . structuring . . . inside the Help Browser for information on adding your own sections in worksheets.

B.5   HYPERLINKS

Many topics and other keywords are provided as *hyperlinks*. Hyperlinks are active text that "jump" to other topics or display information. Maple typically displays hyperlinks as colored, underlined text. Click once with the mouse to activate a hyperlink.

B.6   COMMAND LINE HELP

Regardless of interface, you can enter **?topic** at the Maple prompt (>) for help on **topic**. If you are uncertain of the topic name, which is usually a command-name, just type one or two letters. Maple will display all topic names that start with those letters.

B.7   TOPIC SEARCH

Select Help→TopicSearch . . . to search for topics such as command names. You should type a few letters of the topic name in the box next to Topic. As long as the Auto-Search feature is activated, Maple will automatically search for matching topics as you type the letters. For instance, try searching for **dis**. Maple will suggest topics that appear below, such as **disassemble** and **discont**. Double-click on the topic names to investigate

Maple's suggestions. If you select **discont**, Maple will pop open the Help Browser directly to the **discont** topic-page.

B.8 TEXT SEARCH

If you are uncertain of a topic or command name, try a text search with Help→FullTextSearch . . . . In the box next to Word(s), type the words for which you are searching and press the Search button. Maple will suggest topics that might match your inquiry. Double-click on a topic to open the Help page associated with the topic.

B.9 EXAMPLES

Maple provides many example worksheets that cover a wide variety of topics and applications. Check out **?examples[index]** and **?share[contents]** after you have become familiar with Maple. Also, consult the multitude of web resources, some of which are listed in Appendix I, for further examples of using Maple.

C

Worksheet and File Management

This appendix reviews common techniques for importing and exporting data into and out of Maple. Typical operations include file saving and printing of Maple worksheets. You should also consult **?worksheet[managing]** and Worksheet Interface... for further details.

C.1 RUNNING MAPLE

Consult Chapter 2 for the rudiments of starting the graphical user interface (GUI) version of Maple. You should also consult Section 4.3 and **?configuring** for a discussion of Maple's shared- and parallel-kernel modes of operation.

C.2 NEW WORKSHEETS

Suppose that you wish to continue your calculations on a different worksheet. Create new worksheets by selecting the icon ☐ or menu File→New. During a session, Maple labels each worksheet as "Untitled [number]" on the title bar in ascending order according to newness.

C.3 WORKSPACE

Select Window options to organize and rearrange worksheets inside your workspace. For instance, try opening a few worksheets inside a Maple workspace. You may then select Window→Tile to display all windows next to one another in a tile-pattern.

C.4 SAVING WORKSHEETS

Save your work! You never know when the system might crash. Select the icon ☐ or the menu File→SaveAs... to name and save worksheets, as shown in Figure C.1:

- Folders or Directory: Change folders and directories by double-clicking on the folder name.
- File name: Delete the asterisk (*) and type a name that ends with ".mws", like "hw1.mws".
- Save file as type or Filetype: Leave the type on Maple Worksheet. Worksheets saved in this format preserve the entire contents in Maple format (MWS). See Section C.6 for more information on Maple's worksheet format.

Click on **OK** when your chosen file name satisfies you. The new name will appear on the left side of the title-bar on the worksheet. Once you have named your worksheet, frequently select File→Save to save your work.

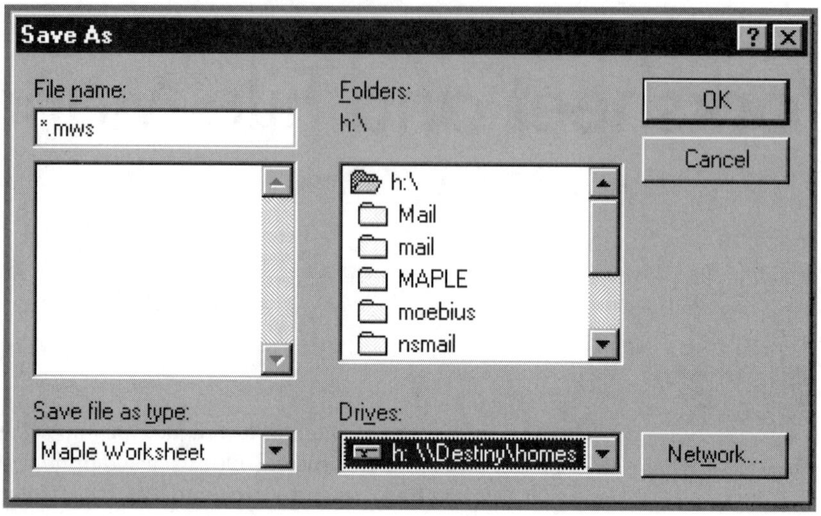

Figure C.1. Save Worksheet

C.5 EXPORTING WORKSHEETS

You can save your work to different formats by selecting File→ExportAs . . . . If you prefer, you can also select File→SaveAs . . . and then save the worksheet to another type of file. Note that exporting a worksheet to another format only exports the current version of your work. You have to export your worksheet again if you wish to incorporate changes inside the saved file. Some common formats include:

- Maple Worksheet (MWS): Maple Worksheet format (See the next section.)
- HTML: Convert your worksheet to HTML for the World Wide Web. See also **?xprt2html** for more details.
- Maple Text: A text-based representation of the Maple worksheet. Save in this format if the worksheet needs to be imported into Maple. The command-line version of Maple typically saves in this format. In general, you should stick to using MWS, instead.

Consult **?saving** for more information about these and other formats.

C.6 WORKSHEET FORMAT (MWS)

When you save a worksheet in the type called "Maple Worksheet," Maple stores that worksheet's contents into a text file that only Maple understands. These files, which typically have the extension ".mws", are written as ASCII, which is a universally understood form of text. However, text written in MWS-format is unintelligible and will produce garbled printouts. You should only print MWS files from within Maple! See also Section C.8.

C.7 OPENING WORKSHEETS

Load previously saved worksheets by selecting the icon 📂 or menu File→Open. The window that pops up, shown in Figure C.2, resembles the "Save As" window. Select a

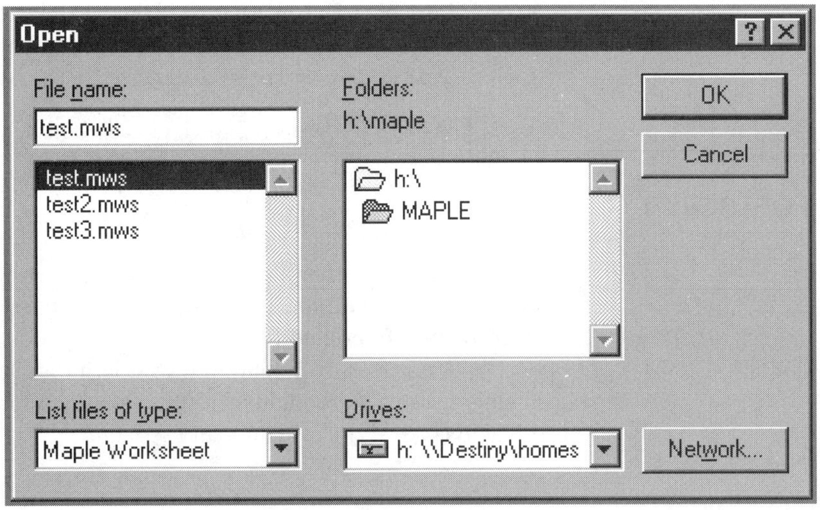

Figure C.2. Open Worksheet

directory by clicking on **Folders** or **Directory**. "Open" automatically lists files with "mws" extensions. Click on an existing file or type the name of a file under **File name**. Click on **OK** to load the worksheet.

C.8 PRINTING

Print your worksheet by selecting the icon ▦ or menu **File→Print** . . . . From the "Print" window shown in Figure C.3, you have two choices for printing:

- File: Click on **Print to file** (Unix users should select **Output to File**.) A check-mark (✔) will appear in the box to the right. (Unix users will see an indented box ◆.) Then, click on **OK**. Maple then creates a PostScript file containing the contents of your worksheet. Maple will then prompt you to enter a file name. Choose a name like "*something*.ps". See the next section for further description of PostScript.

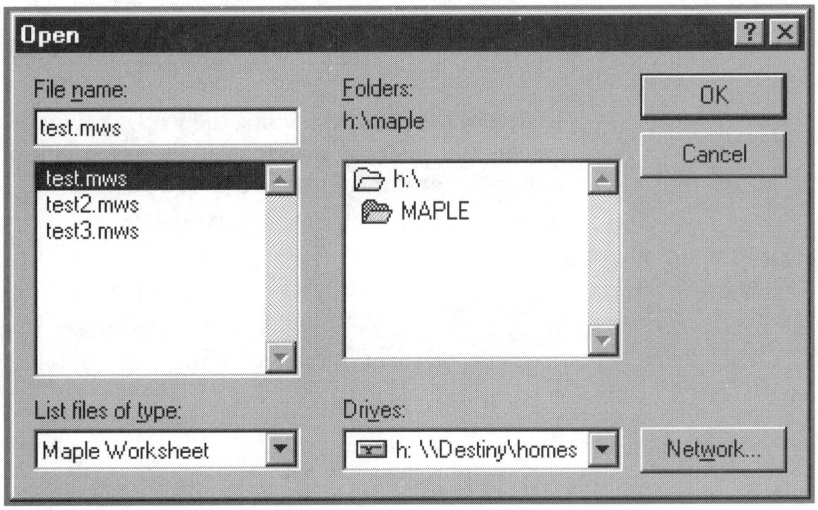

Figure C.3. Print Worksheet

- Hardcopy: Ensure that the "Print to file" box has no checkmark (✔). Then, click on OK. (Unix users should select Print Command and then enter **lpr -P***printer* or **lp -d***printer* in the box to the right.)

Also, try File→PrintPreview. . . to view a file before printing it.

C.9 POSTSCRIPT

PostScript (PS) is another kind of text-based formatting that creates files that print on virtually every kind of printer. The first line in a PS file typically starts with "%!PS-Adobe". Beware of the difference between PostScript and Maple's MWS files! Maple cannot open PostScript files, so retain both PostScript and MWS versions of your worksheets. Remember, also, you should never directly print a file stored in MWS format unless you use Maple's File→Print. . . command sequence!

C.10 FILE I/O

File I/O (input and output) consists of reading input into Maple and printing output to a file. For in-formation on how to input and output numerical data, consult both **?readdata** and **?writedata**. The Help Browser describes further commands inside Programming . . . InputandOutput. . . .

C.11 SAVING AND PRINTING PLOTS

By default, Maple includes plots inside worksheets. If you prefer to display plots in separate windows, select Options→PlotDisplay→Window. Then, execute your plot commands again. New windows containing the plots will appear. Click inside the windows that contain the plots, and select save and print commands as you would a normal worksheet.

You can also redirect plot output to other files. For instance, I have been entering commands, like the following input statements, to create plots inside this text:

```
> with(plots):
> plotsetup(ps,plotoutput='test.ps',plotoptions='height=
         3in, width=4in,color=grey,noborder,portrait'):
```

To display the plots back inside the worksheet, enter **plotsetup(inline)** and then execute your plot commands again. For more information on customizing output, consult **?plotsetup** and **?plot[device]**.

C.12 QUITTING MAPLE

To end your Maple session, enter File→Exit. Maple will then prompt you to save unsaved worksheets. When using the command-line version of Maple, enter **quit**.

D

Maple Library Functions

This appendix briefly discusses how Maple organizes functions stored inside its library.

D.1 MAIN LIBRARY

Other than kernel commands, Maple's *main library* contains the bulk of commonly used functions, sometimes called "demand-loaded functions." Calling one of these functions in an input statement automatically loads the function into memory. If the function's Help file does not indicate any special loading procedure, the function belongs to the main library.

D.2 MISCELLANEOUS LIBRARY

Maple's *miscellaneous library* contains less commonly used functions. To load these functions into memory, you must first enter **readlib(*function*)**. For instance, investigate **?evalr** and **?log10**. Refer to Section 5.6 for an example of **evalr**. In general, the Help files will warn you when to first load a command with **readlib**. Consult **?readlib** for more information.

D.3 LIBRARY PACKAGES

Library packages contain functions for specialized forms of analysis. Examples of library packages used in this book include **plots** and **linalg**. Library packages contain functions that Maple does not automatically recognize as belonging to the main library. Thus, you must load library packages into Maple's memory in order to use functions contained inside those packages. Why doesn't Maple just automatically load the library packages? Many functions that are stored within the packages have names that clash with functions stored within other packages. Also, users might prefer to use names that functions within library packages already use. Consult **?index[package]** for more information on the available library packages. You should also investigate **?share** for other applications.

D.4 LOADING FUNCTIONS FROM LIBRARY PACKAGES

There are three ways by which you may access functions contained in library packages:

1. Enter **with(package)** to define the names of every function contained in **package**. After entering **with(package)**, you may then call any of the functions inside package as you would call functions from the main library:

   > **with(package):**   *Define all functions contained inside a library package.*

   > **function(arguments);**   *You can now directly call functions that are contained in the package that you accessed.*

   By defining the function names, Maple will access **package** for the function names that **package** contains. Those functions then become available for you to use after entering **with(package)**. Furthermore, you do not need to re-enter **with(package)** during the same session, unless you enter **restart** or use parallel-kernel mode.

2. Only access specific functions from a library package in order to avoid conflicts with other names:

   > **with(package,functions):**   *Access only certain functions that are contained inside a library package. Input the function names as a sequence.*

   > **function(arguments);**   *You can now directly call those functions contained in the package that you accessed.*

3. Directly load a function from a package each time you need the function:

   > **package[function](arguments);**   *Directly call a function from its package.*

Beware that library packages contain function names that conflict with function names in Maple's main library or other packages. Maple will warn you upon encountering a conflict, but you must keep track of which version of the function name(s) that you need to use! Consult **?with** for more information.

D.5 FINDING FUNCTIONS

Investigate the following Help pages for information on the following functions:

- Main and miscellaneous library: **?inifcn** and **?index[function]**. See also Index...function in the Help Browser
- Library packages: **?index[package]**. See also Index...packages in the Help Browser.
- Share library: **?share** and **?share[contents]**. See also System...General...Information...Share in the Help Browser.

D.6 VIEWING FUNCTIONS

Maple commands form a programming language with operators, syntax, and functions. In fact, you can view the actual code of library functions with the following commands:

> `interface(verboseproc=2);`   *Tell Maple to print the code for procedures.*

> `readlib(sin);`   *Directly load the code for Maple's sine function.*

Very long output . . .   *Maple loads and displays the entire code for computing the sine of an expression.*

Maple's normal mode of operation abbreviates the display for functions that are loaded with **readlib**:

> `interface(verboseproc=0);`   *Make Maple's reporting mode sparse again.*

> `readlib(sin);`   *Directly load the code for Maple's sine function again.*

proc(*x::algebraic*) . . . **end**   *Maple reports an abbreviated message.*

Consult **?interface** and **?readlib** for more details.

E

Introduction to Programming

This appendix briefly introduces aspects of programming in Maple. Consult Programming . . . and more advanced books on Maple for intensive discussion of Maple's programming features and techniques.

E.1 ADVANCED DATA TYPES

Programming in Maple often requires expression types such as Boolean, relation, array, and table. (Chapter 5 introduces Boolean and relation data types.) Consult Programming . . . Data Types . . . for an extensive list of data types.

E.2 ARRAYS

Arrays organize information into rows and columns much as a spreadsheet does, as shown in Figure E.1. Matrices and vectors are special cases of arrays, as discussed in Chapter 10. Enter arrays with a list of lists as **array([[row1],[row2],...])**, where each row forms a list in the form **[col1,col2,...]**. Because of last-name evaluation, display arrays with **eval(array)** or **print(array)**:

EXAMPLE:
ARRAY

```
> A:=array([[a,1,2,b],[a,3,d,a]]);
```
Assign A to an array of values.

```
> A[1,3];
```
Access A_{13}, the element corresponding to row 1 and column 3 inside A.

$$A := \begin{bmatrix} a & 1 & 2 & b \\ a & 3 & d & a \end{bmatrix}$$

Consult ?array for more information.

$$2$$

Consult ?indices for more information.

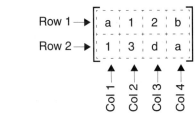

A1 := array([[a,1,2,b]])

One-Dimensional Array

A2 := array([[a,1,2,b],[1,3,d,a]])

Two-Dimensional Array

Figure E.1. Arrays

E.3 TABLES

Tables resemble arrays, with the exception that table indices can use labels other than integers. In general, enter tables as **table([*index1=value,index2=value,...*])**:

EXAMPLE:
TABLE

> **bar:=table([area=10*cm^2,length=1.5*m,material=steel]);**

bar := table([*Create a table. Consult* **?table** *for more information.*

  $material = steel$

  $area = 10cm^2$ *Think of tables as user-defined types, or entities that you can define.*

  $length = 1.5m$

  ])

Access an entry of a table as you would for an array, but use the index label instead of row and column indices:

> **bar[length];**   *Access the value corresponding to bar_{length}.*

                $1.5m$ *Consult* **?indices** *for more information.*

As you would with an array, display tables with **print** or **eval** because of last-name evaluation.

E.4 PROGRAMMING STATEMENTS

Programming involves Maple statements such as repetition and selection. Investigate **?keyword** for a complete list of Maple's reserved words, most of which Maple uses for programming.

E.5 REPETITION STATEMENTS

When you need to repeat a sequence of operations, use repetition statements in two general forms:

GENERAL FORM OF REPETITION STATEMENT

```
> for name from expr by expr to expr while expr
      do statements od;
```

Maple requires only the do statements od portion. All other keywords and expressions are optional.

GENERAL FORM OF REPETITION STATEMENT

```
> for name in expr while expr
      do statements od;
```

Maple requires everything except for the while expr portion.

For example, create an array of squared integers between 1 and 100:

EXAMPLE OF A REPETITION STATEMENT

```
> restart: L:=array(1..10);
```
Assign a 10-element, one-dimensional array.

$$L := \text{array}(1..10, [\,])$$
Maple reports that your array is currently empty.

```
> for i from 1 by 1 to 10 do L[i]:=i^2 od:
```
Find the square of each integer and store in the array.

```
> print(L);
```
Arrays require print or eval to display the contents.

$$[1, 4, 9, 16, 25, 36, 49, 64, 81, 100]$$
Maple reports the array's contents.

Investigate **?repetition** or **?do** for more information.

E.6 SELECTION STATEMENTS

Selection statements test conditions in order to perform certain tasks. Different cases can then activate other statements.

GENERAL FORM OF SELECTION STATEMENT

```
> if expr then statements
```
If expr is true, then perform statements.

```
    elif expr then statements
```
Otherwise, if this expr is true, perform these statements.

```
    elif expr then statements
```
Otherwise, if this expr is true, perform these statements.

```
    ...
```
And so on.

```
    else statements
```
If no exprs are true, then perform these statements.

```
  fi;
```
End the selection statement.

Maple requires everything except for the elif expr then statements portion.

Use Boolean types for each **expr**. If **expr** evaluates as *true*, Maple performs the indicated statements following the **then** keyword. Otherwise, Maple moves to the next **elif** ("else if") condition and tests **expr**. If every **elif** condition fails, Maple activates the statements following the **else** keyword. If all **expr**s fail, Maple takes no action. For instance:

EXAMPLE OF A SELECTION STATEMENT

```
> restart: A:=1:                                  Assign A to an odd value.

> if type(A,even) then print("The value is even.");   Check if A is even.

>     elif type(A,odd) then print("The value is odd.");   Check if A
                                                               is odd.

>     else print("Cannot understand the variable!");    Report an error.

> fi;                                            End selection statement.

              "The value is odd."                  Maple confirms that A is odd.
```

Investigate **?if** for more information. Consult **?ERROR** for producing error messages.

E.7 PROCEDURES

As discussed in **?proc**, you can define your own Maple programs that act as Maple functions by using procedures and Maple's **proc** function:

GENERAL FORM OF PROCEDURES

```
> proc(names)                                      Procedure name and inputs.

      local names:            Declare local variables, which are names used internally by proc.

      global names:           Declare global variables, which are names available
                                                      from outside of proc.

      options names:                            Modify the behavior of proc.

      description string:         Label your procedure with inert commentary.

   statements                             Provide the main body of the procedure.

   end;                                            End the procedure.
```

The **local**, **global**, **options**, and **description** statements are optional. In each statement, specify **names** as a sequence of Maple names separated by commas. The statement sequence **statements** provides the main portion of a procedure. Separate each statement with a semicolon (**;**) or colon (**:**) as you would for normal Maple input. For instance, create a procedure that finds the magnitude of a vector:

EXAMPLE:
VECTOR
MAGNITUDE

```
> restart:
```
Restart Maple.

```
> mag := proc(v)
```
Assign a procedure called **mag** *that has one argument.*

```
>         description "Find vector magnitude":
```
Supply an inert comment.

```
>         local dim, i, temp;
```
List local variables for internal usage.

```
>         if not type(v,vector) then
```
Check the expression type.

```
>             ERROR("You must enter a vector!");
```
If the input is not a vector, produce an error message.

```
>         fi;
```
End the **if** *statement.*

```
>         temp:=0:
```
Initialize your sum to zero.

```
>         dim := linalg[vectdim](v):
```
Determine the vector size. Use the **vectdim** *function contained inside the* **linalg** *library package.*

```
>         for i from 1 by 1 to dim do
```
Start a **for** *loop.*

```
>             temp := temp + v[i]^2:
```
Sum the squares of each vector component.

```
>         od:
```
End the **for** *loop.*

```
>         sqrt(temp);
```
Vector magnitude is the square root of the sum of the squares of a vector.

```
>         end;
```
End the procedure.

Long output...omitted to conserve space.   *Maple reports your procedure back to you here.*

Now, call your procedure as you would a standard Maple function:

```
> with(linalg,vector,norm);
```
Define **vector** *and* **norm** *functions from* **linalg**.

```
Warning, new definition for norm
```
Ignore this warning.

```
> v:=vector([1,2,3,4]):
```
Assign v to a vector.

```
> mag(v);
```
Call the **mag** *procedure to find the magnitude of v.*

$$\sqrt{30}$$
     $\sqrt{1^2+2^2+3^2+4^2} = \sqrt{1+4+9+16} = \sqrt{30}$

```
> norm(v,frobenius);
```
Now, compare your results with that of Maple's **norm** *function.*

$$\sqrt{30}$$
     You can also compare code with **readlib('linalg/norm')**.

```
> mag(1,2,3,4);
```
Deliberately try to make a mistake.

```
Error, (in mag) You must enter a vector!
```
Maple warns you of your error.

F

Spreadsheets

F.1 TUTORIALS

Maple V now sports *spreadsheet* capabilities. Besides providing convenient templates for sorting and organizing data, spreadsheets help you apply the same formulas simultaneously to large amounts of data. This appendix describes basic features of using spreadsheets in Maple. For more information, you should also consult **?spreadsheet** and the following topics in the Help Browser:

- WorksheetInterface...Working with Spreadsheets...Overview
- WorksheetInterface...Reference...Menus...Spreadsheet

You should also refer to Table 1-1 for notation that this appendix employs.

F.2 CREATING A SPREADSHEET

Follow these steps to insert a spreadsheet into your worksheet:

- Inside a worksheet, place your cursor in a fresh execution group.
- Select Insert→Spreadsheet.

Maple will create and insert a new spreadsheet in your worksheet, as shown in Figure F.1. Maple will also activate the Spreadsheet menu and display a new Context Bar. You can also click anywhere on the spreadsheet with your right mouse button to access the same Spreadsheet sub-menus.

F.3 ACTIVATING A SPREADSHEET

Maple draws little black squares around the spreadsheet to indicate that the spreadsheet is *active*, as shown in Figure F.1. Actions such as deleting and resizing (Sections F.4 and F.20) require an activated spreadsheet. When you point the mouse on the border, the cursor will become an open arrow that looks like this: ↖. To activate a previously inserted spreadsheet, click on the outermost edge of the spreadsheet's border.

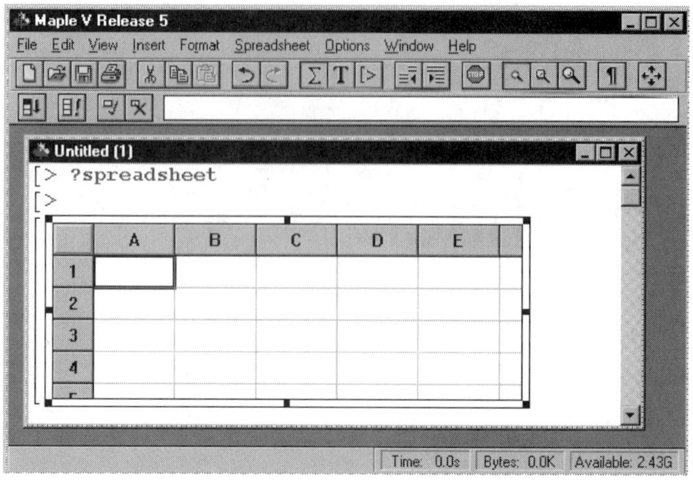

Figure F.1. Spreadsheet

F.4 DELETING A SPREADSHEET

To delete a spreadsheet from your worksheet, follow these steps:

- First, activate a spreadsheet when you see the cursor ⟨cursor⟩ , as discussed in Section F.3.
- Then, select <u>E</u>dit→<u>C</u>u<u>t</u> or <u>E</u>dit→<u>D</u>eleteParagraph to delete a spreadsheet from a worksheet.

Once the spreadsheet is active, you may press the Delete key. Also, try placing the cursor in the paragraph that contains the spreadsheet and press the key-sequence Control-Delete.

F.5 SPREADSHEET COMPONENTS

In general, spreadsheets resemble tables that collect and relate information in a rectangular grid or array. The following elements make up Maple spreadsheets that are illustrated in Figure F.2:

- Vertical *columns* that are labeled with letters in alphabetic order.
- Horizontal *rows* that are labeled with numbers in ascending order.
- Column and row *headers* that label column and row labels, respectively.
- *Cells* that have row and column positions in the spreadsheet grid.

You enter data into the cells (see Section F.8). A *cell address*, which has the syntax *Col-Row*, indicates the location of the cell where you can find the data. For instance, cell A1 has the address of Column A and Row 1.

F.6 MOVING AROUND

To move around your spreadsheet, do one of the following actions:

- Point with your mouse at a cell. Then, click the left mouse button.
- Point and click with your mouse. Then, move up, down, right, and left with the arrow keys.
- Press the Enter key (↵) to move down one cell at a time inside the same column.

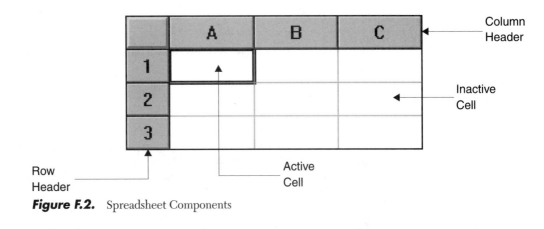

Figure F.2.   Spreadsheet Components

F.7 SELECTING CELLS

A newly inserted spreadsheet starts with one active cell, A1, as shown in Figure F.2. Active cells accept input and menu selections. You can select cells when Maple displays the prompt. Performing the following actions will allow you to select one or many cells:

- *Single cell*: Point your mouse inside any cell. Click once with your left mouse button. Maple will draw a border around the now-active cell.
- *Multiple cells* (basic): Point your mouse inside any cell. Maple considers this cell the *first cell* in a range of multiple cells. Now, click once and hold down your left mouse button. Drag the mouse until you reach the *last cell*. Maple will highlight the selected group of cells. Release the mouse when finished. Try selecting the six cells as shown in Figure F.3: the first cell is A1, and the last cell is B3.
- *Multiple cells* (shortcut): Select the *first cell* by pointing and clicking with your mouse. Then, hold down the shift key, and point and click with your mouse to select the *last cell*. Maple will highlight all cells in all rows and columns that include the first and last cell. To replicate Figure F.3, select cell A1. Then, press the Shift key and click on cell B3.
- *Columns and Rows*: Select a cell from a row or column header. When you see the prompt, drag the mouse to select multiple rows or columns.
- *All cells*: Click on the cell in upper left corner of the spreadsheet (the corner-cell above the header 1 and to the left of the header A).

Figure F.3.   Selecting Multiple Cells

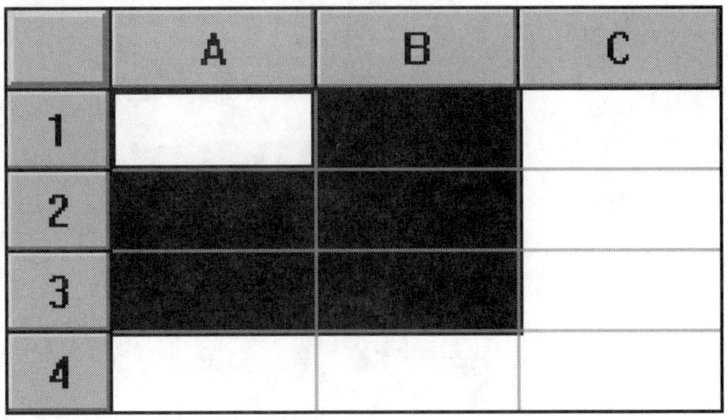

F.8 ENTERING DATA INTO CELLS

You can enter expressions and formulas into Maple's spreadsheet cells. Typical expressions that you would enter include numerical and symbolic data. Formulas that evaluate this data are discussed in the next section. You will need to refer to the context bar and spreadsheet icons shown in Figure F.4.

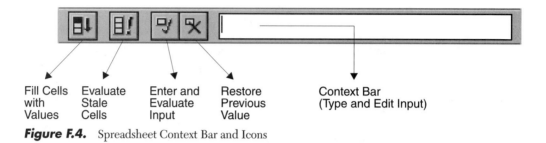

Figure F.4. Spreadsheet Context Bar and Icons

To enter data from the keyboard,

- Select one cell, as discussed in Section F.7.
- Type the data and watch the Context Bar that is shown in Figure F.4. Everything you type will appear there.
- Press ↵ or the ☑ icon.

For instance, consider the sample session that is demonstrated below:

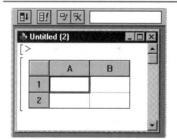

Figure F.5. Select Cell

Selection (Figure F.5):
- Insert a spreadsheet into a worksheet.
- Ensure that cell A1 is selected.

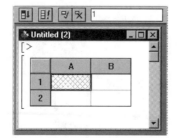

Figure F.6. Type Data

Type data (Figure F.6):
- Type 1 inside cell A1.
- Maple will display 1 in the Context Bar and the cell with crosshatches.

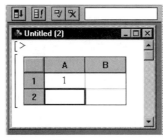

Enter the input (Figure F.7):
- Press ↵ or ☑️.
- Maple displays the output-value of cell A1 in blue.

Figure F.7.   Enter Input

Whenever you enter data from the Context Bar, you must use Maple Notation. However, Maple displays output only in Standard Math notation after you enter your data. Consult **?cellcontent** and **?spreadsheet** for more information.

F.9 COPYING DATA INTO CELLS

You can also copy Maple expressions between a worksheet and spreadsheet. To copy from a worksheet into a Maple spreadsheet cell,

- Highlight a portion of Maple output in order to select an expression.
- Select <u>E</u>dit→<u>C</u>opy or <u>E</u>dit→Cu<u>t</u>.
- Select the desired cell.
- Finally, select <u>E</u>dit→<u>P</u>aste.

Maple displays the new cell contents in the same output format. For instance, try copying the output $\frac{a}{b}$ from the input **a/b** as shown in Figure F.8. If you copy from a spreadsheet cell back into the main worksheet, Maple will convert the expression into input with Maple Notation. Consult **?cellcontent** for other shortcuts that employ the mouse.

Figure F.8.   Copying Maple Output

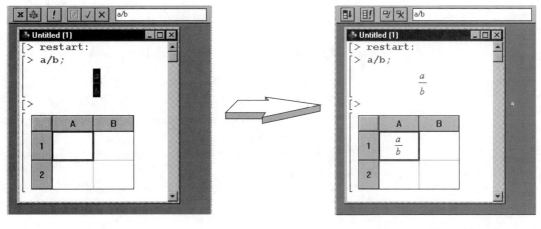

Select Maple Output   Copy and Paste into Cell

F.10 EDITING CELL DATA

If you wish to change a cell's contents,

- Select the cell. Note that Maple displays the cell's contents inside the Context Bar. (Refer to Figure F.4.)
- Inside the Context Bar, delete the text that you wish to change. You can use either the Backspace or Delete keys. You may also highlight the offending portion with your mouse.
- Type the new data.
- Enter the data by pressing either ↵ or the ☑ icon. (Refer to Figure F.4.)
- If you change your mind, press the ☒ icon to restore the original contents. (Refer to Figure F.4.)

To delete cell contents, perform one of the following actions:

- Select the cell(s), and press the Delete key.
- Select an individual cell and delete the data from within the Context Bar.

F.11 AUTOMATIC ENTRY OF DATA

If you would like to automatically generate columns of data, use Spreadsheet→Fill. To fill a row or column with the *same value* as one cell,

- Select a range of cells. The first cell should contain the value that you wish to replicate.
- For a column, select either Spreadsheet→Fill→Down or Spreadsheet→ Fill→Up, depending on whether the last cell is below or above the first cell.
- For a row, select either Spreadsheet→Fill→Right or Spreadsheet→Fill→ Left, depending on whether the last cell is to the left or to the right of the first cell.

You can also increment the values in the cells that you fill. Starting from the first cell, Maple will add an increment to the first cell's value and enter the value in the next cell. Then, Maple will add the same increment to the second cell and store the result in the third cell. Maple repeats this process until Maple reaches the last cell or a user-supplied stop-value. For instance, you can fill a column with a step size of 2 and stop-value of 8, as shown in Figure F.9, by following these steps:

- Select the first cell A1 and enter the value 1.
- Select the range of cells from A1 to A6. (See Section F.7.)
- Click on the ▤ icon or select Spreadsheet→Fill→Detailed.... The Fill Window will pop up.
- Enter the following information: Down for Direction, 2 for StepSize, and 8 for StopValue.
- Click on OK. Maple only fills the cells until reaching cell A4. Why? The next two cells A5 and A6 would contain the values of 9 and 11, respectively, which exceed the stop-value of 8.

For more information, consult `?filling`.

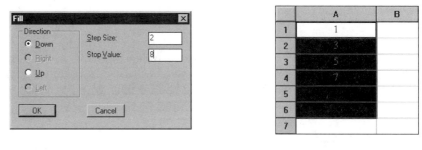

Fill Window   Filled Column

Figure F.9.   Filling Cells

F.12   ENTERING AND EVALUATING FORMULAS

Spreadsheets often refer to expressions as *formulas*. Suppose that you wish to create a formula inside a cell that uses values from other cells within a spreadsheet. You would need, somehow, to refer to different cells that contain values. You can refer to another cell with a *reference*, which is a label that points to a cell address. For instance, the reference **~A1** instructs Maple to access the value stored inside cell A1. Note that you must precede cell references with a tilde (~)! Section F.15 reviews references in more detail.

Why should you bother with references? Cell references enable you to calculate and recalculate a series of formulas without having to re-enter the equations. Consider the following example:

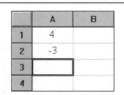

	A	B
1	4	
2	-3	
3		
4		

Figure F.10.   Enter Data

Input some data (Figure F.10):
- Enter the value 4 into cell A1.
- Enter the value −3 into cell A2.

	A	B
1	4	
2	-3	
3		
4		

Figure F.11.   Enter Formula

Enter a formula (Figure F.11):
- Select cell A3.
- Enter the formula **~A1+~A2**.
- Maple will display the formula in the Context Bar and the cell with hash marks.

	A	B
1	4	
2	-3	
3	1	
4		

Figure F.12.   Evaluate Formula

Evaluate the formula (Figure F.12):
- Press ↵ or .
- Maple evaluates the formula **~A1+~A2**.
- Adding the values of cells A1 and A2 yields the value $4 + (−3) = 1$.

For this example, cell A3 contains the value 1 that results from the formula **~A1+~A2**. This formula also belongs to cell A3, though Maple will neither print nor display the formula, except in the Context Bar. This formula instructs Maple to add the values that cells A1 and A2 contain. Although Maple only displays the values of the cells, Maple still remembers any formulas that the cells might contain. Therefore, you can change values throughout the spreadsheet without having to create new formulas to compute new values.

F.13 SPREADSHEET EVALUATION

Recall that pressing ↵ or ☑ evaluates a formula inside a cell. When evaluating spreadsheet cells, Maple follows these steps:

- First, Maple substitutes values for cell references.
- Next, Maple simplifies and evaluates expressions as if the input were entered inside an execution group.
- Finally, Maple reports the output.

Beware that "evaluating a cell" does not mean "forcing evaluation" of an expression! For instance, if you enter **subs(x=0,sin(x))** inside a spreadsheet cell, Maple will still produce sin(0), as discussed in Section 9.2.3. Maple does not produce 0: this output would result from forcing evaluation with **eval**, instead.

What happens if cells change value? You need to recalculate the worksheet, as discussed in the next section. Also, refer to Section F.16 for tips on spreadsheet use and **?calculations** for more information.

F.14 STALE CELLS

Although cell references greatly assist computations, Maple's spreadsheet cells do not gracefully accept changes. When you change data inside cells, Maple will not automatically recalculate cell formulas that depend on cell values that have changed. *Stale* cells have formulas that depend upon other cells with changed values. Maple will warn you of stale cells by drawing cross-hatches in those cells that need re-evaluation. In general, to recalculate stale cells, you may perform any of these actions:

- Single cell: Press ↵ or ☑ to recalculate that cell.
- Multiple cells: Select <u>S</u>preadsheet→<u>E</u>valuateSelection to recalculate several cells.
- All cells: Select 🄱! or <u>S</u>preadsheet→<u>E</u>valuate<u>S</u>preadsheet to recalculate an entire spreadsheet.

Consider the following example that uses the same data shown in Figure F.10:

	A	B
1	2	
2	-3	
3	1	
4		

Change the data (Figure F.13):
- Select cell A1 from the example in Section F.12.
- Delete the value 4 and replace it with the value 2.
- Maple warns you that cell A3 is stale.

Figure F.13.   Change Data

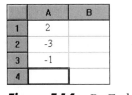

	A	B
1	2	
2	-3	
3	-1	
4		

Figure F.14. Re-Evaluate

Re-evaluate the formula (Figure F.14):
- Select cell A3 and press ↵ or ☑ to recalculate the cell.
- The crosshatches now disappear, so all is well.

Consult **?calculations** for more information.

F.15 ABSOLUTE AND RELATIVE REFERENCES

In order to avoid having to retype data, spreadsheets provide references for formulas. As introduced in Section F.12, a reference points to the value within a cell by using a cell address. Formulas that contain cell references substitute values from these referenced cells. For example, assume that cell A1 has the value 2. When you enter the formula **~A1** inside a cell, say A3, that cell will then have the value 2, as well. In fact, any formula in any cell that uses the reference **~A1** will refer back to the contents of cell A1.

So far, only *relative references* have been introduced. Relative references have the syntax **~ColRow**, where the tilde (~) indicates a reference, and **ColRow** specifies a cell address. When you copy a relative reference to another cell, Maple automatically increments the row and column addresses, as discussed below:

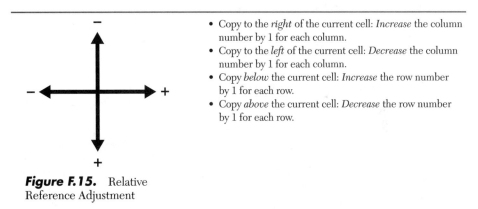

- Copy to the *right* of the current cell: *Increase* the column number by 1 for each column.
- Copy to the *left* of the current cell: *Decrease* the column number by 1 for each column.
- Copy *below* the current cell: *Increase* the row number by 1 for each row.
- Copy *above* the current cell: *Decrease* the row number by 1 for each row.

Figure F.15. Relative Reference Adjustment

Refer to Figure F.15 for a quick reminder of how spreadsheets adjust cell references. For example, assume that you enter the formula **~D4** inside cell B3. Then, you copy the cell contents of B3 to cell A6, which is 1 cell above and 3 cells to the right of B3. Therefore, the new formula inside cell A6 will be ~(D–1)(4+3), which means **~C7**.

To turn off the automatic adjustment of cell references, use *absolute references* with the dollar sign (**$**) operator. Entering a **$** before a row or column address, or both, instructs Maple not to change the address when you copy the formula elsewhere in the spreadsheet. For example, assume that you enter the formula **~D4** inside cell B3. No matter where you copy the cell contents of B3, the formula **~D4** will not change. Overall, there are four possible forms of cell references:

- **~ColRow**: *Complete relative reference*: Change both column and row addresses when copying a cell.

- **~ColRow**: *Complete absolute reference*: Maintain the same column and row addresses when copying a cell.

- ~$**ColRow**: *Absolute column, relative row reference*: Maintain the same column address, but change the row address when copying a cell.
- ~**Col**$**Row**: *Relative column, absolute row reference*: Change the column address, but maintain the row address when copying a cell.

Consider the following session that demonstrates all four forms of cell references:

	A	B	C	D
1	1	2		
2	3	4		

Figure F.16. Cell Data

Enter data (Figure F.16):
- Insert a spreadsheet.
- Enter the numbers as shown.

	A	B	C	D
1	1	2	1	2
2	3	4	3	4

Figure F.17. Relative Column— Relative Row

Use relative references (Figure F.17):
- Enter the formula ~**A1** in cell C1.
- Copy cell C1 into cells C2, D1, and D2.
- Maple makes these formulas: Cell C2 has ~**A2**; cell D1 has ~**B1**; cell D2 has ~**B2**.

	A	B	C	D
1	1	2	1	1
2	3	4	1	1

Figure F.18. Absolute Column— Absolute Row

Use absolute references (Figure F.18):
- Enter the formula ~$**A**$**1** in cell C1.
- Copy cell C1 into cells C2, D1, and D2.
- Maple makes these formulas: Cells C1, C2, D1, and D2 all have the formula ~$**A**$**1**.

	A	B	C	D
1	1	2	1	1
2	3	4	3	3

Figure F.19. Absolute Column— Relative Row

Use mixed references (Figure F.19):
- Enter the formula ~$**A1** in cell C1.
- Copy cell C1 into cells C2, D1, and D2.
- Maple makes these formulas: Cells C1 and D1 have ~$**A1**; cells C2 and D2 have ~$**A2**.

	A	B	C	D
1	1	2	1	2
2	3	4	1	2

Figure F.20. Relative Column— Absolute Row

Use mixed references (Figure F.20):
- Enter the formula ~**A**$**1** in cell C1.
- Copy cell C1 into cells C2, D1, and D2.
- Maple makes these formulas: Cells C1 and C2 have ~**A**$**1**; cells D1 and D2 have ~**B**$**1**.

Never forget to precede all Maple cell references with a tilde (~)! Also, although Maple does not distinguish between uppercase and lowercase column labels, you should generally avoid mixing cases—stick to uppercase letters. Consult **?references** for more information.

F.16 SPREADSHEET TIPS

When evaluating cells, remember that you are still using Maple expressions. Take note of the following suggestions:

- Never terminate or separate expressions in cells with semicolons and colons. If you do, Maple will report an error message, like "22, ';' *unexpected*". Consequently, use separate cells for distinct statements. See Chapter 4 for a discussion on statements.

- Never assign expressions within a cell using the assignment operator `:=`. If you do, Maple will report an error message, like "24, ':=' *unexpected*". However, Maple will permit `assign(Name, value)`. See Section F.17 for more details.

- Beware that Maple may often replace a blank space in the Context Bar with a multiplication operator (`*`). For instance, if you enter `1 a`, Maple converts the input to `1*a`.

- Access library packages outside of the spreadsheet before using functions from those packages. See `?with` for more details.

- By default, all "blank," or inactive, Maple cells have the value 0. For instance, try entering `evalb(~A2=0)` inside a cell A1 of a newly inserted spreadsheet. Maple will report the output *true*.

- Avoid *circular references*, which are cells that refer to themselves. For instance, try entering `~A1` inside cell A1. Maple will report that your expressions is illegal with the error message, `Circular reference in ~A1`. Click inside the Context Bar to delete this travesty of referencing.

F.17 EXTRACTING DATA FROM SPREADSHEETS

Currently, two methods transfer data from a spreadsheet back into an execution group outside of the spreadsheet. The quickest method involves the following steps:

- Select a range of cells inside a spreadsheet.
- Select Edit→Copy.
- Place your cursor in an execution group.
- Select Edit→Paste.

If you copy only one cell, Maple will simply replicate the cell output as a single statement of Maple input. If you copy multiple cells, Maple tabulates the data as a matrix. Maple will insert the expression `MATRIX([list1, list2,...])` into your current execution group, assuming that you are using Maple Notation. Each list represents a row from your selected range of cells. Maple will automatically fill "gaps," or empty cells, with the value 0. You can then access individual elements by extracting the matrix components.

Currently, you cannot assign expressions inside an execution group with the assignment operator `:=`. Thus, you may wish to create a small Maple procedure called **ssa**, as follows:

ASSIGN SPREADSHEET VALUES

Transfer information between spreadsheets and execution groups.

```
> ssa := proc(variable,expression)          Assign a procedure called ssa.

       assign(variable,expression);     Assign variable to expression.

       variable = expression;      Show the output variable = expression.

  end:                                            End the procedure.
```

When you use the "Spreadsheet Assign" procedure, or **ssa**, Maple will assign cell contents to another name. You may then use the name elsewhere outside of the spreadsheet. Consider the following example:

	A	B	C
1	1	12	
2	2	-1	
3	3	*a*	

Figure F.21.   Data Entry

Enter some data (Figure F.21):
- Restart your worksheet.
- Assign the **ssa** procedure in an execution group.
- Enter a spreadsheet with the data as shown to the left.

	A	B	C
1	1	12	▨
2	2	-1	■
3	3	*a*	

Figure F.22.   Assign First Entry

Type a formula (Figure F.22):
- Type the following formula into cell C1 (do not press ↵!): **ssa(X[~$A1],~$B1])**.
- Crosshatches will appear in cell C1, assuming you did not press ↵. (If you did press ↵, start over again.).
- Select the cells C1, C2, and C3 with your mouse.

	A	B	C
1	1	12	$X_1 = 12$
2	2	-1	$X_2 = -1$
3	3	*a*	$X_3 = a$

Figure F.23.   Assign Column

Assign a column (Figure F.23):
- Select Spreadsheet→Fill→Down. Maple will fill in the sequence of values.
- If Maple reports the error message, "*Error, (in , assign,) ,invalid arguments*", unassign X: Enter **X:='X'** inside an execution group and try again.

To demonstrate that Maple assigned *X*, try the following execution group:

CHECK SPREADSHEET VALUES

> `seq(X[i],i=1..3);`

Click inside an execution group.

Produce the sequence X_1, X_2, X_3.

$$12, -1, a$$

Maple correctly accessed the spreadsheet cells.

Consult **?matrix**, **?selection**, and Appendix E for more information.

F.18 SHARING DATA FROM EXECUTION GROUPS

Spreadsheets "remember" names that you have assigned in a worksheet. For instance, do not enter **x:=1** inside an execution group unless you intend for your spreadsheets to replace *x* with the value of 1.

In order to access a list that you entered outside of a spreadsheet, first assign a list, such as **L:=[1,-2,b]**:

ASSIGN A LIST

Assign a list inside an execution group.

```
> restart:
```
Restart Maple.

```
> L:=[1,-2,b]:
```
Assign L to the list $[1, -2, b]$.

Insert a spreadsheet, and then, follow these steps:

	A	B
1	1	
2	2	
3	3	

Figure F.24.   Data Entry

<u>Enter some data</u> (Figure F.24):
- Restart your worksheet.
- Enter the data as shown to the left.

	A	B
1	1	1
2	2	
3	3	

Figure F.25.   Assign First Entry

<u>Enter a formula</u> (Figure F.25):
- Enter this formula into cell B1:
  `L[~A1]`.
- Select cells B1, B2, and B3.

	A	B
1	1	1
2	2	-2
3	3	b

Figure F.26.   Enter Column

<u>Enter the column</u> (Figure F.26):
- Select <u>S</u>preadsheet→<u>F</u>ill→<u>D</u>own for the cells in column B.
- Maple automatically accessed the list values that were stored in *L*.

You should check the formulas inside cells B1, B2, and B3. By filling down, Maple automatically adjusted the relative references from `~A1` to `~A2`, for cell B2, and `~A3`, for cell B3. Consult `?selection` for more information.

F.19 CELL PROPERTIES

Maple's spreadsheet cells have four properties that you can modify: *cell alignment, color, evaluation method*, and *precision*. For each of these properties, perform these steps:

- Select the cells that you wish to modify.
- Select <u>S</u>preadsheet→<u>P</u>roperties . . . .
- Change the properties of the cell(s) inside the Spreadsheet Properties window.
- Click on **Apply** to test the effects of your changes. Click on **OK** when finished.

Modify these properties with the following selections in the Spreadsheet Properties window:

- *Alignment*: To change where Maple displays contents of a cell, choose either **Left**, **Center**, or **Right** under the **Alignment** category.
- *Color*: To change cell color, choose another color under **CellColor**.

- *Evaluation Method*: To change how Maple evaluates and displays expressions, select either Symbolic or FloatingPoint. However, if your input contains decimal points, Maple will use floating-point evaluation regardless of your choice. Be sure to set Precision for floating-point computations.
- *Precision*: To change how many significant figures, or just digits, Maple uses during floating-point evaluations, change the DuringCalculation field. Complicated numerical-analysis might require a higher setting than the DisplayedDecimals field. This field determines the number of digits Maple displays to the right of the decimal point.

Consult **?properties** for more information. Other modifications you can make to a spreadsheet's appearance are discussed in the next section.

F.20 CUSTOMIZING APPEARANCE

To resize a spreadsheet,

- Activate the spreadsheet such that you see the ↖ cursor. Then, drag on one on the black squares with your mouse.
- Or, select Spreadsheet→ResizeToGrid if you prefer to have only whole cells shown.

To resize rows and columns using the headers,

- Point your mouse to the right of a column header or the bottom of a row header. The ⇕ or ⇔ cursor will appear.
- Click and drag your mouse. Release the mouse button when finished resizing.

To resize rows and columns using the menus,

- Select cells from the rows and/or columns whose height and/or width that you wish to change.
- Rows: Select Spreadsheet→Row→Height.... Change the value of height in pixels that appears in the window that pops up and click OK.
- Columns: Select Spreadsheet→Column→Width.... Change the value of width in pixels that appears in the window that pops up and click OK.

To insert rows and columns,

- Rows: Place your cursor below the position where you wish to insert a row. Select Spreadsheet→Row→Insert.
- Columns: Place your cursor to the right of the position where you wish to insert a column. Select Spreadsheet→Column→Insert.

To delete rows and columns,

- Select cells from the row(s) or column(s) that you wish to delete.
- Select either Spreadsheet→Row→Delete or Spreadsheet→Column→Delete.

To remove the spreadsheet headers,

- Activate the spreadsheet.
- Select Spreadsheet→ShowBorder.

Consult **?appearance** for more information.

F.21 PRINTING

When you print your Maple worksheet, Maple will also print all inserted spreadsheets according to these features:

- Currently, you cannot print spreadsheets separately from Maple worksheets.
- Maple prints only the cell values, not the formulas with cell references.
- Blank cells are printed as empty boxes.
- The cells with the highest row and/or column addresses define the area that Maple will print. That is, the cells that are "farthest" from cell A1 define the outer boundary of the print area.
- Blank spaces (space-bar) are considered valid entries. So, to add "white-space" to your spreadsheet, enter spaces in the cells along the right-hand and bottom borders.
- To change the font in the spreadsheet cells, change the 2D Output font to another style. First, select Format→Style.... Under Style, choose "P Maple Output". Click on Modify... and enter new formats. When finished click on OK, and then, Done. However, you cannot view the changed font until you select File→PrintPreview..., or print the worksheet.

G

Additional Features

This section introduces special features available on some platforms.

G.1 MATLAB INTERFACE

MATLAB is a popular program for numerical analysis. You may call MATLAB routines from within Maple, assuming that you have MATLAB installed. Consult **?matlab** for instructions on how to do so.

G.2 WEB PUBLISHING

You can export worksheets to a HyperText Markup Language (HTML) format. Moreover, Maple will automatically convert plots and animations. Consult Worksheet Interface . . . Managing Files and Worksheets . . . export to HTML in Maple's Help Browser for a full description of features. Also, investigate **?vrml** for creating special three-dimensional graphics that can be read by browsers with Virtual Reality Modeling Language (VRML) capabilities.

G.3 SMARTPLOTS

Smartplots provide initial plots of functions without much initial tinkering on your part. Select Insert→Plot→2D or 3D to insert a smartplot. After entering a smartplot, you can then enhance various features of it. Consult **?smartplot** for more information.

H

Transition to New Maple

H.1 GENERAL INFORMATION

Experienced users of Maple V Release 4 (VR4) should select Help→What'sNew or What'sNew . . . Overview to review the recent changes in Maple. For a summary of basic changes, select

- What'sNew . . . R4andR5Compatibility
- What'sNew . . . significantchanges

Common changes that Maple V Release 5 (VR5) implements are briefly reviewed in this appendix. For access to files that contain updates from previous releases, consult **?update**.

H.2 STRINGS

In VR4 and earlier versions of Maple, names were a special case of strings. Strings were defined as any group of characters surrounded by backquotes, such as **'I was a string'**. VR5 now defines strings with double quotation marks (**""**), such as **"I am now a string"**. Note that backquotes now define symbols, as discussed in Chapter 3. In general, you can still use symbols in many places that once required strings. However, in functions such as **plot**, you should now employ strings. Consult **?string** and **?symbol** for more information.

H.3 DITTOS

In previous releases, double quotation marks (**"**, **""**, **"""**) represented Maple's dittos. Because the double-quotes are now reserved for strings, percent signs (**%**, **%%**, **%%%**) now represent dittos. Consult **?ditto** for more information.

H.4 LABELS

In previous versions of Maple, long expressions were abbreviated by a label, such as **%1**, where the number indicated a new label. You may now start names with the **%** character.

Beware that Maple might not accept a number as the second character, however, because of potential conflicts with other labels. Consult **?name** and **?labeling** for more information.

H.5 PLOTS

In VR4, when using 3D plots, the user had to continually redraw the plot in order to view changes after spinning the bounding box. With releases after 5.0, users can spin a bounding box without having to worry about redrawing the plot. Consult What'sNew . . . graphics for further changes.

H.6 PACKAGES

Consult What'sNew . . . packages . . . Introduction for a list of recent changes to Maple's library packages. See **?with** and **?index[packages]** for more information.

Suggested Web Resources

Check out the following Web sites for more information on the topics introduced in this text.

I.1 MAPLE INFORMATION

http://www.maplesoft.com
http://www.birkhauser.com/journals/mapletech/summary.htm

I.2 MATHEMATICS

http://e-math.ams.org
http://euclid.math.fsu.edu/Science/math.html
http://www.ams.org/mathscinet

I.3 CHAPTER SPOTLIGHTS AND APPLICATIONS

1. Petronas Towers: http://www.petronas.com
2. Zebra Mussels: http://www.glsc.nbs.gov and http://www.ansc.purdue.edu/sgnis
3. Unicode: http://www.unicode.org
4. Hewlett-Packard: http://www.hp.com
5. Interval Analysis: http://cs.utep.edu/interval-comp/main.html
6. Niagara Falls: http://www.dams.org and http://www.niagara-usa.com
7. Ford: http://www.ford.com
8. Pipelines: http://www.coastalcorp.com, http://www.anrpl.com, and http://www.aga.org
9. Construction Safety: http://osh.net
10. Boundary Elements: http://www.gpbest.com and http://www.ce.udel.edu/faculty/cheng/benet/
11. MCEER: http://mceer.buffalo.edu

J

Complete Solutions to Practice! Problems

J.1 WARNING!

Many practice problems assume or require you to:

- Clear variable assignments by unassignment (see Section 4.2), or
- Refresh your worksheet with the **restart** command (see Section 4.3).

J.2 CHAPTER 2: MAPLE OVERVIEW

1. Select Help→AboutMapleV.... Then, click OK.
2. Select Help→NewUser'sTour.
3. Ensure that the menu selection has either a check mark (✔) or a depressed box to the left. Little help windows pop-up.
4. Save your current Maple options for future sessions.
5. Open with File→New. Close with File→Close.
6. Type **?** and then press the Enter key (↵).
7. According to Maple's on-line glossary, the Window menu "contains commands to arrange, close, or list worksheets in the current Maple session."
8. Select File→CloseHelpTopic.
9. Select WorksheetInterface...Reference...Glossary.
10. In Maple Notation, enter **1/2** to produce $\frac{1}{2}$.
11. Check Options→InputDisplay→MapleNotation.
12. Enter **1+2+3**.
13. Enter **1+1: 2*2;**.
14. Maple will ignore the text that follows the # character.
15. You see normally invisible characters that denote spaces (·) and paragraphs (¶).
16. Try Insert→TextInput for one method of text entry.
17. Enter **1+1**, **1-1**, and **1*2** inside separate execution groups. Try pressing the F4 key for a shortcut for joining execution groups. Press Enter (↵) when finished.
18. Enter **x:=2;X:=1;**.
19. Enter **x; X;**. Maple is case sensitive.

20. Enter **restart; x; X;**. Entering **restart** erased the values of *x* and *X*.
21. Enter **y:=2*sqrt(x)**.
22. Enter **plot(y,x=0..100,title="Hello, I am a plot")**.
23. Click inside the open worksheet and select File→SaveAs....
24. Select File→New. Follow the solution to Problem 23 in order to save.
25. Click inside the open worksheet, and select File→Print.... Use this method to print Maple worksheets. Don't even *think* you can open PostScript files as Maple worksheets.

J.3 CHAPTER 3: MAPLE LANGUAGE

1. **1** is an integer, **+** is an operator, **sin** is a name ("function"), **and** is an operator (and also, a "reserved word"), **:** is punctuation ("statement separator"), **()** is punctuation, **"Test Plot"** is a string.
2. The portion **1+1** is an expression. Entering the entire input **1+1;** creates a statement.
3. Maple classifies **restart** as a statement. (See **?restart** and **?index[statement]**.)
4. The expression $-1 + 2^3$ uses negation (**-**), addition (**+**), and exponentiation (**^**).
5. Enter **a:=1;b:=2;a*b;ab;**. The input **a*b** yields 2, while **ab** yields just *ab*.
6. Enter **4<=5;5>=4;**. Maple shows $4 \leq 5$ for both inputs.
7. First, enter **restart**. Next, enter **(a^2)/(A+(1/a))**.
8. You get an error message. The input misses the last parenthesis: **sin((a+b))** or **sin(a+b)**.
9. Entering **[1+3]/4** does not mean $\frac{(1+3)}{4} = 1$ in Maple! Maple reserves square brackets for other uses, as specified in Chapter 5.
10. Enter **1^(2^3)** to evaluate 1^{2^3} because exponentiation is nonassociative.
11. You can use **'1'** as a Maple name, but not the lone digit **1**.
12. Enter **Success := Practice + Patience**. You could also enter **'Success := Practice + Patience'**.
13. The Maple names *Ira* and *ira* do not match due to case sensitivity.
14. Enter **type(Alpha,protected);type(Beta,protected);**. Maple protects **Beta**, but not **Alpha**.

J.4 CHAPTER 4: EXPRESSIONS AND ASSIGNMENTS

1. All of these items are expressions.
2. The input **x:=10** is an assignment between two expressions, but not an expression itself.
3. The input **J=72** forms an equation expression. The input **J:=72** assigns *J* to 72.
4. Enter **J:=72; J;**.
5. Enter **J:='J';J;**. You should see the corresponding output $J := J$ and *J*.
6. Open two worksheets. Assign a variable inside one worksheet. Check the variable's value in the other worksheet. A shared worksheet will show the value, whereas a parallel worksheet will not.
7. Select Parallel Server Maple V or enter **xmaple -km p**, depending on your platform. See Problem 6.
8. Maple should report 3, the third-to-last expression you entered.
9. Maple simplifies $\sin(x + x)$ to $\sin(2x)$, assuming that you have not assigned *x* to a very complicated expression.
10. Enter **A:=x+y; (2*A)/(4*A);**.
11. Maple does not know whether *x* is positive or negative. Enter **x:='x': assume(x>=0);** **sqrt(x^2);**. Maple reports *x~*, where the tilde (~) indicates that *x* now carries an assumption.

12. Input 1: Maple reports in succession B, 1, and then 1.
    Input 2: Maple reports in succession A, 1, and then 2.

13. Maple computes $\frac{2^2}{4}$ primarily by automatic simplification. Maple reduces 2^2 to 4 and then, $\frac{4}{4}$ to 1.

14. Although the forward quotes ($'\,'$) delay evaluation, automatic simplification typically activates before evaluation. Therefore, the input $'1+2'$ produces the value 3.

J.5 CHAPTER 5: MAPLE TYPES

1. The surface type is **function**. Check with **type(sin(x+y),function)**. The structured type is **function(addition)**. Check with **type(sin(x+y), function('+'))**.

2. Automatic simplification reduces **1+2** before **whattype** checks the expression.

3. Just enter **72/42**. Maple produces $\frac{12}{7}$.

4. No, Maple cannot compute integers from decimal-number operations.

5. Enter **123.0;**, **1.230e2;**, or **1.230E2;** to produce 123.0.

6. Maple uses integer operations. Enter the expression using decimal points or try the **evalf** function from **evalf(123*10^(-1))**. Consult **?evalf** and Chapter 9.

7. The expressions sin 0 and 10.1 are rational. The expressions $\sqrt{2}$ and e are not.

8. Enter **4^(1/3)** to yield the exact form $4^{\left(\frac{1}{3}\right)}$. Enter **4.0^(1/3)** to yield 1.587401052.

9. Each input evaluates to I.

10. Enter **sqrt(2)** or **I*sqrt(2)**.

11. Enter **(1+2*I)*(-1-I)**.

12. Enter **evalf(Pi,5)**.

13. Enter **false; gamma; infinity; true; Catalan; FAIL; Pi;**.

14. Enter **-infinity**.

15. Enter **beta := 1**.

16. Enter **Beta := 1**. Maple will warn you that **Beta** is protected.

17. You cannot use strings here! Enter **'I love'/'using Maple!'**, instead.

18. Consult **?$**. The statement produces the sequence 0, 1, 4, 9.

19. Enter **i:='i': S:=i^3 $ i=0..3**.

20. Enter **S[1]** for the first element, S_1. Enter **S[2]** for the second element, S_2.

21. Enter **SL:=[S]**.

22. Enter **SS:={S}**.

23. Enter **evalb(SS=SL)**. No, Maple distinguishes between sets and lists, even if they contain the same elements. You can, however, convert the types using **convert**.

J.6 CHAPTER 6: FUNCTIONS

1. Enter **sin(theta)^2+cos(theta)^2**.

2. Enter **simplify(%)** or **simplify(sin(theta)^2+cos(theta)^2)**.

3. Enter **y:=sin(t)**.

4. You cannot use a trigonometric term to construct a polynomial.

5. Enter **x:='x'; A:=x^2-1; B:=x^2+3x+2;**.

6. Enter **C1:=A*A+A*B**.

7. Enter **C2:=A/B**.

8. Enter **expand(C1); factor(C2);**.

9. Enter `r:=rem(P1,P2,x,'q'); q;`.

10. Enter `test:=expand(P2*q)+r; evalb(test=P1);`.

11. Enter `roots(x^3-3*x-2)`. Maple reports [[2, 1], [−1, 2]]. Thus, root 2 factors the polynomial once. Root −1 factors the polynomial twice.

12. Enter `R:=convert(120*degrees,radians); convert(R,degrees);`.

13. Enter `sec(convert(30*degrees,radians))`. Maple produces $\frac{2}{3}\sqrt{3}$.

14. Trick question! tan0 is *undefined*: You cannot divide by zero. Maple produces an error.

15. Enter `convert(arcsin(0.35),degrees)`. The result is approximately 20.5°.

16. Enter `simplify(root(-8,3))` for the complex root $1 + i\sqrt{3}$. Enter `surd(-8,3)` for the real root −2.

17. Enter `log[7](163.0)` or use `evalf(log[7](163))` to find $x = 2.617669875$. Assign x to the result and enter `7^x` to check your answer.

18. Enter `Digits:=6; exp(1.0);` or `evalf(exp(1),6)` to find $e = 2.71828$.

19. Enter `assume(x>0); ln(exp(x));`, and Maple will produce $x\sim$. The natural logarithm and exponential functions are inverse functions. Try also `restart: readlib(invfunc): invfunc[exp](y);`.

20. Enter `abs(-18); abs(0); abs(18);`. Maple will produce 18, 0, and 18.

21. Enter `restart: Re(exp(I*x))+Im(exp(I*x))`. Maple produces $\Re(\mathbf{e}^{(Ix)}) + \Im(\mathbf{e}^{(Ix)})$. To produce $\cos x + \sin x$, use `convert` and `evalc`.

22. Enter `S:=2^i $ i=0..3`. If i is already assigned, Maple will produce an error message. In that case, try either `S:=seq(2^i,i=0..3)` or `S:=2^('i') $ 'i'=0..3`.

23. Enter `k:='k': sum(S[k],k=1..4);` to produce $\sum_{k=1}^{4} S_k = S_1 + S_2 + S_3 + S_4 = 1 + 2 + 4 + 18 = 15$. Why not enter the range `k=0..3`? Because Maple sequence indices start counting from index 1, not 0.

24. Enter `k:='k': product(S[k],k=1..4);` to produce $\prod_{k=1}^{4} S_k = S_1 \times S_2 \times S_3 \times S_4 = 1 \times 2 \times 4 \times 8 = 64$. See also `?mul`.

25. Enter `x:='x': dis := x -> x^3+x^2+x+1;`. You can also enter `x:='x': poly:=x^3+x^2+x+1: dis:=unapply(poly,x);`. See `?unapply` for more details.

26. Enter `dis(-1); dis(1);`. Maple will produce the answers 0 and 4.

27. Enter `plot(dis(x),x=-1..1)`.

28. Enter `restart: f := (x,y,z) -> x+y+z;`.

J.7 CHAPTER 7: MANIPULATING EXPRESSIONS

1. Enter `x:='x': convert(RootOf(x^2+1=0),radical);`. Maple evaluates $\sqrt{x^2} = \sqrt{-1}$ and determines $x = i$.

2. Entering `convert(438,float)` produces 438. (decimal point included).

3. Enter `A:=convert(sin(x),exp)`. Next, enter `simplify(A)`.

4. Enter `A:=sin(x)^2+cos(x)^2: combine(A); simplify(A);`. Maple produces the same result of 1 for both `combine` and `simplify`.

5. Enter `x:='x': y:='y': combine(sin(x)*sin(y));`. Maple produces $\frac{1}{2}\cos(x-y) - \frac{1}{2}\cos(x+y)$.

6. Enter `simplify(x*(x+1)-x^2)` to produce $2x^2 - x$. Try also `normal`.

7. Enter `normal(x+y/x)` to produce factored normal form $\frac{x^2+y}{x}$.

8. Enter `rationalize((x^2-1)/sqrt(x+1))` to produce $\sqrt{x+1}\,(x - 1)$.

9. Entering `expand(factor(x^2+3*x+2))` produces the polynomial $x^2 + 3x + 2$. For polynomials, `expand` and `factor` are inverse functions.

10. Enter `A:=combine(sin(x)*sin(y)); expand(A);` to produce $\sin(x)\sin(y)$.

11. Enter **expand((x+2)/(x+3)^3)** to produce $\dfrac{x}{(x+3)^3} + 2\dfrac{1}{(x+3)^3}$. **normal** is ineffective when used alone.

12. To fully expand $\dfrac{x+2}{(x+3)^3}$, enter **A:=(x+2)/(x+3)^3: Anew := expand(expand (numer(A))/expand(denom(A)));**.

13. Entering **restart: P1:=x*y-(x^2+1)*y; P2:=collect(P1,x); P3:=sort(P2);** produces the output $P1 := xy - (x^2 + 1)y$, $P2 := -yx^2 + xy - y$, and $P3 := -x^2y + xy - y$.

14. Enter **A:=1+sin(x+y): op(0,A); op(A);** to produce the surface-type, plus (+), and operands, 1 and sin($x + y$). You can also enter **whattype(A)** to determine the surface type of expression A.

15. Enter **restart: Spring:=p=k*u; Spring;**.

16. Maple automatically converts greater-than (>) expressions into less-than (<) form. Thus, entering **lhs(2>1)** produces 1, and entering **rhs(2>1)** produces 2.

J.8 CHAPTER 8: GRAPHICS

1. Enter **plot(x,x=0..10)**.

2. Point the mouse on the plot and click the left mouse button. Point the cursor of the mouse at one of the corners of the selected plot.

3. Click the mouse button and drag the corner of the plot.

4. Make sure that you have first selected the plot. Next, select Edit→Copy. Move the cursor to the new position. Then, select Edit→Paste.

5. Enter **restart: plot(y^2-1,y=0..1);**. The variable y is independent, whereas the variable x is dependent.

6. Enter **plot(1/x,x,y=-10..10,discont=true)**. Without the range of the vertical axis, your plot might appear very flat. Note how Maple automatically supplied a horizontal range.

7. Enter **f := x -> x*sin(x); plot(f(x),x=0..Pi);**.

8. Enter **plot(exp(-x²),x=-inifinity..infinity)**.

9. Enter **plot(tan(x),x=-Pi..Pi,-10..10,discont=true, labels=["x", "tan(x)"], title="Tangent")**. Without a vertical range of **-10..10** your plot will not illustrate important features of the tangent function.

10. Enter **plot({x+1,-x-1},x=-2..2)** to display a multiple plot of the functions $f_1(x)$ and $f_2(x)$.

11. Enter **A:=plot(x+1,x=-2..2): B:=plot(-x-1,x=-2..2):**.

12. Enter **with(plots)** to access **display** if you have not already done so. Next, enter **display({A,B})**.

13. Enter **plot([cos(t),sin(t),t=0..2*Pi],scaling=CONSTRAINED)**. You drew a circle of radius unity. (Why? The equation $x^2 + y^2 = \cos^2 t + \sin^2 t = 1$ is the equation for a circle with a radius of 1.)

14. Enter **plot({cos(t),sin(t)},t=0..2*Pi)**. This input instructs Maple to plot both sine and cosine functions on the same plot. The previous problem plotted only one function that was expressed as two parametric functions.

15. Enter **plot3d(exp(x^2-y^2),x=-1..1,y=-1..1)**.

16. Enter **plot3d(x+y,x=-1..1,y=-1..1)**. This surface is a plane.

17. Enter **plot3d(log(x-y^2),x=1..1.5,y=1..1.1, orientation=[135,45])**.

18. Enter this sequence of Maple inputs:

```
[> with(plots): x:='x': r:=0..10:
[> P1:=plot(x,x=r): P2:=plot(x^2,x=r):
[> TP1:=textplot([8,15,"x"]): TP2:=textplot([8,80,"x^2"]):
[> display({P1,P2,TP1,TP2});
```

19. Enter **plot([[0,0],[1,1],[2,0],[0,0]],axes=none)**. Why enter the second "**[0,0]**"? Maple needs to know where to connect the previous point (**[2,0]**).

20. You are plotting in cylindrical coordinates. Enter **plot3d(z-theta^2, theta=0..100, z=-1..1, coords=cylindrical)**.

21. The library package **plots** contains the function **implicitplot**. If you have not already entered **with(plots)**, try **with(plots,implicitplot)**, as described in Appendix D. Then, enter **implicitplot(x^2+y^2=1,x=-1..1,y=-1..1)**. (The equation $x^2 + y^2 = 1$ describes a circle of radius unity.) When using **implicitplot**, you should experiment with different range sizes to cover portions of the implicit function that you might otherwise miss.

22. Enter **with(plottools,circle); display(circle([1,1]));**.

23. Enter these Maple input statements:

```
[> restart:with(plots):
[> opts:=frames=10,view=-20..20,axes=none,labels=["",""]:
[> A:=animate(tan(x*t),x=0..100,t=0..1,opts):
[> display(A,insequence=false);
```

J.9 CHAPTER 9: SUBSTITUTING, EVALUATING, AND SOLVING

1. Enter **restart: EQN:=y=m*x+b;**. Recall that the name *EQN* stores an equation.

2. Entering **subs({x=1,m=2,b=0},EQN)** produces the output $y = 2$. Enter just **y** to check *y*'s value. Maple should produce only *y* because **subs** does not assign.

3. Although $\sin 0 = 0$, **subs** does not evaluate expressions. Thus, entering **subs(x=0, sin(x))** produces just sin(0). Investigate **eval** later in Chapter 9 for details on evaluating substituted expressions.

4. Entering **subs(a*b=c,a*b*c)** will not produce c^2 because the expression *ab* is not a surface-type operand of *abc*. (Enter **op(a*b*c)** to check.) Instead, enter **algsubs (a*b=c,a*b*c)**.

5. Entering **eval(x^2+cos(x),x=2)** produces $4 + \cos(2)$.

6. Entering **eval((x^2-y^2)/(x+y),{x=2,y=3})** yields -1.

7. Entering **eval(x*y^2*sin(x*t),x*y=1)** does not directly evaluate the expression because *xy* is not an operand. Instead, you can trick Maple by entering **eval(x*y^2*sin(x*t),x=1/y)** to produce $y \sin\left(\frac{t}{y}\right)$.

8. Entering **solve(sin(x)=(1/2)*sqrt(3),x)** yields $\frac{1}{3}\pi$.

9. Entering **S:=solve(a*x^2+b*x+c=0,{x})** yields the solution set

$$S := \left\{ x = \frac{1}{2}\frac{-b + \sqrt{b^2 - 4ac}}{a} \right\}, \left\{ x = \frac{1}{2}\frac{-b - \sqrt{b^2 - 4ac}}{a} \right\}.$$

10. Enter **x1:=S[1]; x2:=S[2];**.

11. Entering **_EnvAllSolutions:=true: solve(sin(x)=0,x);** yields $\pi\_Z1\sim$. Maple uses the environment variable $\_Z1\sim$ to indicate the set of all integers.

12. Enter either **fsolve(x^x=2,x)** or **solve(x^x=2.0)** to produce 1.559610470.

13. Enter **fsolve(sin(x)=0,x,x=10..20)**. Note that you should always check your results! Although Maple produces 15.70796327, other answers still satisfy the equation.

14. Entering **fsolve(sin(x)=0,x,avoid={x=0,x=Pi,x=-Pi})** produces $-6.283...$ (approximately 2π).

15. Enter the following Maple input statements:

```
[> x:='x': P:=x^2+4*x+3=0:
[> S:=solve(P,{x});
[> eval(P,S[1]); eval(P,S[2]);
```

Maple produces the output $S := \{x = -3\}, \{x = -1\}$ for **solve**, and $0 = 0$ for both **eval** statements.

16. Entering **map(subs, [S], P)** produces $[0 = 0, 0 = 0]$. Because you produced identities, you verified your solution set.

17. Entering **allvalues(RootOf(_Z^2+1))** yields the complex numbers I and $-I$.

18. Entering **S:=solve(x^5+x+1=0,{x}): evalf(S,2);** yields the output $\{x = -.50 + 85I\}$, $\{x = -.50 - .85I\}$, $\{x = -.77\}$, $\{x = .87 - .75I\}$, and $\{x = .87 + 75I\}$.

19. Entering **solve(x^2>1,x)** produces the lengthy output RealRange($-\infty$, Open(-1)), RealRange(Open(-1), ∞), which translates to $(-\infty < x < -1) \cup (1 < x < \infty)$, or just the intervals $(-\infty, -1) \cup (1, \infty)$. (The symbol $\cup$ means a union between two sets.)

20. Enter **minimize(cos(x));maximize(cos(x));** to produce the extrema -1 and 1. Enter **minimize(tan(x));maximize(tan(x));** to produce the extrema $-\infty$ and ∞.

J.10 CHAPTER 10: SYSTEMS OF EQUATIONS

1. Enter the following Maple input statements:

```
[> restart:
[> P1:=2*x+3*y+z=0:  P2:=2*y+z=-1:  P3:=x+z=2:
[> S:=solve({P1,P2,P3},{x,y,z});
```

Maple produces the solution set $S := \{x = 1, y = -1, z = 1\}$.

2. Entering **subs(S,{P1,P2,P3})** produces the verification $\{0 = 0, -1 = -1, 2 = 2\}$. Assign the solutions with **assign(S)**. Now, enter **x;y;z;** to display the values of $x, y,$ and z.

3. First, enter **x:='x':y:='y':** to erase assigned values. Then, enter **solve({x+y=Pi, sin(x)=y},{x,y})** to produce the solution set $\{x = \pi, y = 0\}$.

4. Enter **solve({x+y=1,2*x+2*y=2},{x,y})**. Maple reports the solution $\{y = y, x = -y + 1\}$ because the equations are multiples of one another, and thus, are linearly dependent. While you can still solve the equations, no unique solution exists.

5. Enter **with(plots): implicitplot({3*x+2*y=-4,-x+3*y=5}, x=-5..5, y=-5..5)**. Check your results with **solve**.

6. Enter **implicitplot({x^2+y^2=1,y=1},x=-2..2,y=-2..2)**. The equations do not intersect on the real plane. However, **solve** will determine an intersection with complex values. Try **complexplot3d** for graphically viewing the results. The real variables x and y form a plane, whereas the imaginary component of the solution set plots perpendicular to that plane.

7. Ensure that you have first entered **with(linalg)**. Enter **p:=vector([p1,p2])**.

8. Enter **type(p,vector)**.

9. Enter **p[1]:=10;p[2]:=20;**.

10. Enter **A:=matrix([[1,2,3],[4,5,6]])**.

11. Matrix A has two rows and three columns.

12. Enter **A[1,2]; A[2,3];**. Maple will produce 2 and 6, respectively.

13. Enter **A:=matrix([[1,2],[2,1]]) + 2*matrix([[-1,0],[0,-1]]) - matrix ([[3,1],[1,3]])**. Next, enter **evalm(A)** to produce the result $\begin{bmatrix} -4 & 1 \\ 1 & -4 \end{bmatrix}$.

14. Enter the following Maple input statements:

```
[> x:='x':y:='y':
[> A:=matrix([[1,2],[2,1]]):
[> b:=vector([x,y]): c:=vector([-1,1]):
[> Ac:=evalm(A&*c);
[> bAc:=evalm(b&*Ac);
```

Maple reports $Ac = [1, -1]$ and $bAc = x - y$.

15. Enter `restart: A:=x+y=2: B:=x-y=0: solve({A,B},{x,y});`. Maple produces the solution set $\{x = 1, y = 1\}$.

16. Enter `with(plots): implicitplot({A,B},x=0..2,y=0..2);`.

17. Enter the following Maple input statements:

    ```
    [> restart:with(linalg):
    [> A:=matrix([[1,1],[1,-1]]):
    [> b:=vector([2,0]):
    [> x:=linsolve(A,b);
    ```

    Maple reports the solution vector $x := [1, 1]$. Also, consult `?genmatrix` to convert your equations to matrix form.

18. Entering `Ax:=multiply(A,x)` yields the result $Ax := [2, 0]$, which is identical to b. To double-check, you can now enter `equal(Ax,b)`. Also, try entering `multiply(inverse(A),b)`.

J.11   CHAPTER 11: INTRODUCTION TO CALCULUS

1. Enter `plot(tan(x),x=0..2*Pi,y=-10..10,discont=true)`.

2. From the previous problem, $\tan \frac{\pi}{2}$ produces a discontinuity that might be positive or negative. Thus, Maple reports *undefined* if you enter `limit(tan(x),x=Pi/2)`. You must specify the direction with which to take the limit—either `limit(tan(x),x=Pi/2, right)` $(-\infty)$ or `limit(tan(x),x=Pi/2,left)` (∞).

3. Enter `readlib(discont):discont(tan(x),x);`. Maple reports $\left\{ \pi\_Z1\sim + \frac{1}{2}\pi \right\}$.

    Thus, values of $x = \frac{n\pi}{2}$ for odd integer-values of n cause discontinuity with $\tan x$. (As shown in Chapter 9, Maple uses environment variables called _Z as placeholders for other values and variables. In this case, variable names that begin with _Z represent integers.)

4. Enter `with(student):h:=-2*Pi..2*Pi: v:=-2..2: showtangent(sin(x), x=Pi/3,x=h,v);`.

5. To use `slope`, you sometimes need to specify the dependent and independent variables, especially for equations with multiple variables. Since a, b, and c are parameters, enter `slope(y=a*x^2+b*x+c,y,x)`. Maple reports $2ax + b$.

6. Entering `Q:=a*x^2+b*x+c; diff(Q,x);` yields the equation of the slope, $2ax + b$.

7. Enter `subs(x=2,diff(Q,x))` to produce $4a + b$.

8. Enter `diff(Q,x,x)` to produce the second derivative $\frac{d^2Q}{dx^2} = 2a$.

9. Entering `diff(x*y^2+x^2*y,x)` yields $\frac{\partial}{\partial x}(xy^2 + x^2y) = y^2 + 2xy$.

10. Enter `int(sin(x),x=0..Pi/2)` to produce $\int_0^{\pi/2} \sin x dx = 1$.

11. Entering `int(sin(x),x)` produces $\int \sin x dx = -\cos(x)$.

12. Along $0 \leq x \leq \pi$, $\sin x$ is above the x-axis. However, along $\pi \leq x \leq 2\pi$, $\sin x$ is below the x-axis. Thus, entering `int(sin(x),x=0..2*Pi)` yields zero. To compute the total area, enter instead `int(sin(x),x=0..Pi) - int(sin(x), x=Pi..2*Pi)`. Maple will produce 4.

13. Entering `int(k,u=0..u)` yields the function ku, whereas entering `diff(k*u,u)` yields the parameter k.

14. Entering `F:=int(sin(x),x)` yields the function $-\cos(x)$. Now, you can compute the integral by entering `-cos(2*Pi)-(-cos(0))`. Maple will produce the result 0.

K
Command Summary

K.1 MISCELLANEOUS CHARACTERS

SYMBOL	DESCRIPTION	EXAMPLE	SECTIONS
?	Find help on a topic or function.	`?help`	2.2, 2.4, 3.1, App. B
#	Provide inert comment.	`# Comment`	2.2, 3.1
\	Continue input; insert control character.	`A \ B;`	3.1
!	Escape to operating system. See `?escape`.	`!dir`	3.1
;	Statement separator (show output).	`1+1;`	2.2
:	Statement separator (suppress output).	`1+1:`	2.2
"	String.	`"string"`	2.4, 3.1, 4.2, 5.5, App. H
'	Delay evaluation.	`A:='A'`	4.2, 4.4, 11.5
`	Form symbols and names.	`` `variable 1` ``	2.4, 3.3, 4.2, App. H
~	Indicate that variable carries an assumption. Spreadsheet variable.	$x\sim$ `~A1`	4.4, App. F
( )	Separate expressions and other Maple-language elements.	`A*(B+C)`	2.4, 3.1, 3.2, 6.1
[ ]	Lists; e.g., $[a, b, c]$. Indexing and selection; e.g., L_1, L_2, L_3.	`L:=[a,b,c]` `L[1],L[2],L[3]`	5.5, 6.5, 9.4, 10.4
{ }	Sets.	`S:={a,1}`	5.5

K.2 MAPLE OPERATORS

OPERATOR	DESCRIPTION	EXAMPLE	SECTIONS
%	Ditto; i.e., repeat previous expressions.	%; %%; %%%	4.3, App. H
!	Factorial; e.g., $3!$.	3!	6.5
^, **	Exponentiation; e.g., x^2.	x^2	3.2, 6.1, 6.4
@@	Find inverse function; e.g., $f^{-1}(x)$.	f@@(-1)	6.5
*	Multiply; e.g., $x \times y$.	x*y	2.2, 2.4, 3.2, 6.2
&*	Multiply matrices; e.g., AB.	A&*B	10.4
/	Divide; fraction; e.g., $x \div y = \dfrac{x}{y}$.	x/y	2.4, 3.2, 5.2
intersect	Set intersection; e.g., $A \cap B$.	A intersect B	5.6, 6.5
+	Addition; e.g., $x + y$.	x+y	2.2, 2.4, 3.2, 6.2, 10.4
-	Subtraction; e.g., $x - y$.	x-y	2.4, 3.2, 10.4
union	Set union; e.g., $A \cup B$.	A union B	5.6, 6.5
minus	Set subtraction; e.g., $A - B$.	A minus B	6.5
..	Range; e.g., $a \le x \le b$.	x:=a..b	2.4, 5.5, 8.2
<	Less than; e.g., $1 < 2$.	1 < 2	5.5, 7.5
<=	Less than or equal to; e.g., $1 \le 2$.	1 <= 2	3.2, 5.5
>	Greater than; e.g., $2 > 1$.	2 > 1	5.5, 7.5, 9.6
>=	Greater than or equal to; e.g., $2 \ge 1$.	2 >= 1	3.2, 5.5
=	Equal to; equation; e.g., $y = mx + b$.	y=m*x+b	2.4, 4.2, 5.5, 7.5
<>	Not equal to; e.g., $1 \ne 2$.	1 <> 2	5.5
$	Sequence; e.g., $2^i = 1, 2, 4$ for $i = 0, 1, 2$.	2^i $ i=0..2	5.5, 6.5, 10.6, 11.4
not	Logical negation; e.g., $\neg P$.	not P	5.5
and	Logical "and"; e.g., $P \wedge Q$.	P and Q	5.5, 6.5
or	Logical "or"; e.g., $P \vee Q$.	P or Q	5.5, 6.5
->	Functional notation; e.g., $f(x) = x^2$.	f := x->x^2	6.6, 9.1, 11.3
,	Expression sequence; e.g., $x, y, 2^a$.	x, y, 2^a	4.4, 5.5, 6.1
:=	Assignment; e.g., $x := 2$.	x := 2	2.4, 4.2

K.3 MAPLE RESERVED WORDS AND STATEMENTS

COMMAND	DESCRIPTION	EXAMPLE	SECTIONS
description, options	Label and customize a procedure.	description "this was created by me"	App. E
end	End a procedure.	end	App. E, App. F
ERROR	Supply an error message.	ERROR("wrong!")	App. E
for, from, by, to, in, while, do, od	Repetition statements.	for i from 1 by 1 to 10 do L[i]:=i^2 od;	App. E
if, then, elif, else, fi	Selection statements.	if type(A,even) then print("The value is even.") fi;	App. E
local, global	Declare variables.	local i, temp;	5.4, App. E
proc	Procedure.	proc(A) if(type(A),numeric) then A^2; 2*A; fi; end;	5.4, App. E, App. F
quit, stop, done	Exit Maple.	quit;	2.1
restart	Restart a Maple session without exiting.	restart;	2.4, 3.2, 4.3

K.4 MISCELLANEOUS VARIABLES AND ALIASES

NAME	DESCRIPTION	EXAMPLE	SECTIONS
constants	Print Maple constants: $false$, γ, ∞, $true$, $Catalan$, $FAIL$, π.	constants	5.4
Digits	Number of digits that Maple uses in numerical evaluations; resembles significant figures.	Digits := 3	5.2, 5.4, 9.6
FAIL	Logical "fail".	FAIL	5.4, 5.5
false	Logical "false"; e.g., F.	evalb(1=2)	5.4, 5.5
gamma	Euler's constant, γ.	gamma	5.4, 9.7, App. A
I	Imaginary number, $\sqrt{-1} = i$.	I	5.3, 6.5
infinity	Infinite value, ∞.	infinity	5.4
Pi	Mathematical constant Pi, π.	Pi	5.4, 6.3, App. A
true	Logical "true"; e.g., T.	evalb(1=1)	5.4, 5.5

K.5 MAPLE FUNCTIONS

FUNCTION	DESCRIPTION	EXAMPLE	SECTIONS
abs	Absolute value; e.g., $|x|$.	abs(x)	6.5, 9.6
algsubs	Algebraic substitution.	algsubs(x*y=c,x*y*z)	9.2
alias	Abbreviate Maple names.	alias(I=I,j=sqrt(-1))	5.3, 10.4
allvalues	Find all solutions from a RootOf expression.	allvalues(RootOf(_Z^2+1))	9.6, 9.7
anames	Display currently assigned names.	anames()	4.3, 6.1
angle	Find the angle between two vectors.	with(linalg): angle(A,B)	10.4
animate	Animate a Maple plot.	with(plots): animate(cos(x*t)^2, x=0..10,t=0..10)	8.1, 8.5
arcsin	Inverse of sine function.	arcsin(y/r)	6.3
array	Assign an array.	A:=array(0..10)	App. E
assign	Assign a name.	assign(c=4)	10.2, App. F
assume	Restrict or constrain a variable.	assume(x>0)	4.4, 6.4, 6.7
circle	Plot a circle.	with(plottools): circle([0,0])	10.3
combine	Combine expressions.	combine(sin(x)^2+cos(x)^2)	7.3, 7.4
collect	Collect like-terms inside an expression.	collect(x*(x^2-x*y),x)	7.5, 7.6
convert	Convert expression types.	convert([1,2],set)	5.6, 6.3, 7.2, 7.3
cos	Cosine.	cos(Pi/4)	6.3
cosh	Hyperbolic cosine.	cosh(Pi/4)	7.6
cot	Cotangent.	cot(Pi/4)	6.3
crossprod	Cross product.	with(linalg):crossprod(v1,v2)	10.4
csc	Cosecant.	csc(Pi/4)	6.3
denom	Extract the denominator of a fraction.	denom(a/b)	7.5
det	Determinant of matrix; e.g., $|A|$.	det(A)	10.4
diff	Differentiation.	diff(y(x),x)	7.5, 11.4
display	Display 2D plot structures.	with(plots): display({P1,P2})	8.1, 8.3, 8.5, 10.3
display3d	Display 3D plot structures.	with(plots): display3d({P1,P2})	8.4
dotprod	Dot product.	with(linalg): dotprod(v1,v2)	10.4
dsolve	Solve differential equation.	dsolve(diff(f(x),x)=C)	7.5
equal	Test equality of vectors and matrices.	with(linalg):equal(A,B)	10.4, 10.5
eval	Evaluate an expression.	eval(x^2,x=a)	9.3, 9.4, 9.5, App. E
evalb	Evaluate the Boolean value of an expression.	evalb(1<2)	5.5, 6.5, 9.3
evalc	Evaluate complex expressions.	evalc(2*I+I^3)	6.5, 9.3
evalf	Evaluate a floating-point value of an expression.	evalf(2*Pi)	5.2, 5.4, 6.5, 9.3, 9.6

continued on next page

FUNCTION	DESCRIPTION	EXAMPLE	SECTIONS
evalm	Evaluate an array, like a matrix or vector.	evalm(A+B)	9.3, 10.4
evaln	Evaluate to a name.	A:=evaln(A)	9.3
evalr	Evaluate a range.	readlib(evalr): evalr(INTERVAL(1..2) + INTERVAL(3..4))	5.6, 9.3, App. D
exp	Exponential function; e.g., e^x.	exp(x)	2.5, 6.4
expand	Expand an expression.	expand(x*(x+1))	6.2, 7.4
factor	Factor an expression.	factor(x^2+3*x+2)	6.2, 7.4
Float	Create a floating-point number.	Float(2,3)	5.2
fsolve	Numerically solve an equation.	fsolve(x^3+17*x-3=0,x)	9.4, 10.2
ifactor	Find integer factors of an expression.	ifactor(72)	6.5
Im	Extract the imaginary component of a complex expression.	Im(exp(2*I))	6.5
implicitplot	Plot an implicit function.	with(plots): implicitplot(x^2+y^2=1, x=-1..1,y=-1..1)	8.5, 10.3
int	Integrate an expression.	int(x^2,x=0..1)	11.6
interface	Modify a user-interface variable.	interface(verboseproc=2)	App. D
INTERVAL	Create an interval; e.g., [1, 2].	readlib(evalr): INTERVAL(1..2)	5.6
inverse	Invert a matrix; e.g., A^{-1}.	with(linalg): inverse(A)	10.4, 10.5
lhs	Extract the left-hand side of an expression.	lhs(y=m*x+b)	7.5, 9.4
limit	Find the limit of a function.	limit(tan(x),x=Pi/2,left)	11.2
linsolve	Solve a linear system of equations.	with(linalg):linsolve(A,b)	10.5
ln	Natural logarithm.	ln(x)	6.4
log	Natural logarithm.	log(x)	6.4
log[]	General logarithm.	log[10](x)	6.4
log10	Base-10 logarithm.	readlib(log10): log10(x)	6.4
map	Apply a procedure to each operand in an expression.	map(sin,[0,Pi/2,Pi])	6.5, 9.5
matadd	Add matrices.	with(linalg): matadd(A,B)	10.4
matrix	Create a matrix.	with(linalg): matrix([[1,2],[2,1]])	10.4, 10.5
max	Find a maximum value from a sequence.	max(1,2,3)	5.6
maximize	Find a maximum value of an expression.	maximize(sin(x))	9.6
middlebox	Draw an approximate area below a curve with rectangular boxes.	with(student): middlebox(x^2,x=0..2,n=3)	11.5
middlesum	Evaluate an approximate area below a curve from middle boxes.	with(student): middlesum(x^2,x=0..2,n=3)	11.5
min	Find a minimum value from a sequence.	min(1,2,3)	5.6, 10.6
minimize	Find a minimum value of an expression.	minimize(sin(x))	9.6
multiply	Multiply matrices.	with(linalg): multiply(A,B)	10.4, 10.5

continued on next page

FUNCTION	DESCRIPTION	EXAMPLE	SECTIONS
norm	Evaluate vector or matrix norm.	`with(linalg):` `norm(v,frobenius)`	10.4, App. E
normal	Reduce rational functions.	`normal((x^2-1)/(x+1))`	7.3
numer	Extract the numerator of a fraction.	`numer(a,b)`	7.5
op	Display operands of an expression's surface type.	`op(sin(x+y))`	5.1, 7.5, 9.2
piecewise	Create a piecewise function.	`piecewise(0<x,exp(x))`	6.5, 11.2

pointplot3d	Plot points in 3D.	`with(plots):`
		`pointplot3d([[1,1,1],`
		`[2,2,2]],connect=true)`
			10.6

plot	Plot an expression.	`plot(x^2,x=0..1,y=1..2)`	2.4, 2.5, 8.1, 8.2, 8.3, 8.5
plot3d	Plot a 3D expression.	`plot3d(x*y,x=0..1,y=0..1)`	8.4, 8.5
plotsetup	Customize a plot display.	`plotsetup(ps,` `plotoutput=`test.ps`)`	App. C
print	Print a string, name, or expression.	`print("Ira was here!")`	10.4, App. E
product	Multiply a sequence of values.	`product(x[i],i=1..n)`	6.5
protect	Prevent variable assignment.	`protect(A)`	5.6, 9.7
quo	Evaluate the quotient from polynomial division.	`quo(a,b,x,'r')`	6.2
rationalize	Remove radicals from a denominator.	`rationalize(1/sqrt(2))`	7.3
Re	Extract the real component from a complex expression.	`Re(exp(2*I))`	6.5
readlib	Load a function into Maple's memory.	`readlib(discont)`	5.6, 6.4, App. D
rem	Evaluate the remainder from polynomial division.	`rem(a,b,x,'q')`	6.2
rhs	Extract the right-hand side of an equation.	`rhs(y=m*x+b)`	7.5, 9.4
root	Evaluate the nth root of an expression; e.g., $\sqrt[n]{x}$.	`root(x,n)`	6.4
RootOf	Placeholder for roots of an expression.	`RootOf(x^2+1)`	7.2, 9.6
roots	Evaluate roots of a polynomial.	`roots(x^2+3*x+2)`	6.2, 9.4
scalarmul	Multiply a vector or matrix by a scalar quantity.	`scalarmul(A,c)`	10.4
sec	Secant.	`sec(x)`	6.3
seq	Generate sequence of expressions.	`seq(i^2,i=0..1)`	6.5, 10.6
series	Expand an expression into a series.	`series(cos(x),x=0,6)`	6.5
showtangent	Draw a tangent to a function.	`with(student):` `showtangent(sin(x),x=Pi)`	11.3
simplify	Simplify an expression.	`simplify(sqrt(x^2),symbolic)`	6.4, 6.7, 7.3, 9.2
sin	Sine.	`sin(x)`	6.3
sinh	Hyperbolic sine.	`sinh(x)`	7.6
slope	Evaluate the slope of a polynomial function.	`with(student):` `slope(y=m*x,y,x)`	11.3
smartplot	Create a plot to tinker with.	`smartplot(cos(x))`	8.1, App. G
sort	Sort operands of a list or polynomial.	`sort([b,a])`	7.5

continued on next page

FUNCTION	DESCRIPTION	EXAMPLE	SECTIONS
`solve`	Solve an equation.	`solve(y=m*x+b,x)`	9.4, 9.5, 9.6, 10.2
`sqrt`	Square root; e.g., $\sqrt{x}$.	`sqrt(x)`	2.4, 6.4, 7.3
`subs`	Substitute expressions for operands in another expression.	`subs(x=a,x*y)`	7.6, 9.2, 9.3, 10.2
`sum`	Sum a sequence of expressions.	`sum(x[i],i=1..n)`	6.5, 11.5
`surd`	Find real-number roots.	`surd(-1,3)`	6.4
`table`	Create a table expression.	`me:=table([name1="Dave", name2="Schwartz"])`	App. E
`tan`	Tangent.	`tan(x)`	6.3
`textplot`	Label plots with text strings.	`with(plots): textplot([0,1,"Hello"])`	8.5, 10.3
`transpose`	Transpose a vector or matrix.	`with(linalg): transpose(A)`	10.4
`type`	Check an expression's type.	`type(1,integer)`	3.3, 5.1, 5.5, 6.2, App. A
`value`	Evaluate inert functions.	`with(student): value(Int(x^2,x))`	11.4, 11.5
`vector`	Create a vector.	`with(linalg): vector([1,2])`	10.4, 10.5
`whattype`	Determine an expression's type.	`whattype(sin(x))`	5.1, 5.5
`with`	Access a library package.	`with(linalg)`	8.1, 8.3, 10.3, 10.4, 11.1, App. D, App. E

Bibliography

MAPLE RERERENCES

Adams, S. G. *Maple Talk*. New Jersey: Prentice Hall, 1997.

Heal, K. M, M. L. Hansen, and K. M. Rickard. *Maple V: Learning Guide*. New York: Springer, 1998.

Monagan, M. B., K. O Geddes, K. M. Heal, G. Labahn, and S. M. Vorkoetter. *Maple V: Programming Guide*. New York: Springer, 1998.

Nicolaides, R. and N. Walkington. *Maple: A Comprehensive Introduction*. Melbourne, Australia: Cambridge University Press, 1996.

ENGINEERING, MATHEMATICS, AND SCIENCE RERERENCES

Throughout your education, your professors will advise you to keep your books. As I discovered, you just never know when they will become handy. . . .

American Institute of Steel Construction (AISC). *Torsional Analysis of Steel Members*. Chicago: AISC, 1983.

American Society of Civil Engineers (ASCE). *Pipeline Design for Hydrocarbon Gases and Liquids*. New York: ASCE, 1975.

Blank, L. T. and A. J. Tarquin. *Engineering Economy*. New York: WCB/McGraw-Hill, 1998.

Boyce, W. E. and R. C. DiPrima. *Elementary Differential Equations and Boundary Value Problems*. New York: John Wiley & Sons, 1986.

Das, B. M. *Principles of Foundation Engineering*. Boston: PWS-Kent Publishing Company, 1990.

Hwang, N. H. C. and C. E. Hita. *Fundamentals of Hydraulic Engineering Systems*. New Jersey: Prentice Hall, 1987.

Lindeburg, M. R. *Engineer-in-Training Reference Manual*. Belmont, CA: Professional Publications, Inc., 1998.

Neumaier, A. *Interval Methods for Systems of Equations*. New York: Cambridge University Press, 1990.

Paquette, R. J., N. J. Ashford, and P. H. Wright. *Transportation Engineering: Planning and Design*. New York: John Wiley & Sons, Inc., 1982.

Purcell, E. J. and D. Varberg. *Calculus with Analytic Geometry*. New Jersey: Prentice Hall, 1984.

Serway, R. A. *Physics for Scientists and Engineers*. New York: Saunders College Publishing, 1986.

Shames, I. H. *Engineering Mechanics*. New Jersey: Prentice Hall, 1990.

Shames, I. H. *Introduction to Solid Mechanics*. New Jersey: Prentice Hall, 1989.

Soong, T. T. *Probabilistic Modeling and Analysis in Science and Engineering*. New York: John Wiley & Sons, 1981.

Spiegel, M. R. *Mathematical Handbook of Formulas and Tables*. New York: McGraw-Hill, 1968.

Van Vlack, L. H. *Elements of Materials Science and Engineering*. New York: Addison Wesley, 1985.

Van Wylen, G. J. and R. E. Sonntag. *Fundamentals of Classical Thermodynamics*. New York: John Wiley & Sons, 1985.

Index

nullary operators: 40 (see also dittos)
numbers: see real numbers, rational numbers, integers, floating-point numbers, irrational numbers, and imaginary numbers
numer (numerator): 89
numerator: 87
numerical
   analysis: 3, 51
   constants: 54
   evaluation: see evaluation
   methods: 3
   solutions: 125-126, 139

O

objects: see types
od
Ohm's Law: 44
one dimensional input: see Maple Notation
op (operands): 48, 58-59, 90
open-channel flow: 79
operands: 26-27, 49, 89-90, 118, 120
operator associativity: 28
operator precedence: 27, 35
operators: 15, 25-28, 30, 69
options
or: 56, 78
Order: 78
ordinary differential equation (ODE): 172
orientation: see plots
output: see Maple output and computer output

P

palettes: (see also expression palette, symbol palette, and matrix palette)
paragraph: 14-15
parameter: 66
parametric
   functions: 104
   plots: 104
   solutions
Pi: 54-55, 73 (see also π)
piecewise: 78
piecewise: 78 (see also functions)
piles: 129
pipeline flow: 111
placeholders: 36-37, 127
plot: 17, 98-105
plot structures: 103-104
plot3d: 98, 105-106, 108, 110
plots (library package): 97, 103, 106-110, 128
plots: 17, 97-113
   animated: 109-110
   customizing: 99-101, 103
   editing: 99
   functions: 100
   library packages: 97
   multiple expressions: see multiple plots
   options: 101
   orientation: 103
   parametric: see parametric plots
   points: 107

printing: 99
range: see range
resizing: 98
saving: 99
structures: see plot structures
superimposing: 103 (see also multiple plots)
text: 107
title: 18, 99(see also string)
tutorials: 97
two dimensional: 98-105, 109
three dimensional: 98, 105, 109, 112
plotsetup
plottools (library package): 97, 108, 110
pointplot
pointplot3d
polynomials: 70-73, 87, 124, 129
   arithmetic: 69-72
   definition: 70
   division: 72
   expanding: see expanding
   factoring: see factoring
   factors: 71
   roots: 124
PostScript (PS): 18
powseries (power series): 78
powers: 74
predefined: see protected names
print
printer
problem solving: 1, 5
   methodology: 5-6
problems: 1
proc
procedural Maple functions: 77
procedures: 53 (see also **proc**)
product: 78
product: 78
programming statements
prompt: see Maple prompt and ">"
protect: 29-30, 63
protected names: 29-30, 53, 55, 77
pvac (print vectors): 142 (see also **share**)
punctuation: 25
purchase price: 31
Pythagorean Theorem

Q

qualitative: 97, 102
quit: 9
quo (quotient): 72
quotes: see Maple quotes
quotient: 71 (see also **quo** and polynomials)

R

radical: 87
radical expression: 87-88
radians: 73
radnormal (normalize radical): 88
radsimp (simplify radical): 88
range: 18, 57-58, 99-100, 126
range brackets: 15
ratio: see fraction and rational numbers

rational functions: 87, 89
rational numbers: 50
rationalize: 87
ratpoly: 69
Re: 53, 78
readdata
readlib: 62, 76, 78
real numbers: 50
real roots: 75
realroot: 73, 76
references
   absolute
   absolute column, relative row
   automatic adjustment
   circular
   complete absolute
   complete relative
   mixed
   relative
   relative column, absolute row
relational operators: 57 (see also <, <=, >, >=, =, and <>)
relations: 57, 90, 127
rem (remainder)
remainder: 72 (see also **rem** and polynomials)
repetition statements
reserved words: 25, 30
resistor: 43-44
restart: 17, 33, 39-40
right hand side (RHS): 91, 93, 126
rhs (right hand side): 91, 125
root: 73, 75
RootOf: see RootOf
RootOf: 85, 127
Roots: 73
roots: 73, 124
roots: 72-74, 81, 124, 127
   complex: 76
   finding: 72
   multiplicity: 72-73
   non-principal: 75
   principal: 75
   real number: 75
round: 51
row
row reduction

S

salvage value: 31
scalar equation: 124
scalarmul
science: 1
sec (secant): 74
section
select: 78
selecting: 59 (see also "[and]")
selection statements
semantics: 23
semicolon: see (";")
separable ODE
seq (sequence): 58, 77-78
sequences: 58-59, 66, 78, 90, 124-126 (see also "," and "$")
series: 78
series: 78